RATIONALITY, RELATIVISM AND INCOMMENSURABILITY

Pour Noëlle

Rationality, Relativism and Incommensurability

HOWARD SANKEY
Department of History and Philosophy of Science
University of Melbourne
Victoria, Australia

Routledge
Taylor & Francis Group
LONDON AND NEW YORK

First published 1997 by Ashgate Publishing

Reissued 2018 by Routledge
2 Park Square, Milton Park, Abingdon, Oxon, OX14 4RN
52 Vanderbilt Avenue, New York, NY 10017

Routledge is an imprint of the Taylor & Francis Group, an informa business

Publisher's Note
The publisher has gone to great lengths to ensure the quality of this reprint but points out that some imperfections in the original copies may be apparent.

A Library of Congress record exists under LC control number: 97071712

ISBN 13: 978-1-138-36414-1 (hbk)
ISBN 13: 978-1-138-36416-5 (pbk)
ISBN 13: 978-0-429-43148-7 (ebk)

Contents

Acknowledgements

This book brings together a series of essays which I have written in the last several years on a number of interconnected topics in the philosophy of science. While I have been at work on these essays I have enjoyed the support of a number of institutions. My chief material debt is to the Department of History and Philosophy of Science at the University of Melbourne, where the bulk of this work has been conceived and written. I am also indebted to the Leverhulme Trust for a postdoctoral fellowship during academic year 1989-90, which initially supported my stint at Saint David's University College, University of Wales, Lampeter. In addition, I am grateful to the Center for Philosophy of Science at the University of Pittsburgh for a visiting fellowship during the first part of 1995. Three of the essays were completed at the Center during what was for me a remarkably rewarding and productive experience.

The papers included here have been given in various colloquia. For discussion, I am indebted to audiences at Kansas State and La Trobe Universities, the Universities of Illinois, Melbourne and Pittsburgh, Saint David's University College, the 1993 Australasian Association of Philosophy conference in Adelaide, and the Pittsburgh Center's International Fellows Conference in Castiglioncello, Italy in May 1996.

In my experience, the activity of philosophy crucially involves the critical exchange of ideas. For their comments, objections, correspondence and interest, I wish to record a warm debt of gratitude to all of the following: Paulo Abrantes, Harold Brown, Steve Clarke, John Clendinnen, David Cockburn, John Collier, Brian Ellis, John Fox, Dimitri Ginev, Allen Hazen, Paul Hoyningen-Huene, O. R. Jones, Henry Krips, Hugh Lacey, Larry Laudan, Homer LeGrand, Oscar Manhal, Graeme Marshall, Michele Marsonet, Alan Musgrave, Robert

Nola, Nick Rescher, R. R. Rockingham Gill, Bob Sharpe, Barry Taylor and Neil Thomason.

All but one of the essays included here have appeared elsewhere. Accordingly, I wish to thank the editors and publishers of the following publications for permission to reproduce this material here: 'In Defence of Untranslatability', *Australasian Journal of Philosophy*, 68 (1990), pp. 1-21; 'Incommensurability and the Indeterminacy of Translation', *Australasian Journal of Philosophy*, 69 (1991), pp. 219-23; 'Incommensurability, Translation and Understanding', *The Philosophical Quarterly*, 41 (1991), pp. 414-26; 'Translation and Languagehood', *Philosophia*, 21 (1992), pp. 335-7; 'Kuhn's Changing Concept of Incommensurability', *British Journal for the Philosophy of Science*, 44 (1993), pp. 775-91; 'Five Varieties of Cognitive Relativism', *Cogito*, 7 (1993), pp. 106-11; 'Judgement and Rational Theory-Choice', *Methodology and Science*, 27 (1994), pp. 167-82; 'The Problem of Rational Theory-Choice', *Epistemologia*, 18 (1995), pp. 299-312; 'Normative Naturalism and the Challenge of Relativism: Laudan versus Worrall on the Justification of Methodological Principles', *International Studies in the Philosophy of Science*, 10 (1996), pp. 37-51; 'Rationality, Relativism and Methodological Pluralism', *Explorations in Knowledge*, XIII (1996), pp. 18-36; 'Kuhn's Ontological Relativism', in R. S. Cohen and D. Ginev (eds), *Issues and Images in the Philosophy of Science*, *Boston Studies in Philosophy of Science*, Kluwer Academic Publishers, Dordrecht, 1996; 'Taxonomic Incommensurability', *International Studies in the Philosophy of Science*, forthcoming 1997.

Introduction

As was not the case earlier this century, philosophers of science of the past four decades have repeatedly confronted the problems of relativism, the rationality of science and the incommensurability of theories. By the end of the 1950s, empiricist models of science and its method had come under sustained scrutiny and many common assumptions about the nature of science were the target of criticism. During the 1960s, a new historical movement in the philosophy of science emerged which laid great stress on the extent to which the practice and methodology of science evolves historically.

The picture of science as an essentially unchanging enterprise, driven by a universal method and couched in a neutral linguistic medium, came to be seen as a distorted image, based on a static, ahistorical conception of science. Attention soon shifted to the manner in which scientific activity is conducted in a variety of different social, intellectual and historical contexts, and the ways in which these contexts undergo a continual process of transformation. Where formerly the method of science had been assumed to be invariant, it became fashionable to suppose that the methods scientists actually employ undergo variation in the history of science. And where formerly observation had been taken to provide a secure epistemic foundation as well as a neutral source of empirical meaning, it became common to argue that the observational and theoretical language of science evolves as the concepts employed by theories also change.

The denial of both a stable methodology and a common language for science gave rise to what has been described as a 'crisis of rationality'.[1] For without an invariant language or a fixed methodology, choice of scientific theory seemed unable to be based on objective rational grounds. Absence of a common language suggested that alternative theories might be incommensurable in the sense that claims made by theories about the world might be unable to be compared with each other. Absence of a common methodology suggested that, even if theories might be compared, there would still be no neutral ground, independent of theory, on which to base any given choice of theory.

Philosophers and other analysts of science were quick to detect the relativistic and antirationalist tendencies of the historical movement. Indeed, some philosophers — and numerous sociologists and social historians — of science not only detected such tendencies, but positively embraced them. However, there has been prolonged discussion in the literature of the philosophy of science of various attempts to avoid these conclusions. Some have attempted to defend traditional empiricist ideas against the newer approach. Some have proposed modified versions of the historical approach, on which relativism and antirationalism may be avoided. Still others have suggested that the perception of crisis is ill-founded: rather than lead inexorably to relativism, the new philosophy of science contains the germs of a new way of thinking about rationality and conceptual change in science.

My sympathies lie in large measure with the latter approach. Far from leading inexorably to relativism and antirationalism, I hold that important insights about scientific methodology and rationality may be gleaned from the historical movement. The existence of profound conceptual change in science, as well as the absence of a neutral observation language, are important findings which may be credited to proponents of this approach. However, once the phenomenon of conceptual change is properly understood, few of the dire consequences to which it initially seemed to lead actually do follow from it. As for the absence of a universal method, and the resulting variation of method, the extreme consequences of radical relativism and lack of scientific rationality do not follow on this front either. We must readjust our concept of rationality to cohere with variation in scientific methodology. The result of coming to grips with methodological variation is not total relativism, but a more sophisticated view of objective rationality.

The essays included in this book develop a number of these themes. About half of the essays concentrate specifically on the thesis, proposed by Thomas Kuhn and Paul Feyerabend, that alternative scientific theories are incommensurable due to semantic differences between the vocabulary in which they are expressed. Several other of the essays seek to characterize a new way of thinking about scientific rationality, which can be derived from the historical critique of the idea of a fixed scientific method. In a number of the others, I attempt to show how some seemingly relativistic themes of the historical approach may be embraced in a non-relativistic manner within the context of a pluralistic and naturalistic theory of scientific methodology and rationality.

The book is divided into five parts. Part I contains a single essay, which proposes a taxonomy of relativistic doctrines that is employed throughout the remaining chapters. The three essays in Part II all deal with various aspects and refinements of Kuhn's version of the incommensurability thesis. The essays in Part III defend the idea of translation failure between incommensurable theories against the objection, due to Donald Davidson and Hilary Putnam, that the idea of translation failure, or of an untranslatable language, is incoherent or even unintelligible. Part IV develops the idea that the work of Kuhn and Feyerabend contains within it a new conception of scientific rationality. In Part V, I explore the claim due to Larry Laudan that a broadly naturalistic conception of rational justification can account for methodological variation in a manner which does not lead to epistemic relativism.

To set the stage, the book opens with a taxonomy of relativistic doctrines. I have often been struck by how philosophers characterize positions as relativistic for a variety of rather different reasons. One who says that languages 'carve up the world in different ways' will be branded a relativist just as readily as one who says that criteria of rationality vary with culture, or that truth depends on whatever conceptual framework one happens to adopt. Yet very different arguments are required in order to establish and develop such claims. And while the positions associated with such claims may all be relativistic in some quite general sense of the term, they nevertheless constitute importantly distinct philosophical positions.

Thus, to deal properly with relativism, it is crucial to distinguish between a number of significantly different doctrines. Accordingly, I distinguish relativism which takes what is rational to believe to be relative to context from relativism which takes the truth of substantive claims about the world to be relative to context. If combined, these two forms of relativism yield an epistemological relativism, according to which rationally justified true belief may also be relative. Philosophers have traditionally taken relativism about truth to be incoherent. Yet support for the thesis of relative truth may be found in the idea that languages or conceptual schemes 'carve up the world in different ways'. To spell this out somewhat, I propose a distinction between conceptual relativism, according to which there may be alternative, equally acceptable, conceptual schemes, and ontological relativism, according to which, in some sense remaining to be specified, the world depends on our conceptual and epistemic contribution.

The latter two forms of relativism are of particular relevance to the essays in Parts II and III, which address the topic of incommensurability. The essays in Part II take Kuhn's version of the incommensurability thesis as their target. Kuhn's views have evolved continuously since their original presentation in *The Structure of Scientific Revolutions*. Hence, they present a moving target. Thus, in Chapter 2, the first of these essays, I plot the development of Kuhn's views, and argue that three distinct stages in this development may be distinguished. Kuhn has sometimes assimilated incommensurability to Quinean indeterminacy of translation. Yet I argue in an appendix to this chapter that there are significant differences between the two notions. Chapters 3 and 4 focus on Kuhn's later treatment of incommensurability, which involves localized translation failure between theories which employ alternative taxonomic systems. I argue in Chapter 3 that the overall position which emerges in Kuhn's later work is a form of ontological relativism, on which the world experienced by the scientist depends on the taxonomic structure of the theory accepted by the scientist. Yet in Chapter 4 I argue that the thesis of 'taxonomic incommensurability' does not itself pose a threat to the usual epistemic and ontological commitments of the scientific realist.

One of the more controversial aspects of the incommensurability thesis is failure of translation between the vocabulary employed by alternative theories. This aspect of the thesis has been exposed to searching critique by Donald Davidson, who argued in his justly famous paper, 'On the Very Idea of a Conceptual Scheme', that coherent sense cannot be made of the idea of a totally untranslatable language. In Part III, I examine Davidson's arguments in detail, as well as related objections due to Hilary Putnam. In Chapter 5 I defend the idea of untranslatability between the special vocabularies of theories against the objections of Davidson and Putnam to the untranslatability of total languages. In an appendix to Chapter 5 I also suggest, against Davidson, that evidence of languagehood must ultimately depend on extralinguistic factors, rather than translation. In both Chapters 5 and 6, I employ and defend a distinction made by Kuhn and Feyerabend between understanding what is said in a language and translating into some other language.

Given the focus of the essays in Parts II and III on incommensurability, there is some overlap between these two parts of the book and my earlier book, *The Incommensurability Thesis*. In that book, I sought to show that the semantic variance which gives rise to the idea of incommensurability may be dealt with in an entirely satisfactory manner within the framework of scientific realism. My main strategy was to set the problem of incommensurability within the context of a modified causal theory of reference, and to treat semantic variance as a matter of divergent linguistic relations which alternative theories may bear to a mind-independent world. I employed a 'causal descriptivist' account of reference, which grants a supplemental role to description in reference determination, to argue that translation fails due to limits on the way reference may be determined in alternative theories. Yet, despite untranslatability, there may nonetheless be sufficient continuity of reference between theories to allow detailed comparison of content on the basis of shared and overlapping reference.

After completing *The Incommensurability Thesis*, I continued to work on several topics related to the problem of incommensurability. The present book contains five of the papers which I subsequently wrote on these topics, as well as two papers, versions of which are found in the earlier book.[2] One topic of particular interest, given my realism, is the antirealist metaphysics which Kuhn developed with increasing refinement in his later work. In Chapters 3 and 4, I critically examine several aspects of Kuhn's later position, which I did not have the opportunity to discuss in *The Incommensurability Thesis*. I also continued to ponder the issues arising from the idea that one may understand a language which cannot be translated into one's native tongue. My further thoughts on these matters may be found in Chapter 6, as well as in the Appendix to Chapter 5. Where the present treatment of incommensurability most differs from the earlier book is in a shift of focus away from details of the relation between reference and incommensurability. Readers interested in detailed analysis of the theory of reference in relation to the problem of incommensurability, or in my positive argument for translation failure between theories, are encouraged to consult the earlier book.[3]

From such broadly semantic concerns, I turn in Parts IV and V to the epistemological issues of rational theory choice, methodological variance and epistemic justification. The two essays which make up Part IV explore the idea that the basis of a new conception of scientific rationality may be found in the work of Kuhn and Feyerabend. This idea occurs, for example, in Richard Bernstein's suggestion, in his book *Beyond Objectivism and Relativism*, that Kuhn and Feyerabend should be understood as calling for a liberalized view of scientific rationality, akin to the deliberative forms of reason associated with the rationality of practical action. With this thought in mind, in Chapter 7 I briefly state the leading elements of a non-algorithmic, methodological pluralist account of the nature of rational scientific theory choice, all of which may be found in the writings of Kuhn and Feyerabend. Such an account requires, however, that rational choice involve a considerable measure of deliberative judgement, which cannot be dictated by algorithmic rules. Thus, in Chapter 8 I argue that an account of rational judgement must play a central role in the theory of scientific rationality. However, lacking a theory of judgement of my own, I adopt the characterization of judgement as an acquired, expert capacity to arrive at decisions in the absence of rules, which has been cogently developed by Harold Brown in his book, *Rationality*.

The major problem facing any account of scientific reason derived from the views of Kuhn and Feyerabend is precisely the problem which has confronted their own work: the problem of relativism. Thus, in Part V, I attempt to show that a pluralistic, non-algorithmic account of rational theory choice need not lapse into an epistemological relativism of contextually variant methodological standards. My position on this issue has been heavily influenced by the work of Larry Laudan, particularly his book *Science and Values* and subsequent writings. Laudan has argued strongly for the view that a naturalistic account of the warrant of methodological rules enables a pluralistic view of method to evade the threat of relativism. This issue is the unifying theme of Part V.

In Chapter 9, I argue that neither the denial of an invariant scientific method nor the assertion of a plurality of methodological standards leads to a relativist account of the rationality of theory choice. I trace the idea that relativism follows from variation of method to the assumption that mere compliance with operative standards suffices for rational justification, and I argue against a number of possible defences which might be given of this assumption. The objection that methodological variance leads to relativism has also been levelled against the position developed by Laudan in *Science and Values*. In Chapter 10 I defend Laudan's 'normative naturalist' account of the epistemic warrant of methodological standards against one of the main proponents of this line of criticism, John Worrall. Finally, in Chapter 11, I take up Laudan's challenging claim that the roots of contemporary epistemological relativism may be found in the metamethodological views of earlier empiricist philosophers of science. I examine this claim in the context of Karl Popper's thesis of the conventional status of methodological rules, and argue that in fact such conventionalism leaves Popper fully exposed to the charge of relativism.

With the exception of Chapter 4 and occasional remarks in other chapters, the issue of scientific realism figures only marginally in this book. In some respects, this is because I take the issue of realism to be independent of many of the epistemic and semantic issues with which the essays in this book are concerned. Yet, in other respects, the essays have been written from the standpoint of a firm commitment to scientific realism. Thus, while I have not made the connections explicit, the overall picture which I seek to articulate here is one which I take to be entirely consonant with a rather robust form of realism. In future work, I hope to provide a fuller elaboration of the relationship which I see between scientific realism, and the views about rationality and conceptual change presented here.

Notes

1. Hacking (1983, pp. 1-2); cf. Hacking (1979, p. 228).
2. Somewhat different versions of Chapters 2 and 5, both of which appeared in their present form as articles, were contained in *The Incommensurability Thesis*. I include them here, each equipped with an appendix, because they complement the discussion in the remaining chapters of Parts II and III, which were not contained in the earlier book.
3. See, in particular, Chapters 2, 3 and 5. For a compressed version of the argument for translation failure between theories, see my (1991).

Part I

RELATIVISM

1 Five varieties of cognitive relativism

1.1 The issue of relativism

The doctrine of relativism was once widely dismissed as incoherent. Yet recent philosophy abounds with relativistic claims. It is now common for philosophers of science to deny that there are invariant standards for the assessment of scientific theories. Antirealist philosophers of language suggest that truth is internal to language or conceptual scheme. Some contemporary metaphysicians tell us much the same thing about reality. And reflection on the vast variety of beliefs and practices found among the numerous peoples of the world has led many to think that what it is right to do and believe depends on the culture to which one belongs.

But despite its recent popularity, claims of relativism continue to be controversial. There are still those who think that without universal standards there can be no objective difference between a good idea and a lunatic one. There are still those who think that without an absolute standard against which to judge our beliefs and actions, any belief or act is as good, or as rational, as any other. And there are still those who see relativism as a profound challenge to human reason, which threatens to undermine all the progress that has been made over the centuries by serious thinkers devoted to rational thought.

When controversy surrounds a doctrine, an important philosophical task is to clarify the issue by making relevant distinctions. The aim of this first chapter is the simple taxonomic task of bringing out the range of possible relativist positions. To this end, I will distinguish five varieties of cognitive relativism. By cognitive relativism I mean, roughly speaking, those forms of relativism which have to do with knowledge and with what we have knowledge of. In concentrating on such forms of relativism, I will be setting aside various non-cognitive forms of relativism, such as moral or aesthetic relativism and certain relativistic views about cultural practices. It will emerge in the course of my analysis that there are deep problems with cognitive relativism. But the main point I seek to establish is that there is a range of possible relativist positions, so one cannot talk simply of relativism without qualification.

1.2 Rationality relativism

The first form of relativism is relativism about rationality, or more specifically, relativism about rational belief. One place in which the issue of relativism about rationality has emerged is in recent work in the philosophy of science. Starting in the 1950s and 1960s, traditional objectivist assumptions within the philosophy of science have increasingly been put in question. With the rejection of many of the assumptions on which traditional objectivist philosophy of science rested, a variety of positions has emerged which suggest that scientific rationality is relative to context or has no higher epistemic status than any other mode of thought.

On at least one traditional view, associated in this century with assorted empiricist philosophers of science, such as Popper and the logical empiricists, science was thought to be governed by a uniform scientific method, which was common to all scientists working in different subject areas. Opinions diverged among empiricists over the precise details of the scientific method, for example over whether it was based on induction or deduction, or whether observation functions primarily to confirm or to disconfirm theories. But it was generally assumed that the characteristic methodology of science involves the use of observation and rationally grounded patterns of inference. And, whatever the particular conception of method involved, philosophers tended to assume that the scientific method provides objective criteria, which could be used in the rational evaluation of scientific theories, and which might serve as a neutral court of appeal in matters of theory choice.

As against this traditional view of the objectivity of science, much recent work in the philosophy of science rejects the idea that science is governed by a stable scientific method applicable in all fields of science and in all time periods in the history of science. Recent philosophy of science has tended, instead, to make the standards employed in science vary with the theoretical framework, context or tradition of research within which scientists operate. Here one of the main influences has been work in the history of science. Historical research has suggested that actual science bears little resemblance to the picture of science presented by traditional monomethodological orthodoxy in the philosophy of science. Rather than fixity of method, the history of science reveals that the procedures, standards and evaluative criteria used in science are just as much subject to variation as are substantive scientific beliefs and theories themselves.

Particularly influential in applying the lessons of the history of science to the philosophy of science have been Paul Feyerabend and Thomas Kuhn. In *Against Method* (1975), Feyerabend has argued that, at one time or another, all methodological rules have legitimately been broken by the practice of actual scientists. If Feyerabend is right, there is no fixed scientific methodology, since every methodological rule has justifiably been violated at some stage by scientists. In *The Structure of Scientific Revolutions* (1970a), Kuhn argued that many of the standards used to evaluate proposed solutions of scientific problems are internal to the large scale theoretical structures he called 'paradigms'. He also denied the existence of a fixed set of methodological criteria standing outside of paradigms, which would be capable of providing unequivocal judgment on which of rival paradigms is rationally to be preferred.[1] This rejection of a fixed method, or fixed set of standards, capable of neutrally arbitrating disputes between theories is now fairly widespread, though by no means universal, among philosophers of science.

Often the denial that there is a fixed scientific method is taken to imply relativism about scientific rationality. For example, in a recent exchange with Larry Laudan, John Worrall has claimed that:

> If no principles of evaluation stay fixed, then there is no 'objective viewpoint' from which we can show that progress has occurred and we can say only that progress has occurred *relative to the standards that we happen to accept now*. However this may be dressed up, it is relativism. (1988, p. 274)

This picture of the relation between relativism and the denial of a fixed methodology is also found in Alan Chalmers' discussion of the issue in *What is this thing called Science?* (1982), where Chalmers writes that:

> The extreme rationalist asserts that there is a single, timeless, universal criterion with reference to which the relative merits of rival theories are to be assessed ... The relativist denies that there is a universal, ahistorical standard of rationality with respect to

which one theory can be judged better than another. (1982, p. 101-2)

This picture is well captured by Worrall's concluding claim against Laudan that 'either there is an invariant core ... of methodological principles or everything is open to change ... *without* such [an invariant core Laudan's] model collapses into relativism' (Worrall, 1988, p. 275).

The picture of the relation between relativism and methodology presented in these quotes reflects a widespread assumption. It is commonly assumed that, without fixed methodological principles, rational scientific belief must be relative to changing standards, which vary with respect to the theoretical, conceptual or historical contexts within which scientists operate. On such a view, it is thought to follow from variation of accepted methodological standards within science that beliefs which are certified by the standards of one context are rationally on a par with beliefs which are certified by the standards of another context.

But while such relativism about rationality is frequently thought to follow from variation of methodological standards, it is important to note that standard variance is not by itself sufficient to relativize rationality in this way. For it is one thing to say that the principles or standards which are actually employed in science vary with historical or other context. It is quite another thing to infer rationality relativism from variation of such principles and standards. To infer that rationality is relative to context from the existence of standard variance is to make a move which violates the distinction between 'is' and 'ought'.

This is because to say that the standards scientists employ vary from context to context is to make a factual claim about what scientists do. As such, it is to make a descriptive claim which is lacking in normative force. But to make the relativistic claim that rationality is relative to context due to standard variance is to go beyond this and make a normative claim rather than a descriptive one. This is because to claim that a belief is rational relative to some context is to claim that the belief is rational. And to claim that a belief is rational is to judge it worthy of acceptance, which is to make a normative evaluation of it.

Given this gap between the descriptive claim of standard variance and the normative claim of rationality relativism, something further needs to be added to the argument for relativism. In particular, it needs to be added that in order for rationality to be relative, not only must standards vary, but the satisfaction of some set of standards must itself constitute rational belief worthiness. If this were the case, rationality would be relative to context in the sense that a belief certified by standards operative in some context would thereby be rational. But, since any belief is presumably certifiable by some possible standards, the apparent upshot of such relativity is that one belief is as rational as any other.

Thus, the vital premise in the argument for relativism about rationality is not that standards vary, but that there is nothing to rationality beyond adherence to a set of standards. Taken by itself, therefore, the denial of fixed methodological standards in favour of variant ones falls short of a full-blown relativism of rational belief. For it does not entail the further claim that a belief that accords with one set of standards is as worthy of belief as one that accords with any other set of standards. Rather, the denial of a stable methodology only denies that the principles which are accepted as governing rational thought remain fixed. It does not follow from this that the rationality of a belief is insured by the existence of some set of standards with which it accords.

1.3 Relativism about truth

The second form of relativism is relativism about truth. Some relativists might wish to dispense with talk of truth altogether, and would presumably deny that there is a distinct doctrine of relativism about truth. However, there is, at least conceptually, an important distinction to be drawn between relativism about truth and relativism about rationality. The latter says that rationality depends on theoretical or historical context, and is relative to such context. The former says that the truth of a given belief, sentence or proposition depends on and is relative to the historical, theoretical or social context in which it occurs. Whatever the merits of relativism about rationality, relativism about truth is still widely dismissed by philosophers as incoherent or self-refuting.

To see why truth relativism has seemed inconsistent, suppose that the truth of some proposition is said to be relative to context. For concreteness, suppose the truth of the proposition 'The Earth is flat' is said to be relative to the context in which it is asserted. The claim that truth is relative in this way would seem to entail that the proposition that the Earth is flat might be true if asserted in one context but false if asserted in another. On the face of it, such a claim of relativity is incoherent since it leads straight to contradiction: it implies both that the Earth is flat and that it is not flat. Because it seems to imply a contradiction, such relativism appears to be incoherent.

As against this, however, the relativist may reply that the charge of incoherence begs the question against truth relativism. For a contradiction only arises from variation of truth value relative to context if truth is understood in an absolute sense. No contradiction arises if truth is understood in a relative sense. For a proposition that is true relative to a context is not true independent of that context. So the truth of a proposition relative to a context does not conflict with its falsity relative to some other context.

The trouble with this reply is that if relative truth is understood in such a way that the truth of a proposition relative to one context fails to conflict with its falsity relative to another, the notion of relative truth must be understood in a rather weak sense. In particular, if the truth of 'The Earth is flat' relative to one context is not to conflict with the falsity of 'The Earth is flat' relative to another, the relative truth of the proposition can entail little more than that one is entitled to assert the proposition in some context. It cannot follow from relative truth that the state of affairs described by a proposition actually obtains independently of a given context. For if that followed, then there would be a conflict between the truth of a proposition relative to one context and the falsity of the very same proposition relative to some other context.

But if truth relativism reduces truth to context relative warranted assertability, then it is difficult to see how truth relativism is to be distinguished from rationality relativism. In short, a stronger notion of relative truth than mere assertability in a context is required if truth relativism is not to collapse into rationality relativism. As we will see in Section 1.6, a stronger notion of relative truth is available, but this will require introduction of a further, ontological, form of relativism.

A second objection that is often raised against relativism about truth is that it is self-refuting. The truth relativist asserts that truth is relative. But then the question immediately arises of how the assertion, made by the truth relativist, that truth is relative is itself to be understood. Here the truth relativist faces a dilemma. Either, in asserting truth to be relative, the truth relativist asserts that the doctrine of truth relativism is itself true in an absolute sense. Or else the relativist asserts that the doctrine of truth relativism is true in a relative sense.

Consider the first possibility. Suppose that the doctrine of relativism about truth is asserted by the truth relativist as an absolute claim. That is, suppose that truth relativism is asserted to be true without its own truth being relative to any context, as a truth which applies to all contexts. But if the truth relativist asserts that truth relativism is true in an absolute sense, then truth relativism denies what it asserts. For it asserts that truth is relative while asserting that the very assertion that truth is relative is itself true in a non-relative sense.

Now consider the second possibility. Suppose that truth relativism is asserted to be true relative to context. In that case, the doctrine of truth relativism is true for the truth relativist. But, given that the non-relativist about truth denies that truth is relative, truth relativism is false for the non-relativist. But if the view that truth is relative is false for the non-relativist, then it follows that the view that truth is non-relative is true for the non-relativist. But if truth is non-relative, then truth relativism is false. So the claim that truth relativism is true relatively also leads to the denial of what the relativist asserts.

Philosophers have tended to assume that relativism about truth is fatally undermined by the objection that it is incoherent and self-refuting. For that reason such relativism has a bad reputation in philosophy. However, there is a suggestion found in the work of Kuhn and Feyerabend, which may enable partial sense to be made of truth relativism. The suggestion can be derived from the claim, made by both authors, that some pairs of scientific theories are semantically incommensurable due to conceptual variance.

According to Kuhn and Feyerabend, some successive or competing scientific theories employ radically divergent conceptual apparatus. In the transition between such conceptually variant theories, a semantic shift in the vocabulary employed by the theories takes place. Such semantic change results in the inability to fully or precisely translate the expressions used by one theory by means of the expressions employed by the other. The claim of incommensurability is that, given translation failure between theories, the content of such theories is unable to be compared, since no consequence of one theory agrees or disagrees with any consequence of the other.

The idea of a translation failure between two theories contains, I suggest, the basis for a minimal relativity of truth. To see this, let us suppose that some proposition 'P' of theory T is such that neither it nor its denial can be translated from T into another theory T*. If 'P' were true, then there is a sense in which its truth is relative to T. For while the truth of 'P' may not depend on T, 'P' cannot be removed from T and transplanted into T*. Nor can '~P' be formulated in T*. The truth of 'P' is therefore relative to T in the minimal sense that 'P' is asserted by T and is true, while neither 'P' nor '~P' can be asserted by T*.

This falls short of full-blown relativism about truth, where the latter is understood as the doctrine that 'P' is true in one theory and false in another. But the idea that there may be a true proposition which is only available from a particular theoretical standpoint captures something that the truth relativist may want to say. For such a relativist wishes to deny that truth is independent of theory. And incommensurability ties truths closely to the theory in which they are asserted, so that there is a sense in which truth is not independent of theory.[2]

1.4 Epistemological relativism

The third variety of relativism I wish to distinguish is a hybrid of the preceding two. It arises by combining the idea that truth is relative with the idea that rationality is relative. Philosophers have traditionally conceived knowledge as justified true belief, meaning that a belief that is rationally held and true constitutes knowledge. By combining truth relativism and rationality relativism with a justified true belief account of knowledge, we obtain epistemological relativism, or relativism about knowledge.[3]

According to epistemological relativism, knowledge is relative to the context in which the knower is situated. What is knowledge for members of one culture, or for proponents of a given scientific theory, depends upon their cultural or theoretical context. Thus, what constitutes knowledge is not jointly determined by objective rational considerations and the way the world really is, independently of how it is thought to be within a given cultural or theoretical context. Rather, what constitutes knowledge is determined by what, in a given context, counts as a rational consideration and what, in that context, counts as truth.

On the assumption that truth and rational belief are relative to context, the belief that P constitutes knowledge if, relative to a given context, 'P' is both rationally believed and true. It follows that a belief that constitutes knowledge in one context may not be knowledge in another. For example, the belief that the Earth is flat might be true and rationally believed to be true relative to one context, yet false and rationally believed to be false relative to another context. According to epistemological relativism, the Earth would be known to be flat in the former context, and known not to be flat in the latter.

Interestingly, whatever plausibility this form of relativism has with regard to rationality, it inherits a high degree of implausibility from relativism about truth. For it can be argued in terms precisely analogous to those used against truth relativism that epistemological relativism is both incoherent and self-refuting. This does not bode well for the epistemological relativist. However, the situation may begin to seem more promising for epistemological relativism, as well as for the truth relativist, if support is sought from the next doctrine that I will discuss.

1.5 Ontological relativism

Sometimes it is said that the way the world is, reality itself, depends upon or is in part influenced by the beliefs, theories or conceptual apparatus we operate with. Something like this is hinted at by Kuhn's talk of change of world in the revolutionary transition between scientific paradigms. Kuhn says, for example, that 'when paradigms change, the world itself changes with them' (1970a, p. 111). Such talk can make the transition between paradigms sound like space travel: 'It is rather as if', Kuhn says, 'the professional community had been suddenly transported to another planet' (1970a, p. 111). Talk of world change is a constant theme in Kuhn's discussion of scientific revolutions, e.g., 'after a revolution scientists are responding to a different world' (1970a, p. 111), and 'the proponents of competing paradigms practice their trades in different worlds' (1970a, p. 150).

The idea that in some sense the very world we inhabit depends on and varies relative to the way we think, talk or conceive of it is the key to the fourth variety of relativism, which is a metaphysical thesis one might call ontological relativism. The view that is suggested by Kuhn's talk of world change between paradigms would make the world or reality that is investigated by scientists depend upon the theory or paradigm they accept. Such ontological relativism is a difficult view to make sense of. For it comes close to the absurd claim that reality goes in and out of existence whenever scientists change theories. Worse, it suggests that there is a whole multitude of alternative realities constantly popping in and out of existence with theory change.

Ordinarily, a view such as the one suggested by Kuhn's talk of world change would not be described as a form of relativism at all. Since such a view makes reality depend upon human thought, it seems to have rather more in common with doctrines that philosophers have traditionally called idealism. Idealism, roughly, is the view that what exists either is itself made up of mental substance, or else depends for its existence on some form of mental activity, such as thought or experience. Such an idealist approach rejects the idea of an objective reality whose properties, structure, and existence is independent of human thought and experience.

There is, however, no need to make sense of such a radically idealistic form of relativism, since it is possible to distinguish a weaker position which is more intelligible than world change idealism. This weaker position admits the existence of an external reality that is independent of human thought and experience. But it denies that this reality itself can be known by us.

On such a view, the only world which is epistemically accessible to us is a made-up world, a construction. Such a constructed world is a partial product of human thought and practice, and can change when human thought and practice change. But it is not produced by human thought and activity alone. Rather, the mind independent reality that lies beyond human knowledge exercises indirect constraint on our constructed world by impinging on us in the form of sense experience. On such a view, we mould our constructed world to fit the rough shape of things as they are disclosed to us by our senses.

The main difficulty which faces this weaker constructivist form of ontological relativism is to avoid slipping into an extravagant world change idealism which dispenses with the existence of a mind independent reality altogether. On the one hand, such relativism must avoid giving too great a role to experience in fixing our belief schemes. For if excessive control is granted to sense experience in constraining belief formation, there is reduced scope for variation of constructed world. On the other hand, the moorings to reality by way of experience must not be cut completely. For without any connection between experience and reality there would be little difference between the constructed reality of the constructive ontological relativist and the mind dependent reality of the world change idealist.

1.6 Ontological relativism, incoherence, self-refutation

In Section 1.4, I said that truth relativism and epistemological relativism might gain support from ontological relativism. Let us see what follows about truth and knowledge from constructive ontological relativism. On such a view, knowledge and truth may be taken to be relative to constructed world. A proposition is true if it is true in a given constructed world. A belief constitutes knowledge if it is rationally justified given the standards operative in some context, and if it is true in the constructed world associated with that context.

To see whether constructive ontological relativism supports truth relativism and epistemological relativism, we must ask whether such relativism escapes the charges of incoherence and self-refutation which were earlier levelled against relativism about truth. The answer to this question is not straightforward. But there are *prima facie* grounds for thinking that the charges may be avoided.

Consider the charge that truth relativism is incoherent. Here the objection was that truth relativism entails a contradiction, since it implies that one and the same proposition may be both true and false.

Provided that propositions can be identified across constructed worlds, it is not clear that such incoherence arises.[4] For a proposition whose truth value varies with context is not held, by the truth relativist, to be capable of being both true and false with respect to the same constructed world. Rather, the proposition is said to be true relative to the constructed world associated with one context, and false relative to the constructed world associated with another context. But, given that the proposition varies in truth value relative to different constructed worlds, no conflict arises between its truth relative to one world and its falsity relative to another.

Now consider the charge that truth relativism is self-refuting. Here the objection was that truth relativism faces a dilemma. Either an absolute assertion of truth relativism denies what it asserts, or else a relativized assertion allows truth to be absolute for the non-relativist. But by situating truth relativism within the context of ontological relativism, the claim of truth relativism appears to have shifted enough to avoid self-refutation. Within the context of ontological relativism, truth is relative to constructed world because reality itself is epistemically inaccessible, and neither propositions nor rationally justified beliefs can be made true by such a reality.

Still, it might be objected that the claim that there is no absolute truth, but only truth relative to constructed world, is itself an absolute claim. Thus, precisely as with the original objection, truth relativism asserts what it denies. But things are not so simple this time. The relativist claim presently under consideration is not simply the claim that truth is relative. It is the claim that, because of the nature of our relation to reality, we are unable to formulate truths about reality itself; we can only formulate truths relative to a constructed world. This claim is not itself put forward as a claim whose truth is relative to constructed world. Rather, this claim is a general epistemological and metaphysical claim about our lack of epistemic access to reality itself.[5] As such, it is explicitly put forward as an absolute claim, which is perfectly consistent with being one.

Nor is the argument from the relativity of truth relativism to truth being absolute for the non-relativist available. For the present claim is not that truth relativism is asserted in a relative sense. As we have just seen, the claim is that we are epistemically so related to reality that we cannot formulate truths with respect to it. But, since that claim is not put forward as a relative claim, it is not possible to claim that truth is therefore absolute relative to the non-relativist.

1.7 Conceptual relativism

One way to retain a mind independent reality while holding it at an epistemic remove is conceptual relativism. This doctrine is often closely associated with constructivist forms of ontological relativism of the kind we have just been considering. Conceptual relativism is the view that there is, or might be, a multiplicity of alternative conceptual schemes, none of which is, or can be shown to be, superior to any other. On such a view, reality is a Kantian thing-in-itself, lost behind a veil of appearances. Truth and reality are what is taken as such by those who employ a given conceptual scheme. As a result, beliefs and theories elaborated within a given conceptual scheme are, from an epistemological point of view, no better or worse than radically differing beliefs and theories elaborated within some other. But what is a conceptual scheme?

What precisely a conceptual scheme is depends on the form of conceptual relativism in question. In general, a conceptual scheme is a set of concepts, ordinarily associated with a particular descriptive vocabulary. Sometimes conceptual schemes are taken as the fundamental systems of categories by means of which the world is partitioned into various kinds of things. Sometimes, in a nominalist vein, they are identified with the set of predicates of some natural language, or of closely related languages.

Conceptual schemes may also be more localized entities, such as the conceptual apparatus of a particular theory. An example of alternative conceptual apparatus is that of phlogistic versus oxygen chemistry. Eighteenth century phlogistic chemists spoke of such things as phlogiston, phlogisticated air, dephlogisticated air, and light inflammable air. Oxygen chemists, following Lavoisier, employed more familiar concepts, such as oxygen, hydrogen and nitrogen. The phlogiston and oxygen theories are examples of different scientific theories which applied distinct conceptual apparatus to a common set of phenomena.

Conceptual relativism arises from reflection on multiple conceptual schemes, as well as on the role of concepts in cognition. Both when one describes an observed fact and when one makes an observation, a conceptual scheme is interposed between observer and reality. It is impossible to remove oneself altogether from all conceptual apparatus and view or describe reality in its pure form. Reality in itself, stripped of conceptual overlay, is not something to which we have direct access. Since it is impossible to remove oneself entirely from all conceptual schemes, it is impossible to take up a neutral God's eye position outside one's own conceptual scheme to compare it with reality.

Similarly, one can never get outside of conceptual schemes altogether to compare alternative conceptual schemes with reality.

As a result, it is impossible ever to be in a position to tell whether some conceptual scheme better matches the world's own categorial structure than another scheme. That is, it is impossible to check conceptual schemes against reality to see which scheme correctly represents reality itself. Therefore, it is impossible to know if one theory with one conceptual scheme is correct and another theory with a different conceptual scheme is incorrect.

Similarly, since it is impossible to shed conceptual scheme, it is impossible for there to be any neutral means of comparing rival theories which have alternative conceptual schemes. Adherents of rival theories cannot appeal to neutral statements of evidence or standards of appraisal to comparatively evaluate the rival theories. For adherents of rival theories will accept observation statements and standards couched in terms of their conceptual schemes. Given this, there will be no access to neutral observation described in neutral terms, or to neutral standards of appraisal. So there will be no objective way of deciding which theory to accept.

The major drawback with conceptual relativism is its assumption that an objective critical appraisal of a theory requires one to shed all of one's conceptual baggage. Here the case of phlogistic and oxygen chemistry serves as counter-example. Advocates of both the phlogiston and oxygen theories of chemistry were able to see the gain in weight of oxidized metals as a problem for phlogistic chemistry, though they described the process of oxidation in different terms. It took some time for this and other empirical and conceptual difficulties to wear away support for phlogistic chemistry, but in the end the oxygen theory won out.

It may be impossible to calibrate a conceptual scheme directly with reality. Yet where experience and prediction conflict, or where data otherwise fail to mesh with theory, it remains possible to test our views — albeit it fallibly — against reality. A discredited philosophy of science empiricism may be, but that does not mean that experience plays no epistemic role.

1.8 Conclusion

My main aim in this chapter has been to stress the range of available forms of cognitive relativism. Along the way, however, I have indicated difficulties which arise for various forms of the doctrine. One influential form of relativism about rational belief suffers due to lack of argument from standard variation to standard-relative rationality. Relativism about truth courts paradox, as, by implication, does relativism about knowledge. Relativism about reality risks collapse into an absurd idealism, while conceptual relativism implausibly diminishes the role of empirical evidence.

It will hardly have escaped notice that the various forms of relativism I have distinguished may stand in different relations. They may be held separately, or combined in a variety of ways. For example, one might defend relativism about rationality but reject truth, ontological and conceptual relativism. Or, as discussed in Section 1.6, one might combine truth relativism with some form of ontological relativism, thinking thereby to rescue the former from incoherence and self-refutation.

But I suspect that one particular combination of forms of relativism is of most contemporary relevance. This is a concoction blended from rationality relativism, a limited relativism about truth based on incommensurability, and a conceptual relativism which admits the existence of a mind independent reality. For such relativists, as for their adversaries, the crucial issue remains that of the extent to which variation of rational belief is subject to objective constraints.

Notes

1. It is important to note that while Kuhn originally seemed to deny the existence of such fixed criteria, in later work he admits the existence of a set of criteria which remain more or less invariant throughout the history of science. However, such criteria are incapable, according to Kuhn, of unequivocally determining a choice between alternative theories. Cf. the 'Postscript' to Kuhn (1970a) as well as his (1977c). I will return to this point repeatedly in subsequent chapters.
2. In his later work, Kuhn combined the thesis of semantic incommensurability with a limited relativism about truth roughly along the lines sketched here (see Sections 3.8 and 4.6).
3. Weaker forms of epistemological relativism may also be arrived at by combining a non-relativist view of rationality with truth relativism, or by combining rationality relativism with a non-relativist view of truth. But I will focus on the stronger form of epistemological relativism on which both truth and rationality are relative.
4. Of course, the assumption that propositions can be identified across constructed worlds is problematic. One might argue, following Putnam (1975c), that reference is fixed by environment, and that propositional identity requires identity of environment.

But then, if a constructed world constitutes an environment in the appropriate sense, there can be no propositional identity across constructed worlds. It would follow, too, that truth is not relative to constructed world, since there are no shared propositions whose truth value may vary with world.

5. It might be objected that such a general claim is, if true, a counterexample to the relativistic claim that truth is relative to constructed world. Here the relativist has two choices: either to say that the general claim is a truth which is true relative to all contexts, or to say that not all truths are relative to constructed worlds.

Part II

INCOMMENSURABILITY

2 Kuhn's changing concept of incommensurability

2.1 Introduction

The year 1962 saw the introduction by Kuhn and Feyerabend of the thesis of the incommensurability of scientific theories.[1] Since then, the thesis has been widely debated and attracted much criticism. Yet it has enjoyed considerable influence, particularly in the area of the history and philosophy of science concerned with scientific theory change and choice. This influence is in large part due to the immense popularity of Kuhn's masterwork, *The Structure of Scientific Revolutions*, which ensures that the idea of incommensurability continues to reach a broad audience. It is, however, less widely appreciated that Kuhn's version of the idea has, in the meantime, undergone a process of continual revision and clarification. As a result, the version of the thesis for which Kuhn is best known differs markedly from the version which he later came to espouse. In this chapter I present a study of the process of change which chronicles the key stages of the developments of Kuhn's concept of incommensurability.[2]

Kuhn's treatment of incommensurability divides into early and late positions, separated by a transitional stage.[3] Originally, Kuhn's notion of incommensurability involved semantic, observational and methodological differences between global theories or paradigms. His initial discussion suggested that proponents of incommensurable theories are unable to communicate, and that there is no recourse to neutral experience or objective standards to adjudicate between theories. In subsequent efforts to clarify his position he restricted incommensurability to semantic differences, and assimilated it to Quinean indeterminacy of translation. During this intermediate stage

Kuhn's treatment of the issues tended to be incomplete, often resulting in cursory discussion.[4] However, in recent years he began to develop his position in more refined form. His later view was that there is translation failure between a localized cluster of interdefined terms within the languages of theories.

The views of Feyerabend, the other main advocate of the incommensurability thesis, will be dealt with here only to the extent that consideration of them illuminates some aspect of Kuhn's position. However, it is worth briefly indicating the key differences between their views. Unlike Kuhn, whose notion of incommensurability initially included non-semantic factors, Feyerabend always restricted his use of the notion to the semantic sphere (cf. Feyerabend, 1978, pp. 66-7). Feyerabend originally developed his idea of incommensurability as an objection to the reductionist account of theory succession, according to which earlier theories are deductively subsumed by the later theories which replace them (see his 1981b). He argued that because of conceptual disparity between theories, successive theories may fail to have common semantic content, in which case the overlap of consequence classes necessary for reduction would not obtain. His idea of incommensurability differs from Kuhn's in that semantic variance between theories extends to the entirety of the observational and theoretical terms employed by incommensurable theories, whereas for Kuhn such semantic variance tends to be confined to central subsets of the terms which occur in such theories. Moreover, apart from some early clarifications (1981c and 1981d), and an apparent extension of incommensurability to world views (1975, chapter 17), Feyerabend's idea remained fundamentally unchanged since originally being developed.

2.2 Kuhn's early position

Incommensurability figures integrally in Kuhn's account of revolutionary scientific change in *The Structure of Scientific Revolutions*. According to Kuhn, scientific activity divides into periods of 'normal science' punctuated at intervals by episodes of 'revolution'. Normal science is 'research firmly based upon one or more past scientific achievements' (1970a, p. 10), and scientific revolutions occur when 'an older paradigm is replaced in whole or in part by an incompatible new one' (1970a, p. 92). The pivotal notion here is that of a 'paradigm'. Kuhn takes paradigms to be 'universally recognized scientific achievements that for a time provide model problems and solutions to a community of practitioners' (1970a, p. viii); as such, they 'provide models from which spring particular coherent traditions of scientific research' (1970a, p. 10). However, Kuhn also uses 'paradigm' in the broader sense of a global theoretical structure embracing the 'network of commitments — conceptual, theoretical, instrumental, and methodological' (1970a, p. 42) of a normal research tradition.[5] Besides 'tell[ing] us different things about the population of the universe and about that population's behaviour', paradigms 'are the source of the methods, problem-field, and standards of solution accepted by any mature scientific community at any given time' (1970a, p. 103).

Revolutionary transition between paradigms is at the heart of Kuhn's account and is the point at which incommensurability enters. As it figures in Kuhn's account, incommensurability constitutes an impediment to choice of paradigm: 'Just because it is a transition between incommensurables, the transition between competing paradigms cannot be made a step at a time, forced by logic and neutral experience' (1970a, p. 150). Because of incommensurability, the decision between rival paradigms does not admit of a neat resolution. Kuhn likens the process of choice to a 'gestalt switch' (1970a, p. 150), and says 'the transfer of allegiance from paradigm to paradigm is a conversion experience' (1970a, p. 151).

The influence of incommensurability is mainly apparent in paradigm debate: 'the proponents of competing paradigms are always at least slightly at cross-purposes', and 'fail to make complete contact with each other's viewpoints' (1970a, p. 148). The incommensurability which thus besets paradigm debate is due 'collectively', Kuhn says, to the following three factors:

> [T]he proponents of competing paradigms will often disagree about the list of problems that any candidate for paradigm must resolve. Their standards or their definitions of science are not the same. (1970a, p. 148)

> Within the new paradigm, old terms, concepts, and experiments fall into new relationships one with the other. The inevitable result is ... a misunderstanding between the two competing schools... To make the transition to Einstein's universe, the whole conceptual web whose strands are space, time, matter, force, and so on, had to be shifted and laid down again on nature whole... Communication across the revolutionary divide is inevitably partial. (1970a, p. 149)

> In a sense that I am unable to explicate further, the proponents of competing paradigms practice their trades in different worlds... practicing in different worlds, the two groups of scientists see

different things when they look from the same point in the same direction. (1970a, p. 150)

Incommensurability thus emerges as a complex relation between paradigms consisting, at least, of standard variance, conceptual disparity, and theory dependence of observation.

The thesis that there may be no appeal to neutral observation and that standards of theory appraisal are internal to paradigm suggests a relativistic view of the epistemic merits of paradigms.[6] For if, in the absence of independent means of evaluating paradigms, a paradigm is to be assessed by standards dictated by the paradigm itself, such appraisal is relative to acceptance of paradigm. Yet Kuhn has subsequently resisted the charge of relativism, maintaining instead that there are shared scientific values independent of paradigms.[7] However, he insists that such values fail to unambiguously determine choice of theory. This enables him, in the 'Postscript', to restate the problem of deciding between paradigms:

> There is no neutral algorithm of theory-choice, no systematic decision procedure which, properly applied, must lead each individual in the group to the same decision. (1970a, p. 200)

Since Kuhn later separates such methodological issues from incommensurability proper, I will not pursue the theme of standard variation at this stage.[8] Instead, I will now focus upon the semantic and conceptual aspects of Kuhn's early account of incommensurability.

The second factor contributing to incommensurability involves change of conceptual apparatus: 'to make the transition to Einstein's universe, the whole conceptual web whose strands are space, time, matter, force, and so on, had to be shifted and laid down again on nature whole' (1970a, p. 149). Kuhn takes such conceptual change to prevent the laws of a displaced paradigm from being derived from the paradigm which replaces it.

Kuhn argues that the analogues of Newton's laws that follow from Einstein's physics as a special case are not identical with those laws. This is because the statements of Einsteinian versions of the laws employ relativistic concepts which 'represent Einsteinian space, time, and mass', and so differ in meaning from the statements which express Newton's laws:

> the physical referents of these Einsteinian concepts are by no means identical with those of the Newtonian concepts that bear the same name. (Newtonian mass is conserved; Einsteinian is convertible with energy. Only at low relative velocities may the

two be measured in the same way, and even then they must not be conceived to be the same.) Unless we change the definitions of the variables in the [Einsteinian versions of the laws], the statements we have derived are not Newtonian... [T]he argument has ... not done what it purported to do. It has not, that is, shown Newton's Laws to be a limiting case of Einstein's. For in the passage to the limit it is not only the forms of the laws that have changed. Simultaneously we have had to alter the fundamental structural elements of which the universe to which they apply is composed. (1970a, pp. 101-2)

This passage reveals a fundamental convergence between Kuhn's and Feyerabend's notions of incommensurability. As with Feyerabend's original use of the notion (1981b, pp. 62-9), Kuhn's argument against the derivation of Newton's laws from Einstein's is directed against the reductionist account of theory replacement. Indeed, since the failure of derivability is due to conceptual disparity between the theories, Kuhn's notion of incommensurability may even appear to coincide with Feyerabend's exactly.[9] The equivalence of their views is further suggested by the fact that Kuhn combines the claim of conceptual disparity with a rejection of the empiricists' neutral observation language (1970a, pp. 125-9). For this suggests that for Kuhn, as for Feyerabend, incommensurability does not consist simply in difference of the basic concepts of theories. It also involves dependence of the meaning of observational terms upon the theory in which they occur.

However, Kuhn later claimed only to have meant that part of the languages of incommensurable theories differ in meaning.[10] This attenuates the parallel between Kuhn's original notion of semantic incommensurability and Feyerabend's. For it suggests that the language used to report observations, while not being theory neutral, is only in part semantically variant between theories.

While this implies that incommensurable paradigms are not altogether unrelated semantically, Kuhn is sometimes drawn toward a far stronger thesis. This is apparent from the third constitutive element of incommensurability: viz., that 'proponents of competing paradigms practice their trades in different worlds' (1970a, p. 150). *The Structure of Scientific Revolutions* contains numerous comments to the effect that 'when paradigms change, the world itself changes with them' (1970a, p. 111), and 'after a revolution scientists work in a different world' (1970a, p. 135). Although the image of a 'world change' is usually qualified in some way, it suggests that the transition between incommensurable paradigms is a transition from the 'world' of one paradigm to the 'world' of another.

Often, such remarks are meant only to emphasize the influence of conceptual framework on perception, as in this comment on the failure to derive Newton's laws from Einstein's:

> the transition from Newtonian to Einsteinian mechanics illustrates with particular clarity the scientific revolution as a displacement of the conceptual network through which scientists view the world. (1970a, p. 102)

At other times, Kuhn intends the difference to go beyond difference of perception:

> paradigm changes do cause scientists to see the world of their research-engagement differently. In so far as their only recourse to that world is through what they see and do, we may want to say that after a revolution scientists are responding to a different world. (1970a, p. 111)

> in the absence of some recourse to that hypothetical fixed nature that he 'saw differently,' the principle of economy will urge us to say that after discovering oxygen Lavoisier worked in a different world. (1970a, p. 118)

In such passages, Kuhn seems inclined to view the world independent of scientific belief and perception as disposable.

Kuhn wishes to say that incommensurable paradigms present scientists with different 'visual gestalts' of the same world (cf. pp. 111-2). And he insists that 'though the world does not change with change of paradigm, the scientist afterward works in a different world' (1970a, p. 121). Yet his tendency to dispense with the world beyond the perceptual and epistemic states of the scientist strongly suggests that there is nothing over and above the 'world' presented by the gestalt of a paradigm, or at least that the world in itself is of no relevance to science. The tension between admitting an independent reality and discarding it is never clearly resolved in Kuhn's original account, and has resulted in the widespread impression that his version of incommensurability involves some form of idealism.[11]

However, the 'world change' image may also be interpreted in a weaker sense as expressing a thesis about reference. It may be taken as the idea that there is a major difference in reference between paradigms. This interpretation is suggested by Kuhn's previously quoted discussion of Newtonian and Einsteinian concepts (1970a, pp. 101-2). In that passage Kuhn asserts that 'the physical referents of these Einsteinian concepts are by no means identical with those of the

Newtonian concepts that bear the same name'. And he remarks that 'Newtonian mass is conserved; Einsteinian is convertible with energy', which suggests that the terms for mass in the two theories do not have the same reference. In the light of such remarks, the 'world change' image may be taken to mean that in the transition between incommensurable paradigms there is a wholesale change in what is referred to. Thus, talk of the 'world' of a theory may be construed as talk about the set of entities to whose existence the theory is committed and to which its terms purportedly refer.

In sum, not even the conceptual component of Kuhn's original diffuse notion of incommensurability admits of unified analysis. Paradigms which are incommensurable due to conceptual variance are not derivable from one another; in some sense, they may even be about different worlds; or perhaps they simply fail to have common reference. These disparate elements begin to coalesce during Kuhn's transitional phase, which we will now consider.

2.3 The transitional phase

In subsequent development of his views, three general points emerge as basic to Kuhn's position. First, direct comparison of theories requires their formulation in a common language: 'The point-by-point comparison of two successive theories demands a language into which at least the empirical consequences of both can be translated without loss or change' (1970b, p. 266). Second, no such common language is available: 'There is no neutral language into which both of the theories as well as the relevant data may be translated for purposes of comparison' (1979, p. 416). Third, exact translation between the languages of theories is impossible: 'translation of one theory into the language of another depends ... upon compromises ... whence incommensurability' (1976, p. 191). Thus, in clarifying incommensurability, the issue of translation failure between theories becomes the dominant theme.

Reflection on translation led Kuhn to draw a connection between incommensurability and Quine's thesis of the indeterminacy of translation.[12] Quine's thesis, in brief, is that 'manuals for translating one language into another can be set up in divergent ways, all compatible with the totality of speech dispositions, yet incompatible with one another' (Quine, 1960, p. 27). The thesis stems from a behaviourist critique of meaning: Quine holds that verbal behaviour leaves meaning indeterminate; and he denies that there are facts about meaning beyond what is evident in such behaviour. The key to the thesis is an indeterminacy in the reference of sortal predicates, as illustrated by Quine's imagined native word 'gavagai' (1960, p. 52). Quine argues that the reference of 'gavagai' is inscrutable: ostension does not determine whether it refers to rabbits, rabbit stages, or undetached rabbit parts (Quine, 1969, p. 30), while the translation of the native 'individuative apparatus' needed for fine discrimination of reference is also indeterminate (1969, p. 33). Inscrutability of reference renders the translation of sentences containing such terms indeterminate.

At times Kuhn draws support from the indeterminacy thesis. In arguing that translation 'always involves compromises', Kuhn cites Quine's discussion of indeterminacy as evidence that 'it is today a deep and open question what a perfect translation would be and how nearly an actual translation can approach the ideal' (1970b, p. 268). He appeals to Quine's 'gavagai' example to indicate the epistemological difficulties of translating a language with different concepts:

> Quine points out that, though the linguist engaged in radical translation can readily discover that his native informant utters 'Gavagai' because he has seen a rabbit, it is more difficult to discover how 'Gavagai' should be translated... Evidence relevant to choice among ... alternatives will emerge from further investigation, and the result will be a reasonable analytic hypothesis... But it will be only a hypothesis... [T]he result of any error may be later difficulties in communication; when it occurs, it will be far from clear whether the problem is with translation and, if so, where the root difficulty lies. (1970b, p. 268)

At a later stage, however, Kuhn seeks to distance his position from Quine's. In the following passage he explains how his views on reference and translation diverge from those of Quine:

> Unlike Quine, I do not believe that reference in natural or scientific languages is ultimately inscrutable, only that it is very difficult to discover and that one may never be absolutely certain one has succeeded. But identifying reference in a foreign language is not equivalent to producing a systematic translation manual for that language. Reference and translation are two problems, not one, and the two will not be resolved together. Translation always and necessarily involves imperfection and compromise; the best compromise for one purpose may not be the best for another; the able translator, moving through a single text, does not proceed fully systematically, but must repeatedly shift his choice of word and phrase, depending on which aspect of the original it seems most important to preserve. (1976, p. 191)

As opposed to Quine, Kuhn holds that while it may be determined what the terms of another language or theory refer to, they may prove not to be translatable in a faithful or uniform manner.

Kuhn's appeal to Quine is somewhat misleading, since it tends to suggest that incommensurability is a form of the indeterminacy of translation. For Quine, translation is indeterminate in the sense that there is no fact of the matter about how to translate from one language into another: indeterminacy means no sense can be made of correct translation. Kuhn's claim that translation involves compromise and imperfection runs counter to indeterminacy since it presupposes that, at least in principle, correct translation is possible: translation is only compromised if there is something to be right about.[13] As will become clear in the sequel, for Kuhn incommensurability implies failure of exact translation between theories: terms of one theory have meaning which cannot be expressed within the language of another theory. As such, the claim of incommensurability denies translation in a manner which is impossible if translation is indeterminate in Quine's sense.

Despite treating translation as the basic issue, Kuhn does not provide a detailed analysis of translation failure between theories during this transitional period. What little he does say amounts at most to a general indication of the cause and extent of such failure. Kuhn explains that translation is problematic, 'whether between theories or languages', because 'languages cut up the world in different ways' (1970b, p. 268). Theories employ different systems of 'ontological categories' (1970b, p. 270) in order to classify the objects in their domain of application. In the transition between theories classificatory schemes change:

> One aspect of every revolution is, then, that some of the similarity relations change. Objects which were grouped in the same set before are grouped in different sets afterwards and vice versa. Think of the sun, moon, Mars, and earth before and after Copernicus; of free fall, pendular, and planetary motion before and after Galileo; or of salts, alloys, and a sulphur-iron filing mix before and after Dalton. Since most objects within even the altered sets continue to be grouped together, the names of the sets are generally preserved. (1970b, p. 275)

Such categorial change involves change in the meaning, and even the reference,[14] of the retained terms:

> In the transition from one theory to the next words change their meanings or conditions of applicability in subtle ways. Though

> most of the same signs are used before and after a revolution — e.g. force, mass, element, compound, cell — the ways in which some of them attach to nature has somehow changed. Successive theories are thus ... incommensurable. (1970b, p. 267)

Since it is only some of the 'similarity-sets' that change, and only some terms 'attach to nature' differently, the translation failure resulting from such conceptual change is of limited scope.

Apart from the claim that translation between theories involves compromise and imperfection, Kuhn does little at this stage to clarify the semantic aspects of such translation failure. On occasion Kuhn oversimplifies the issue by writing as if change in meaning of retained terms were in itself sufficient for untranslatability. In the preceding quotation, for example, Kuhn's inference from change of meaning to incommensurability is direct and without qualification. Elsewhere he claims that scientists who 'perceive the same situation differently' while using common vocabulary 'must be using words differently', and hence speak from 'incommensurable viewpoints' (1970a, p. 200). Such a pattern of inference suggests that assigning different meanings to old terms is all that is required for incommensurability to occur.

But this makes the connection between change of meaning and incommensurability too direct. If incommensurability involves failure to translate from one theory into another, mere change in the meaning assigned to shared words does not in itself suffice for incommensurability. The point is simply that a vocabulary can undergo change of meaning without necessarily resulting in failure to translate. For one thing, such a change in the meaning of words can occur in a trivial manner: words may have their meanings switched around. A fixed stock of meanings may be reassigned to different terms of a given vocabulary without leading to translation failure between the alternative interpretations of the vocabulary.

Less trivially, single words with identical meanings are unnecessary for translation: translation need not be word-for-word. Even if there are terms in one language not matched by individual words the same in meaning in the other language, it may still be possible to translate them by combinations of terms, or phrases, of the other language. Hence a change in the meaning of some of the terms which are retained between theories need not lead to an inability to translate from the language of one theory into that of another.

The general point is that what is needed for translation failure is something more than mere change of meaning. At the very least, Kuhn's claim of partial translation failure requires an inability on the part of some theory to define terms which are employed within another theory.[15]

A further source of unclarity is Kuhn's treatment of the relation between translation and comparison of content. As we noted earlier, Kuhn takes 'point-by-point comparison' of theories to require formulation in a common language (1970b, p. 266). And he takes incommensurability to imply that theories are unable to be compared in such a manner:

> In applying the term 'incommensurability' to theories, I had intended only to insist that there was no common language within which both could be fully expressed and which could therefore be used in a point-by-point comparison between them. (1976, p. 191)

Yet Kuhn also denies that incommensurability is to be construed as incomparability:

> Most readers ... have supposed that when I spoke of theories as incommensurable, I meant that they could not be compared. But 'incommensurability' is a term borrowed from mathematics, and it there has no such implication. The hypotenuse of an isosceles right triangle is incommensurable with its side, but the two can be compared to any required degree of precision. What is lacking is not comparability but a unit of length in terms of which both can be measured directly and exactly. (1976, p. 191)

This is puzzling, for it raises the question of how the content of theories inexpressible in a common language can be compared, if not in point-by-point manner.[16]

However, while denying comparison in a common language, Kuhn notes that 'comparing theories ... demands only the identification of reference' (1976, p. 191), and that 'systematic theory comparison requires determination of the referents of incommensurable terms' (1976, p. 198, note 11). Although he fails to elaborate, Kuhn is implicitly contrasting 'point-by-point' comparison with comparison by means of reference. He does not explain what 'point-by-point' comparison is, but he seems to be operating with a distinction between direct comparison of statements expressed in a common vocabulary and comparison of statements which differ in meaning via overlapping reference.

More specifically, two theories which share a common vocabulary invariant in meaning may diverge simply with respect to the truth values they assign to a common set of statements. Such theories may be compared 'point-by-point' in the sense that one theory asserts precisely the same statement that the other denies. By contrast, theories expressed in vocabulary which is variant with respect to meaning may still be compared by means of overlapping reference. Such theories do not assert or deny a common set of statements. But even if their statements do not have the same meaning, they may be compared if the constituent terms of their statements have the same reference. Such a comparison fails to be 'point-by-point' because it does not consist in pairing a statement asserted by one theory with its denial drawn from another theory. It may also fail to be 'point-by-point' in another sense: since not all terms of one theory need co-refer with terms of the other, not all statements of the theories may be brought into conflict by means of relations of co-reference.[17]

To conclude discussion of Kuhn's middle period, recall the disparate elements of his original position mentioned earlier. Kuhn's original conception involved failure of derivation, 'world change' and wholesale change of reference. The picture which emerges from this transitional phase combines these elements in more coherent fashion. It remains the case that the central statements of a theory are not entailed by a theory with which it is incommensurable. But given Kuhn's restriction of change of meaning and reference to only some of a theory's terms, it follows that incommensurable theories share a modicum of semantically invariant vocabulary. As a result, there is neither complete change of reference, nor does the world which theories are about change. Thus, Kuhn's 'world change' image may be interpreted as change in the basic 'ontological categories' which different theories impose upon the world.[18]

2.4 Kuhn's later position

Incommensurability, as portrayed during Kuhn's middle period, involves partial translation failure between theories committed to different basic categories. Though such broad features of Kuhn's position subsequently remain unaltered, the details are refined in more recent work, especially his 'Commensurability, Comparability, Communicability' (1983). Kuhn's later position is characterized by a more nuanced account of translation failure and its connection with categorial change.

In 'Commensurability, Comparability, Communicability', Kuhn outlines a notion of 'local incommensurability' which he claims to have been his original idea.[19] Local incommensurability consists in failure to translate between localized clusters of interdefined terms:

> The claim that two theories are incommensurable is ... the claim that there is no language, neutral or otherwise, into which both theories, conceived as sets of sentences, can be translated without

residue or loss... Most of the terms common to the two theories function the same way in both; their meanings, whatever they may be, are preserved; their translation is simply homophonic. Only for a small subgroup of (usually interdefined) terms and for sentences containing them do problems of translatability arise. (1983, pp. 670-1)

So construed, incommensurability is a limited inability to translate from a local subgroup of terms of one theory into another local subgroup of terms of another theory. As such, language peripheral to the non-intertranslatable subgroups of terms constitutes semantic common ground between incommensurable theories. Hence, as Kuhn admits (1983, p. 671), at least part of the content of such theories may be directly compared.

Kuhn continues to link translation failure closely with change of classification, maintaining, as previously, that the membership classes of certain key categories are altered in the transition between incommensurable theories. Since the categories are interrelated, such changes are not isolated, but have a holistic effect:

> What characterizes revolutions is ... change in several of the taxonomic categories prerequisite to scientific descriptions and generalizations. That change, furthermore, is an adjustment not only of criteria relevant to categorization, but also of the way in which given objects and situations are distributed among pre-existing categories. Since such redistribution always involves more than one category and since those categories are interdefined, this sort of alteration is necessarily holistic. (1987, p. 20)

Kuhn explains, in his (1983, pp. 682-3), that languages and theories deploy sets of 'taxonomic categories' constitutive of 'taxonomic structures'. In translating between them, it is necessary to preserve categories; and, because of the interconnection of categories, intertranslatable languages must have the same taxonomic structure. Translation problems arise because 'different languages [and theories] impose different structures on the world' (1983, p. 682); for translation to succeed, 'taxonomy must ... be preserved to provide both shared categories and shared relationships between them' (1983, p. 683).

The holistic nature of category change is directly reflected in translation failure: the interconnection of categories is paralleled by the interdefinition of concepts. Kuhn illustrates this with examples, arguing, for instance, that while much language used in phlogistic chemistry is subsequently retained, 'a small group of terms remains for which the modern chemical vocabulary offers no equivalent' (1983,

p. 675). The residual terms, which include 'phlogiston' and its cognates, as well as 'element' and 'principle', constitute an interdefined cluster not definable within later theory. While Kuhn grants that various applications of such terms may be specified in the language of modern theory, he denies that translation is possible:

> Among the phrases which describe how the referents of the term 'phlogiston' are picked out are a number that include other untranslatable terms like 'principle' and 'element'. Together with 'phlogiston', they constitute an interrelated or interdefined set that must be acquired together, as a whole, before any of them can be used, applied to natural phenomena. Only after they have been thus acquired can one recognize eighteenth-century chemistry for what it was, a discipline that differed from its twentieth-century successor not simply in what it had to say about individual substances and processes but in the way it structured and parceled out a large part of the chemical world. (1983, p. 676)

Translation between such local complexes of terms fails because the meaning of such terms is determined in relation to other terms of the interdefined set. Terms which are defined within an integrated set of concepts cannot be translated in piecemeal fashion into an alternative complex in which the necessary conceptual relations do not obtain.

The notion of a localized translation failure between interdefined sets of terms is the central feature of Kuhn's later account of incommensurability and the most significant refinement of his position. As we saw earlier, the thesis of local incommensurability was neither developed in detail nor clearly evident in Kuhn's original discussion of the issue. While the local thesis is suggested obliquely during his middle period, explicit development of the local version constitutes a further step in the overall process of moderation which Kuhn's account of incommensurability has undergone.

Appendix: Incommensurability and the indeterminacy of translation

In a number of publications which date from the 1970s, Kuhn linked the thesis of the incommensurability of scientific theories with Quine's thesis of the indeterminacy of radical translation.[20] Kuhn's thesis is that 'there is no language, neutral or otherwise, into which both [of two incommensurable] theories, conceived as sets of sentences, can be translated without residue or loss'.[21] Quine's thesis, on the other hand, is that behavioural evidence available to a radical translator leaves the translation of alien utterances indeterminate.

In his later work, Kuhn tended to distance his position from Quine's. In his (1983), for example, he distinguishes translation between languages already known to the translator from interpretation of an initially unknown language.[22] In light of this distinction, he claims that 'Quine's "radical translator" is in fact an interpreter, and 'Gavagai' exemplifies the unintelligible material he starts from' (1983, p. 672). The task of such an interpreter is 'in the first instance ... [to] learn a new language', and 'whether that language can be translated into the one with which the interpreter began is an open question' (1983, p. 673). Kuhn also notes that Quine employs a 'theory of translation based on an extensional semantics', and argues that such a theory overlooks conceptual or intensional aspects of meaning which 'are what a perfect translation would preserve' (1983, p. 680). In making points such as these, Kuhn seems to suggest that the interpreter can discover meaning which goes beyond the evidence to which Quine restricts the radical translator, and that it is such meaning which escapes full translation between incommensurable theories.[23]

In this note I seek to establish the following result. The notion of translation failure of relevance to incommensurability is distinct from that of translational indeterminacy in Quine's sense; at most, Kuhnian incommensurability constitutes a weak form of indeterminacy, quite distinct from Quine's. This result lends support to Kuhn's later tendency to distance his position from Quine's. However, I will also suggest that it enables us to see a point of convergence between their views on translation which is perhaps the intended link between incommensurability and indeterminacy.

It follows from Kuhn's denial of full translation into a common language that there may be expressions of one theory which cannot be translated into the language of another. Thus, Kuhn claims that translation between languages fails while Quine says it is indeterminate. The connection is not immediately apparent. One link that might be suggested is that Kuhn's version of incommensurability is a form of Quinean indeterminacy which arises in translating between theories. However, I will now show that this suggestion is mistaken.

Quine considers the case of the linguist faced with determining the meaning of utterances of an unknown language from verbal response to visual stimulation. This leads him to the indeterminacy thesis: 'manuals for translating one language into another can be set up in divergent ways, all compatible with the totality of speech dispositions, yet incompatible with one another' (1960, p. 27). The thesis represents a behaviourist critique of meaning, for Quine holds not only that verbal behaviour fails to determine meaning, but that 'there is nothing to linguistic meaning ... beyond what is to be gleaned from overt behavior in observable circumstances' (1987, p. 5).

For Quine, therefore, there is more than one way to translate between languages: 'indeterminacy means not that there is no acceptable translation, but that there are many' (1987, p. 9). But this directly conflicts with incommensurability. For, strictly speaking, there is not even one translation between the languages of incommensurable theories. The incommensurability thesis would not appear therefore to be a form of Quine's indeterminacy thesis, since it contradicts the claim of translational indeterminacy.

But such emphasis on failure versus indeterminacy of translation may be misplaced, since the key issue raised by Quine is what is to count as admissible evidence for translation. Quine claims that there are multiple translations consistent with the evidence, which he construes as observed verbal behaviour. Kuhn's denial of full translation between incommensurable theories seems to imply that there can be no complete translation which is consistent with the evidence. The question arises of whether such translation failure is to be analyzed in terms of a Quinean assumption that behaviour is the only admissible evidence.

If the claim of incommensurability is construed as the claim that there is no translation consistent with the behavioural evidence, then the theses of indeterminacy and incommensurability do contradict one another, as before. For Quinean indeterminacy entails that multiple translations are consistent with the behavioural evidence. So, on a behaviourist construal, the incommensurability thesis denies indeterminacy, and cannot therefore be a form of Quinean indeterminacy.

If incommensurability is not analyzed in terms of behavioural evidence, a rather different picture emerges. The denial of translation between theories would then imply that there is more to meaning than is evident in behaviour, for it would appeal to a richer form of linguistic evidence. Moreover, the claim of translation failure would be consistent with the claim that verbal behaviour alone is insufficient to determine translation, since a different form of evidence would pertain to the denial of translation. Yet incommensurability would still differ from Quinean indeterminacy in at least three ways: it implies failure rather than indeterminacy of translation; it neither implies nor precludes that behaviour leaves meaning indeterminate; and it imposes no behaviourist constraint on meaning.

There remains a sense in which incommensurability entails translational indeterminacy, though it is not Quine's sense. Consider this passage in which Kuhn explains that translation can neither be faithful nor uniform.

> Translation always and necessarily involves imperfection and compromise; the best compromise for one purpose may not be the best for another; the able translator, moving through a single text, does not proceed fully systematically, but must repeatedly shift his choice of word and phrase, depending on which aspect of the original it seems most important to preserve. The translation of one theory into the language of another depends, I believe, upon compromises of the same sort, whence incommensurability. (1979, p. 191)

The idea of unavoidable compromise and imperfection suggests that, in the absence of exact translation, translation may be indeterminate in the sense that there may be a choice between imperfect translations. For example, it may be impossible to translate a word exactly, but possible to translate it in either of two equally inexact ways.

This form of indeterminacy must be sharply distinguished from Quine's. In the first place, such indeterminacy constitutes an indeterminacy between translations which diverge from correct translation to an equivalent (or near equivalent) degree. Quinean indeterminacy, on the other hand, constitutes an indeterminacy between translations which are fully consistent with the permissible linguistic evidence; it is therefore an indeterminacy between equally correct translations.

In the second place, Quinean indeterminacy implies that there is no fact of the matter (apart from facts about verbal behaviour) for translation to be right or wrong about. Such indeterminacy removes the presupposition of uniqueness which is crucial to the notion of a correct translation. Kuhn's claim that translation involves compromise and imperfection runs counter to Quinean indeterminacy since it presupposes the possibility, in principle, of correct translation. For a translation can only be compromised or imperfect if there is a fact of the matter for translation to be right or wrong about. Hence, the claim of incommensurability constitutes a denial of correct translation of a kind which would be impossible if translation were indeterminate in Quine's sense.

Finally I will consider a further suggestion about the link between incommensurability and Quinean indeterminacy which does not make the former a form of the latter. Notwithstanding the differences outlined above between indeterminacy and incommensurability, there remains a central point of convergence between the views of Kuhn and Quine with respect to translation. In particular, they both hold that there is no single adequate translation between languages, since for Kuhn there is not even one fully adequate translation, while for Quine there is more than one adequate translation. This parallel between their views might explain why Kuhn linked his view with Quine's.

Yet it must be stressed that such convergence does not draw the notions of incommensurability and indeterminacy of translation closer together. For Quine, an adequate translation is one which is consistent with overt verbal behaviour, while for Kuhn a correct translation is one which fully preserves meaning. As I pointed out above, Kuhn's untranslatability involves facts about meaning which do not feature in Quinean indeterminacy.

While this suggestion brings out a point of convergence, it also draws attention to a fundamental point of divergence. Quine's denial that there is more to meaning than manifested in overt verbal behaviour prevents him from saying that translation fails in Kuhn's sense. Kuhn cannot claim that there is nothing to meaning beyond what is evident in overt verbal behaviour, for he wishes to appeal to facts about meaning which lead to translation failure. Where Quine and Kuhn most fundamentally disagree, therefore, is with respect to the issue of whether overt verbal behaviour exhaustively manifests meaning.

Notes

1. Both Kuhn (1970a) and Feyerabend (1981b) originally appeared in 1962.
2. This essay was originally written before the appearance of a number of Kuhn's later writings on incommensurability. As a result, it fails to address several refinements which Kuhn introduced in those writings. However, I discuss these refinements in Chapters 3 and 4.
3. The main body of Kuhn's (1970a) is the source for his early position. The transitional phase is represented by the 'Postscript' to his (1970a), his (1970b), (1976) and (1979). His later position is found in his (1983), (1987) and (1989).
4. Kuhn's first main attempts at clarification were published around 1970. See the 'Postscript' to his (1970a) and his (1970b). Over the next ten years his discussion of incommensurability was confined to brief remarks in his (1976) and (1979).
5. The ambiguity of Kuhn's original use of 'paradigm' has been widely noted; see, for example, Shapere (1984b, p. 39) and Masterman (1970). Kuhn subsequently distinguished the paradigm as 'constellation of beliefs, values, techniques' from the

paradigm as 'shared exemplar', referring to them as 'disciplinary matrix' and 'exemplar' respectively; see the 'Postscript' to his (1970a) as well as his (1977b).

6. Kuhn's seeming denial of extraparadigmatic criteria of theory choice has seemed relativist and irrationalist to many commentators. See, for example, Scheffler (1967, pp. 74ff) and Shapere (1984b, p. 46).
7. Kuhn lists such cognitive values as accuracy, simplicity, fruitfulness, internal and external consistency; see his 'Postscript' (1970a, pp. 185, 199). He discusses the issues raised by differential weighting of values and variant application of the same value in his (1977c).
8. But see the essays in Parts IV and V.
9. Shapere, for example, explicitly equates their views, see his (1984c, p. 83); the equation is implicit in Scheffler (1967, pp. 49-50).
10. In later writings Kuhn is careful to specify that meaning variance is only partial, e.g. (1970b, p. 267). In the following remark he claims always to have meant this: '"some difference in some meanings of some words [theories] have in common" is the most I ever have intended to claim' (Kuhn, 1977d, p. 506). Yet it must be said that this was far from obvious in the original discussion in his (1970a).
11. For the charge of idealism see Scheffler (1967, p. 19); the issue is discussed at length in Nola (1980a). There is, however, strong textual evidence to show that Kuhn is not an idealist who rejects the existence of a reality independent of theory. As a number of authors have pointed out, Kuhn operates with a distinction between the changeable world of theory and nature or the environment, which remains stable between theories (1970a, pp. 111-2, 114, 125); see Brown (1983a, pp. 19-20 and 1983b, p. 97), Devitt (1984, p. 132) and Mandelbaum (1982, pp. 50-2). Yet this does not rule out a weaker form of idealism which contrasts the reality independent of theory with the changing and constructed reality experienced by the scientist.
12. Kuhn pointed to a parallel between incommensurability and translational indeterminacy on several occasions: e.g. (1970a, p. 202), (1970b, p. 268) and (1976, p. 191). Later, however, he distinguished the two notions sharply (1983, pp. 679-81); see also (1989, p. 11).
13. Admittedly, if there is a choice between incorrect translations, one might say that translation is indeterminate. But for Quine indeterminacy implies a choice between equally good translations, not a choice between equally bad ones. His point is that there are

numerous translations consistent with the linguistic evidence, not that there are none. For a full discussion of the contrast between Quinean indeterminacy and Kuhnian incommensurability see the Appendix to the present chapter.

14. For change of reference, cf. Kuhn's remarks that "the line separating the referents of the terms 'mixture' and 'compound' shifted; alloys were compound before Dalton, mixtures after" (1970b, p. 269).
15. The point that more than conceptual difference is required for incommensurability is made with reference to Kuhn by Feyerabend (1981f, p. 154, note 54).
16. Siegel points out that Kuhn's remarks appear self-contradictory: 'unless there is a substantive difference between "comparison" and "point-by-point" comparison, Kuhn is saying that incommensurable paradigms can be compared, but not compared "point-by-point". This is equivalent to saying that they can be compared, but not compared, which does little to illuminate Kuhn's position' (1987, p. 61). Siegel is right that Kuhn's discussion is imperspicuous. Yet he seemingly overlooks the 'substantive difference' provided by Kuhn's explicit mention of comparison by means of reference (see next paragraph in the text).
17. Kuhn's remarks about reference indicate acceptance on his part of the point, originally made in this context by Scheffler (1967), that reference suffices for comparison. This is further apparent in Kuhn (1979, pp. 412, 417) where, with some reservation, he endorses the causal theory of reference as a 'technique for tracing continuities between successive theories and ... for revealing the nature of the differences between them' (1979, pp. 416-7).
18. Cf. Hacking (1979), and Hoyningen-Huene (1989) and (1993, pp. 268-9).
19. Kuhn notes that 'the claim that two theories are incommensurable is more modest than many of its critics have supposed', and says that 'insofar as incommensurability was a claim about language, about meaning change, its local form is my original version' (1983, p. 671). Suffice it to say that, while this may very well have been what he originally intended, it is not what he originally conveyed.
20. Kuhn drew the connection in several places, e.g. (1970a, p. 202), (1970b, p. 268) and (1976, p. 191). Feyerabend, the co-sponsor of the thesis, made no such link; cf. his (1975, p. 287).
21. Kuhn (1983, p. 670). For similar characterizations of incommensurability, see Kuhn (1976, p. 191) and (1979, p. 416). It should be stressed that Kuhn's notion of incommensurability involves only limited translation failure between subsets of the

vocabulary used by theories; cf. his remarks on local incommensurability (1983, pp. 670-1).

22. For further discussion of the issues connected with the distinction between translating and interpreting a language, see Section 5.3 and Chapter 6.
23. Elsewhere Kuhn suggests that 'Quine's arguments for the indeterminacy of translation can, with equal force, be directed to an opposite conclusion: instead of there being an infinite number of translations compatible with all normal dispositions to speech behavior, there are often none at all' (1989, p. 11). While this remark rightly contrasts untranslatability with indeterminacy, it is unclear how Quine's arguments can be directed to such a conclusion without placing a construal on 'dispositions to speech behavior' not in keeping with Quine's behaviourism. In any case, Kuhn resists Quine's 'abandon[ment of] traditional notions of meaning', and abandons instead the idea that 'anything expressible in one language ... can be expressed also in any other' (1989, p. 11). Perhaps the resulting untranslatability would conform to the non-Quinean indeterminacy sketched below.

3 Kuhn's ontological relativism

3.1 Introduction

Ever since Kuhn first proposed his model of scientific theory change, relativism, in one form or another, has been associated with his work. There has, for example, been widespread discussion of Kuhn's suggestion that scientific rationality varies relative to the changing rules and standards employed by different paradigms.[1] There has also been much discussion of his account of conceptual change in science by philosophers who saw in it an extreme conceptual relativism of radically incommensurable conceptual schemes.[2] Yet in later years Kuhn retreated from many of the claims which were responsible for these earlier reactions to his position.[3] His later work presents instead an ontological form of relativism, which involves an antirealist denial of objective natural kinds.[4]

According to the new position which began to take shape late in Kuhn's career, scientific theories are the source of alternative sets of taxonomic categories which are imposed by theories on the world. A set of such categories constitutes a localized complex of interconnected concepts, such that terms for such categories are unable to be translated from one set of categories into another such set. Rather than reflecting reality, these categories constitute, at most, ways of ordering experience; such categories do not reflect reality because it is not possible to do so. Given that there is no objectively right way to represent the world, and that the sets of categories imposed on the world vary with theory, there is a sense in which, as theories change, the world changes with them.

As we saw in Chapter 2, in *The Structure of Scientific Revolutions*, Kuhn distinguished three forms of incommensurability between paradigms.[5] The first is a methodological form of incommensurability which arises because rival paradigms address different sets of problems, and apply different methodological standards in evaluating their solution. Second is a semantic form of incommensurability which is due to variation in the conceptual apparatus deployed by alternative paradigms. The third sense of incommensurability is an ontological form of incommensurability, which Kuhn describes by saying that 'proponents of competing paradigms practice their trades in different worlds' (1970a, p. 150).

These three forms of incommensurability correspond to the three forms of relativism which I distinguished above. Methodological incommensurability has been widely discussed in connection with rational scientific theory choice and relativism due to variation of methodological standards.[6] Semantic forms of incommensurability have been dealt with in the literature on meaning variance, referential stability, and the intelligibility of alternative conceptual schemes.[7] Incommensurability of an ontological variety has received relatively little attention. Yet, given Kuhn's recent development of an ontological form of relativism, there appears to be a return to this third form of incommensurability in Kuhn's later work.

The aim of this chapter is both to document Kuhn's move away from conceptual relativism and rationality relativism, and to provide an analysis of his later tendency toward an ontological form of relativism. I will start by discussing Kuhn's shift away from a relativistic stance about rationality and conceptual schemes. I will then turn to matters of ontology by considering Kuhn's earlier idealist sounding talk of world change and his later idea of changes in the taxonomic categories which theories impose on the world.

3.2 Relativism about rationality

In *The Structure of Scientific Revolutions*, Kuhn made a number of claims about methodological standards, which, when taken together, suggested that the rationality of scientists' epistemic choices is relative to operative paradigm. He claimed that paradigms 'are the source of the methods, problem-field, and standards of solution accepted by any mature scientific community at any given time' (1970a, p. 103). Because of the paradigm dependence of methodology, 'when paradigms change, there are usually significant shifts in the criteria determining the legitimacy of problems and of proposed solutions' (1970a, p. 109). Such criteria and standards cannot, however, be applied to the choice between paradigms, since 'the choice is not and cannot be determined merely by the evaluative procedures characteristic of normal science' (1970a, p. 94). Yet there are no extraparadigmatic standards to govern this choice, since, 'as in political revolutions, so in paradigm choice — there is no standard higher than the assent of the relevant community' (1970a, p. 94).

Critics were quick to object to this combination of the paradigm dependence of methodological standards and the absence of extra-paradigmatic standards. Popper saw Kuhn as an advocate of the 'myth of the framework', according to which 'the rationality of science presupposes a common framework', so that rational choice and communication break down in the absence of a shared framework provided by a paradigm (1970, p. 56).[8] On Lakatos's interpretation of Kuhn, 'each paradigm contains its own standards' and 'there are no super-paradigmatic standards', hence '*scientific revolution is irrational, a matter for mob psychology*' (1970, p. 178). While for Siegel, Kuhn's 'irrationalist portrayal of theory choice makes scientific knowledge relative as well, since judgments of factual and theoretical adequacy are on this picture relative to the incompatible criteria of evaluation fostered by rival paradigms' (1987, p. 54).

The key relativist tendency in Kuhn's position detected by these critics centers upon the combination of the claim of paradigm dependent evaluative criteria with the denial of higher order criteria. For without any possible appeal to paradigm independent criteria of theory choice by means of which to decide between paradigms, there may be no objective, rational basis for the decision to accept one paradigm over another. Thus, if there is any sense in which scientific practice and theory acceptance may be rational, it can at most be dependent on the operative standards of normal science, which vary with and are internal to paradigms. As a result, rationality in science is relative to accepted paradigm, while the decision between paradigms cannot be made on rational grounds.

The relativist tendency of Kuhn's original position is so pronounced that some of those sympathetic to Kuhn have attempted to defend him by presenting a more defensible version of relativism. Gerald Doppelt, for example, criticizes the conceptual relativist interpretation of Kuhn which is presented by Scheffler and Shapere, only to provide a novel interpretation of 'Kuhn's epistemological relativism' (Doppelt, 1982). Doppelt objects to the undue emphasis placed on Kuhn's meaning variance thesis in Shapere's and Scheffler's interpretation, and draws attention instead to the extent to which the problems dealt with by paradigms are incorporated into the evaluative standards employed by scientists. According to Doppelt's interpretation of Kuhn, the incommensurability of paradigms is due to variation in their problem solving agendas, and rationality is relative to paradigm because scientists' standards of evaluation depend on these agendas.

By the early 1970s, however, an apparent change of stance can be found in Kuhn's writings. In several publications dating from about 1970, Kuhn insists on the existence of generally applicable methodological criteria, allows an active yet limited role for rational argument in scientific theory choice, and rejects a mechanical or algorithmic view of such choice.[9] This modified position is developed at greatest length in 'Objectivity, Value Judgment and Theory Choice' (1977c), where Kuhn claims that there is a partially shifting, though broadly invariant set of methodological criteria, which function as values rather than as rules, and which serve to guide or influence scientists in their choices of theory (1977c, pp. 322-5, 335). The set of values he describes (e.g., accuracy, consistency, simplicity) does not, however, unequivocally determine choice between theories, since the values may conflict in application and are not preferentially ordered. Moreover, Kuhn claims, particular values may be subject to variant interpretation, and so do not even themselves yield unambiguous choice of theory.

In the years after publication of *The Structure of Scientific Revolutions*, then, Kuhn progressively moved away from the relativism about scientific rationality which characterized his original position. The position he later developed is one according to which rational factors play an important role in choice between scientific theories, though there are limitations on what rational argument can achieve in the course of such decisions. These limitations are in part due to the intrinsic inability of the various applicable methodological criteria to unambiguously determine choice in favour of one theory as opposed to an alternative. While there is, on this later view, scope for rational disagreement between advocates of rival paradigms, the position avoids a radical relativization of scientific rationality to variant methodological standards which are entirely dependent on paradigm. This successive weakening of his position about rationality is paralleled by a similar weakening of Kuhn's treatment of semantic incommensurability.

3.3 Conceptual relativism

A second form of relativism often attributed to Kuhn is the doctrine sometimes referred to as 'conceptual relativism'.[10] In relation to Kuhn's model of scientific theory change, this doctrine is usually associated with the ideas of meaning variance and semantic incommensurability.[11] Kuhn holds that, in revolutionary transition between paradigms, there is 'a need to change the meaning of established and familiar concepts', which leads to a 'displacement of the conceptual network through which scientists view the world' (1970a, p. 102). A number of different consequences have been held to flow from such meaning variance, such as the inability to translate or communicate between theories, absence of overlap between the consequences of theories and incomparability of theoretical content.[12]

The doctrine of conceptual relativism may be formulated in a variety of different ways. Davidson, for example, presents it as the thesis that there may be totally untranslatable languages, to which reality and truth are relative (cf. Davidson, 1984). However, a version of conceptual relativism appropriate to Kuhn's model requires a close connection between paradigms and the conceptual apparatus which they employ. For, on Kuhn's model, significant conceptual variation occurs in the transition between paradigms, with the result that rival paradigms are the source of divergent conceptual schemes. In light of Kuhn's frequent remarks to the effect that 'when paradigms change, the world itself changes with them' (1970a, p. 111) and that in the transition between paradigms a 'whole conceptual web' had to be 'shifted and laid down again on nature whole' (1970a, p. 149), it is tempting to interpret the conceptual variation involved in paradigm change as a profound change resulting in replacement of an entire conceptual scheme.

If paradigm change is taken to involve wholesale displacement of conceptual scheme, semantic incommensurability may be interpreted as radical incomparability of paradigms due to conceptual disparity. On such an interpretation, there is translation failure between the languages employed by rival paradigms, as well as communication failure between the adherents of such paradigms. As a result of translation failure, incommensurable paradigms are incomparable for content, since no consequence of one paradigm may be matched against an identical consequence of a rival paradigm or the negation of such a consequence. Moreover, the conflict between paradigms which are incomparable for content may not be resolved by means of empirical test, since such paradigms share no observational consequences in common. Indeed, given that observation is itself thoroughly impregnated by theoretical assumptions originating from background paradigm, the very possibility of objective empirical evidence for or against a theory is thrown into serious doubt. Ultimately, the ideas of objective truth and reality also come under threat. For without the possibility of an objective test or comparative evaluation of paradigms, the prospects of obtaining an accurate reflection of theory transcendent reality seem poor.

It is doubtful that Kuhn ever meant to endorse such a radical conceptual relativism. Nevertheless, a number of Kuhn's philosophical commentators have taken such relativism to be a central feature of his work, and have objected to it accordingly. In several influential articles, Dudley Shapere traces the relativism he attributes to Kuhn to the incomparability of paradigms due to meaning variance, and objects that such incomparability makes it inexplicable how incommensurable paradigms are able to constitute genuine rivals.[13] Moreover, in his all out attack on conceptual relativism and the dualism of conceptual scheme and empirical content on which it depends, Donald Davidson places Kuhn among a group of thinkers who are in the clutches of the conceptual scheme idea (Davidson, 1984). In the course of his attack, Davidson raises a number of objections to conceptual relativism, the main thrust of which is to seriously challenge the idea that we may coherently conceive of the possibility of a totally untranslatable language.[14]

Apart from the occasional remark denying total variation of meaning,[15] Kuhn himself shed little light on the issue of conceptual relativism until the early 1980s. In his paper 'Commensurability, Comparability, Communicability' (1983), Kuhn explicitly addresses objections of incoherence raised against the incommensurability thesis by authors such as Davidson and Shapere. Instead of a relativism of radically incommensurable conceptual schemes, Kuhn there endorses a thesis of 'local incommensurability'. According to this thesis, there may be localized failure of exact translation, within the context of an inclusive natural language, between the special languages employed by theories. Such languages, or better, sublanguages, contain complexes of terms, which are holistically interdefined, and which are unable to be translated in piecemeal fashion into another complex of terms in which the relevant semantic relations do not obtain.

The restricted untranslatability thesis enables Kuhn to meet Shapere's rivalry objection, since language peripheral to non-intertranslatable complexes of terms provides sufficient common ground for partial comparison of the content of theories. It also enables Kuhn to meet a key objection of Davidson's that the argument for translation failure typically proceeds within the very language into which translation allegedly fails.[16] For one may argue, within some fragment of a background natural language taken as metalanguage, that a pair of alternative theoretical sublanguages fails to be intertranslatable.[17]

While the local version of the incommensurability thesis permits Kuhn to avoid radical conceptual relativism and various associated objections, the account he offers of the reasons for translation failure contains the seeds of his ontological relativism. For, as I will show in

Section 3.5, Kuhn claims that translation fails due to variation in the taxonomic structures which theories impose on the world. Before turning to that topic, however, I will discuss Kuhn's idealist sounding talk of world changes in his earlier work.

3.4 The world change image

The Structure of Scientific Revolutions contains numerous suggestions that, in a sense Kuhn does not fully specify, the world itself changes in the transition between competing paradigms. Kuhn remarks, for instance, that a historian considering past science might be inclined to say that 'when paradigms change, the world itself changes with them', for 'it is rather as if the professional community had been suddenly transported to another planet' (1970a, p. 111). Remarks such as these are accompanied by talk of new entities coming into existence and scientists seeing different things when they observe the world. For example, Kuhn says that 'pendulums were brought into existence by something very like a paradigm-induced gestalt switch' (1970a, p. 120), and 'Lavoisier ... saw oxygen where Priestley had seen dephlogisticated air' (1970a, p. 118).

Although Kuhn's use of the image of a world change is usually qualified,[18] philosophical critics nevertheless detected a strong idealistic tendency in his views.[19] However, this was not entirely due to Kuhn's use of the world change image. Kuhn endorsed a strong version of the thesis of theory dependence of observation, and denied that empirical factors determine choice of theory. This created the impression that reality does little to constrain theory on his model of science. In addition, the apparent conceptual relativism of Kuhn's original model portrayed scientists as if they were cut off from reality and isolated within radically variant conceptual schemes. Thus, rather than the world change image by itself, it is Kuhn's use of the image conjoined with the anti-empirical, conceptual relativist flavour of his model, which suggests idealism. For they present a picture of science on which a drastically reduced role is played by an independent reality external to human thought and experience.

Such a denial of a role to external reality is consistent with two forms of idealism. The first form of idealism is a mentalistic doctrine which denies altogether the existence of an independent reality beyond thought and experience. There are, however, strong grounds against attributing this form of idealism to Kuhn, since, as has been argued by a number of authors, Kuhn assumes the existence of an independent reality throughout his work.[20] The assumption of such a reality is consistent with a second, 'constructivist' form of idealism, which admits an independent reality but denies the possibility of epistemic access to it. The latter doctrine is a broadly Kantian position, according to which, despite the impinging of external reality on us in sense perception, the world inhabited by human cognizers is at least partly constituted by our own conceptual contribution.

On such a constructivist reading of Kuhn's metaphysical stance, different 'phenomenal worlds' (to use a phrase borrowed from Paul Hoyningen-Huene[21]) are constituted by the conceptual schemes of alternative paradigms. Thus, in the transition between paradigms, the phenomenal world of one paradigm is exchanged for the phenomenal world of another. While the phenomenal world of a paradigm is not reality itself, since reality is inaccessible, the phenomenal world with which a scientist is epistemically engaged depends on the paradigm accepted by the scientist. Such a constructivist reading of Kuhn, therefore, yields a sense in which the way the world is is relative to operative paradigm.

3.5 Taxonomic change and translation failure

The third, ontological, strand of relativism has been a persistent theme throughout Kuhn's work. As we have just seen, the idea that how the world is is somehow relative to paradigm was already present in his idealistic handling of the world change image in *The Structure of Scientific Revolutions*. However, in Kuhn's later work the idea has taken on a novel form as Kuhn has developed the idea that scientific revolution involves changes of taxonomic categories.

Since the early 1970s, Kuhn has repeatedly stressed that scientific revolutions produce changes in the systems of classification employed by scientists. Here I quote an early statement of his view, though numerous similar passages might be cited from his more recent work:[22]

> One aspect of every revolution is, then, that some of the similarity relations change. Objects which were grouped in the same set before are grouped in different sets afterwards and *vice versa*. Think of the sun, moon, Mars, and earth before and after Copernicus; of free fall, pendular, and planetary motion before and after Galileo; or of salts, alloys, and a sulphur-iron filing mix before and after Dalton. Since most objects within even the altered sets continue to be grouped together, the names of the sets are generally preserved. (1970b, p. 275)

Thus, a scientific revolution is not merely a transition between theories which make conflicting claims about entities which they classify in the same way. Rather, entities which are classified as belonging to one category by one theory may be classified as belonging to a different category by another theory. This is because the explanatory purposes of a theory may be best served by classifying the entities in its domain of application differently from previous theories, as, for example, classifying the Earth as a planet served the explanatory purposes of Copernican astronomy.

A number of important features of Kuhn's view of categorial change may be gleaned from the above quotation. First, the categorial change at issue is not a wholesale displacement of classificatory framework. Rather, change in membership is restricted to only some categories within a classificational system. Second, change of category membership is not restricted to redistribution of individual objects among different classes. Rather, sets, or perhaps kinds, of objects may also be assigned to new categories, as, for example, the alloys were shifted from the class of compounds to the class of mixtures (Kuhn, 1970b, p. 269). Third, it is possible to identify at least some of the objects and sets of objects as the same things across classificatory schemes. Thus, there is a common, or at least a broadly overlapping, domain of objects and sets of objects, which is shared between alternative theoretical systems of classification.

Kuhn's views about categorial change have important semantic consequences for the categorial expressions or kind terms implicated in such change. To the extent that there is retention of terminology across classificatory change, there may be extensional, as well as intensional, variation affecting such terminology. As Kuhn comments,

> ... the distinctive character of revolutionary change in language is that it alters not only the criteria by which terms attach to nature but also, massively, the set of objects or situations to which those terms attach. (1987, p. 19)

Because such semantic change involves membership redistribution among interconnected categories, such change is not isolated, but has a holistic effect:

> What characterizes revolutions is, thus, change in several of the taxonomic categories prerequisite to scientific descriptions and generalizations. That change, furthermore, is an adjustment not only of criteria relevant to categorization, but also of the way in which given objects and situations are distributed among preexisting categories. Since such redistribution always involves

more than one category and since those categories are interdefined, this sort of alteration is necessarily holistic. (1987, p. 20)

The holistic nature of the changes brought about by categorial change is, according to Kuhn, directly responsible for failure to translate from the language of one theory into the language of another.

Where I have just spoken of the language of a theory, Kuhn now tends to speak of a lexicon.[23] A lexicon is a 'structured vocabulary' (1990, p. 300), which incorporates a taxonomic structure that is employed in describing the world.[24] Such a taxonomy, which Kuhn sometimes calls a 'lexical structure', is what provides the 'invariants of translation' (1983, pp. 682-3). For, in order to translate a word from the lexicon of one theory into the lexicon of another, there must be a 'homology of lexical structure' (1983, p. 683).[25] Because items are redistributed among categories in revolutionary transition between theories, the categories of one theory are unable to be mapped onto the categories of another. Translation fails because the meaning of a name for a given category depends upon terms which refer to other categories within the taxonomy. Because of the holistic way in which such terms are interdefined, they are unable to be translated into a 'lexical structure' which employs a variant categorial system.[26]

Within the philosophical literature on semantic incommensurability, the claim of meaning variance has met with less resistance than has the claim of referential variance. Thus, a philosopher sympathetic to the claim that terms may shift their meaning in the transition between theories, might nevertheless object to Kuhn's claim that the names of taxonomic categories change their reference in scientific revolutions. For, as has been argued by advocates of the causal theory of reference, the reference of natural kind terms may be fixed, independently of theoretical descriptions of the kinds to which they refer, by means of direct causal relations with members of such kinds.[27] Thus, it might be thought that Kuhn's thesis of translation failure between theories is objectionable because it mistakenly rests on a thesis of the referential variance of natural kind terms.

However, Kuhn's thesis of categorial change is not on as shaky ground as this may suggest. The application to science of the idea of non-descriptive reference fixing at initial naming ceremonies has proven deeply problematic in the context of theoretical terminology. Rather than reference being fixed once and for all at initial naming ceremonies, the reference of terms used in science is subject to variation, and there tends instead to be a shift in the pattern of groundings by which terms are applied to their referents.[28] Moreover, it is necessary to incorporate into the causal theory a role for descriptions in securing reference to unobservable entities, which creates the potential for variation in the reference of theoretical terms with significant variation in descriptive content.[29] Given the need to allow reference change subsequent to original term introduction and to grant a reference determining role to descriptions, the causal theory does not provide a basis on which to reject Kuhn's thesis of referential variance in the course of scientific revolution.

Yet, while there may be reasons internal to the theory of reference for thinking Kuhn's reference change thesis is defensible, the significance of such change to Kuhn's philosophical position is not confined to merely semantic issues. In particular, as I will now argue, his thesis of change of taxonomic structure plays a major role in his ontological relativist position, according to which the existence of natural kinds or categories is relative to the phenomenal world of a theory. In preparation for that topic, I will now discuss Ian Hacking's suggestion that Kuhn's position amounts to a new form of nominalism.

3.6 Revolutionary transcendental nominalism

Ian Hacking has suggested, in a number of places,[30] that Kuhn's views on the nature of scientific categorization amount to a form of nominalism, which he calls 'revolutionary transcendental nominalism' (Hacking, 1983, p. 111). On such an interpretation, Kuhn is not to be read as an idealist who denies that there is a reality existing independently of human thought. Rather, Kuhn denies that the kinds to which individual things belong have any existence prior to thought.

There are, of course, a number of different versions of nominalism. The common thread running through all such versions of nominalism is the thesis that all that exists are individual objects, or, as they are usually called, particulars. Conversely, there are neither Platonic forms existing over and above particulars, nor — which is of greater relevance in the present context — do the kinds or categories to which individual objects belong have any existence independently of human classificatory activity. Understood in a strict sense, nominalism is a distinct doctrine from idealism or constructive idealism. For, rather than deny the mind independent existence of reality or of objects, nominalism denies only that the classification of objects into kinds may represent kinds which exist independently of the mental.

As we saw in the previous section, Kuhn holds that the changes of classificatory scheme which take place in scientific revolution are partial rather than total. Hacking's nominalist rendering of Kuhn preserves this aspect of Kuhn's position:

> Kuhn like some other contemporaries might be called an empirical realist and transcendental nominalist. That is, a great many of our commonplace sortings are a given fact of the interactions of any human group and the world in which it lives. That is the empirical realism... [According to] transcendental nominalism, there is not some uniquely right conceptualization of the world, nor is the world of itself constituted by more than merely superficial "kinds of things." The "kinds" that enter our theoretical speculations are man-made ... (Hacking, 1979, p. 230)

Thus, according to Hacking, Kuhn is an 'empirical realist' because he grants the existence of 'commonplace' kinds:

> many of our prescientific categories *are* natural kinds: people and grass, flesh and horseflesh. The world simply does have horses and grass in it, no matter what we think, and any conceptual scheme will acknowledge that. (1983, p. 110)

However, at a level which transcends such ordinary empirical groupings of things, the world is not itself divided up into kinds of things; at the transempirical level, kinds depend on human classificatory activity. Such a combination of realism and nominalism fits nicely with Kuhn's example of the alloys; they constitute an empirical kind which survives alteration of the higher level categories of compound and mixture (Kuhn, 1970b, p. 269).

A second feature of Hacking's interpretation which accords well with Kuhn involves the instability of transempirical kinds. For Hacking argues that, unlike the classical nominalist, Kuhn holds that human imposed categorial schemes are subject to revision in the course of scientific revolution. This is why Kuhn's is a 'revolutionary' form of transcendental nominalism.

> The old-fashioned nominalist of times gone by held that our systems of classification are products of the human mind. But he did not suppose that they could be radically altered. Kuhn has changed all that. The categories have been altered and may be altered again. (Hacking, 1983, p. 110)

Thus, on the overall picture which emerges from Hacking's reading of Kuhn, while there are empirical kinds, transempirical kinds depend on human classificatory activity, and are subject to variation with change of theory.[31]

Hacking's nominalist rendering of Kuhn permits a novel reading of Kuhn's world change image. For while the world itself may not change, the world of kinds may do so:

> The world does not change, but we work in a new world. The world that does not change is a world of individuals. The world in and with which we work is a world of kinds. The latter changes; the former does not. After a scientific revolution, the scientist works in a world of new kinds. (1993, p. 306)

Since the world of individual objects is unaltered by change of theory, there is a robust sense in which the world is stable. Yet since we must think and interact with the world in terms of categories supplied by us, the world of kinds which we inhabit is a world in flux.

There is, I think, a great deal to be said for Hacking's interpretation of Kuhn as a kind of nominalist. It fits well with much that Kuhn has said about the metaphysics and semantics of paradigm change, particularly with his suggestion that there may be taxonomic change with change of theory, and it makes plausible sense of the world change image. Yet, despite Kuhn's commitment to partial continuity of objects and kinds across categorial change, which we saw in the previous section, there remains in Kuhn's work a strong tendency toward the mind dependence of objects. Recently, for instance, Kuhn suggested that the individuation of things as objects depends on our application of sortal concepts which permit the identification of particular objects.[32] And he has explicitly responded to Hacking that the latter's

> nominalist version of my position — that there are real individuals out there, and we divide them into kinds at will — does not quite face my problems ... I need a notion of 'kinds' ... that will populate the world as well as divide up a preexisting population. (1993, p. 316)

It therefore appears that Kuhn's position differs from Hacking's nominalist interpretation of it by denying that individual objects are to be conceived as existing entirely independently of human conceptual activity.

Nevertheless, Kuhn's apparent commitment to the view that there are both individual objects (e.g., the sun, moon and Earth) and kinds (e.g., alloys, salts), which survive variation of higher order category (e.g., planet, compound), suggests an intermediate view. While ultimately objects and kinds depend for their individuation upon classification, lower level empirical objects and kinds tend, on the whole, to survive changes in higher order, theoretical classification. Thus, Kuhn's transcendental nominalism is combined with a mitigated empirical realism, according to which low level objects and kinds, though by and large resistant to change, are classification dependent.[33]

3.7 Ontological relativism

On the interpretation of Kuhn's ontological relativism which I wish to propose, Hacking's transcendental nominalism provides a key element of Kuhn's position. According to transcendental nominalism, beyond the level of commonplace empirical groupings, the world does not itself contain divisions between naturally occurring kinds of things. Rather, classification of the transempirical world into taxonomic kinds depends entirely on human conceptual contribution. Such classificational systems are developed in the course of scientific theorizing, and they are subject to revision in the transition between theories.

It is tempting to suppose that, according to such nominalism, how the world is differentiated into natural kinds depends on and is relative to categorial scheme. If this were so, then natural kinds would be brought into being by different categorial schemes, so that in the transition between such schemes there is an actual transformation in the way the world itself is constituted. Where formerly the world was itself divided into one set of kinds, later it is divided into a different set of kinds. On such an interpretation of nominalism, there is a robust sense in which the world changes with change of paradigm, and in which the taxonomic structure of the world varies relative to categorial scheme.

There does not, however, appear to be any basis for attributing such a doctrine of the mental differentiation of reality itself to Kuhn. Kuhn denies that the natural kinds picked out by our classificatory schemes have any existence independently of human conceptual activity. And he claims that scientists impose their classificatory schemes upon the world. But he does not hold that the imposition of such schemes transforms reality itself, in the sense of bringing a new set of natural kinds into existence.

Rather, Kuhn's metaphysical stance is a Kantian one close to that I earlier described as constructivism.[34] On such a view, there is indeed a reality independent of all human mental activity. But such a reality is, Kuhn says, 'ineffable, undescribable, undiscussible' (1991a, p. 12). Presumably, it is also largely, if not entirely, unknowable (cf. 1979, p. 418). Instead of such a thoroughly mind independent reality, the world experienced by humans is a 'phenomenal world' (to use

Hoyningen-Huene's phrase once again) that is a joint product of sensory input, deriving ultimately from reality itself,[35] and of our human conceptual contribution. Such a phenomenal world is a constructed world which contains the kinds of entities which are described by the categorial scheme of the operative theory (cf. 1979, p. 418).

It must be emphasized that Kuhn's view is not that the phenomenal world experienced by the scientist is entirely produced by the categorial scheme of a theory. Rather, the taxonomic categories of the scheme provide a structure for possible experience:

> Insofar as the structure of the world can be experienced and the experience communicated, it is constrained by the structure of the lexicon of the community which inhabits it. (1991a, p. 10)

The idea that the lexicon provides a structure which constrains experience is, as Kuhn notes, heavily Kantian: 'like the Kantian categories, the lexicon supplies preconditions of possible experience' (1991a, p. 12). And again,

> Both [lexical structures and Kant's *a priori* categories] are constitutive of *possible experience* of the world, but neither dictates what that experience must be. Rather they are constitutive of the infinite range of possible experiences that might conceivably occur in the actual world to which they give access. (1993, p. 331)

Thus, Kuhn's position is one on which the manner in which incoming sensory input is experienced is determined by categorial scheme, and so the phenomenal world of the scientist varies relative to operative categorial scheme.

Such constructivist variation of phenomenal world with categorial scheme, combined with the transcendental nominalist rejection of mind independent transempirical kinds, provides the basis for my reading of Kuhn's ontological relativism. This interpretation of Kuhn takes over from transcendental nominalism the thesis that there are no higher level transempirical natural kinds for the categorial schemes of theories to reflect accurately or inaccurately. And it conjoins with such nominalism the constructivist thesis that the phenomenal world experienced by the scientist depends on the categorial scheme of the theory employed by the scientist.

On the metaphysical picture yielded by this combination of nominalism and constructivism, the taxonomic structure of the phenomenal world of a theory depends on the categorial scheme employed by the theory. As a result, the phenomenal worlds of scientific theories associated with different categorial schemes contain divergent systems of natural kinds. Thus, the set of natural kinds constitutive of the taxonomic structure of the phenomenal world of a theory depends on the categorial scheme of the theory. Given that such phenomenal worlds vary relative to the categorial scheme of operative theory, the existence of a set of natural kinds which populates the phenomenal world of the scientist is therefore a form of existence which is relative to prior choice of scientific theory.

3.8 Kuhn's view of truth

As further evidence that Kuhn's ontological relativism is a position of the kind I have just outlined, I wish now to discuss Kuhn's views on the nature of truth. As is well known, Kuhn was a long-standing critic of the application of the correspondence theory of truth to the relation between scientific theories and reality.[36] In his later work, Kuhn continued to oppose the correspondence theory, and he also sketched his position about the nature of truth in the context of the idea of variant lexical structures.

According to Kuhn's later views on the subject of truth, the correspondence theory of truth must be rejected,[37] though there remains a necessary role to be played by a weaker conception of truth.[38] The required weaker notion of truth must have an application that is internal to lexical frameworks. For, while a claim may properly be said to be true or false within the context of a given lexicon, the categorial system embedded in the lexicon is not itself capable of being true or false.

In rejecting the correspondence theory of truth, Kuhn wishes to reject the idea that the categorial structure of a theory might accurately reflect the way the world is independently of theory. That such structures cannot themselves be correspondence true appears to be the point of the following passage, in which Kuhn claims that the 'form of life' associated with a given lexicon cannot itself be true or false.

> Experience and description are possible only with the described and describer separated, and the lexical structure which marks that separation can do so in different ways, each resulting in a different, though never wholly different, form of life. Some ways are better suited to some purposes, some to others. But none is to be accepted as true or rejected as false; none gives privileged access to a real, as against an invented, world. The ways of being-

> in-the-world which a lexicon provides are not candidates for true/false. (1991a, p. 12)

Such a denial that the taxonomic structures of theoretical lexicons may even constitute possible candidates for truth or falsity accords well with the reading of Kuhn's ontological relativism which I have suggested. For on such a view, the world itself has no natural kind structure for categorial schemes to correspond with, and taxonomic structures only come into play once one has entered a given phenomenal world.

While Kuhn rejects application of the correspondence theory to the relation between categorial systems and reality, he holds that a weaker notion of truth is required, which may be applied internal to the lexical structures of theories:

> ... lexicons are not ... the sorts of things that can be true or false. A lexicon or lexical structure is the long-term product of tribal experience in the natural and social worlds, but its logical status, like that of word-meanings in general, is that of convention. Each lexicon makes possible a corresponding form of life within which the truth or falsity of propositions may be both claimed and rationally justified, but the justification of lexicons or of lexical change can only be pragmatic. With the Aristotelian lexicon in place it does make sense to speak of the truth or falsity of Aristotelian assertions in which terms like 'force' or 'void' play an essential role, but the truth values arrived at need have no bearing on the truth or falsity of apparently similar assertions made with the Newtonian lexicon. (1993, pp. 330-1)

Kuhn thus allows that there is a notion of truth which has a valid use within the context of a given lexicon. At one point Kuhn suggests that the notion of truth involved may be provided by 'something like a redundancy theory of truth'.[39] Yet at one point in the above quote, as well as in the following passage, application of the notion of truth appears to coincide rather closely with that of rational assertability:

> ... the evaluation of a putatively scientific statement should be conceived as comprising two seldom-separated parts. First, determine the status of the statement: is it a candidate for true/false? To that question ... the answer is lexicon-dependent. And second, supposing a positive answer to the first, is the statement rationally assertable? To that question, given a lexicon, the answer is properly found by something like the normal rules of evidence. (1991a, p. 9)

Kuhn appears to be suggesting that, provided that a statement has a place within a lexical system, its truth value is to be fully determined by considering its evidential credentials. If the connection which Kuhn seems to be drawing here between truth and rational assertability is an indication of his view of truth, then his conception of truth internal to a lexicon would appear to be a verificationist rather than a redundancy conception of truth.[40]

Since Kuhn makes application of the concept of truth internal to lexicon, it might appear that he adopts a relativistic view of truth. However, Kuhn does not go so far as to make the truth of scientific claims relative to operative theory. It is rather the case that a claim which may be true within the lexical framework of one theory fails to correspond to any comparable claim asserted or denied by an alternative theory. This point is closely connected with the incommensurability of such theories:

> Within the world of each practice, true laws must be universal, but some of the laws governing one of these worlds cannot even be stated in the conceptual vocabulary deployed in, and partially constitutive of, another. The same no-overlap principle that necessitates the universality of true laws bars the practitioners resident in one world from importing certain of the laws that govern another. The point is not that laws true in one world may be false in another but that they may be ineffable, unavailable for conceptual or observational scrutiny. It is effability, not truth, that my view relativizes to worlds and practices. (1993, p. 336)

Thus, rather than a relativistic view on which the truth of shared claims about the world varies with theory, Kuhn's view is one on which claims about the world may fail to be shared across such theories. The result is that, not only is truth a notion whose application is internal to theory, it is a notion which cannot be applied in comparisons between theories.[41]

I wish to claim that Kuhn's remarks about the nature of truth are fully consonant with my interpretation of his ontological relativist position. First, consider Kuhn's rejection of the correspondence theory of truth. Kuhn denies that a categorial scheme may accurately reflect reality in the sense of the correspondence theory of truth. This accords with the transcendental nominalist denial that reality is itself divided up into natural kinds independently of human conceptual intervention. Second, Kuhn's notion of truth internal to a lexicon sits well with the constructivist thesis that the phenomenal world of the scientist depends on the categorial scheme of accepted theory. For, given that scientists occupy a particular phenomenal world, they will be able to decide on questions of truth and falsity arising within such a world. Yet, due to differences in the categorial structure of theories, questions of the truth value of a particular claim made by a theory need not arise within the context of a theory with which it is incommensurable.

3.9 Finale

Having now sketched my view of the ontological relativist position which emerges in Kuhn's later work, I wish to conclude by restating some of the central themes which I have developed here. One of my central claims has been a historical one about the development of the relativistic position which characterizes Kuhn's philosophy of science. As originally elaborated in *The Structure of Scientific Revolutions*, Kuhn's position appeared to contain both a relativistic stance towards matters of scientific rationality and a radical conceptual relativism of incommensurable conceptual schemes. However, both of these claims were moderated, as Kuhn admitted the existence of extraparadigmatic methodological factors informing rational theory choice, and reduced the scope of conceptual variation between theories with his thesis of 'local incommensurability'.

However, as we have seen particularly in the last two sections, there continues to be a strong tendency towards relativism in Kuhn's work. This tendency centers on his denial of the existence of a reality which has an inbuilt natural kind structure that is independent of human conceptual intervention. This aspect of Kuhn's relativism places his views in sharp contrast with those scientific realists who hold that there is a mind independent reality, replete with objective natural kinds, the existence and constitution of which are completely independent of human mental activity. A second key feature of Kuhn's ontological relativism is his commitment to the Kantian view that the world phenomenally presented to the scientist is in large part determined by the taxonomic structure which theories impose on the world. This aspect of his position places Kuhn in close proximity to those idealist or idealistically inclined philosophers who have insisted on the impossibility of extracting ourselves from our conceptual frameworks to compare our thoughts and concepts directly with reality. Finally, Kuhn's rejection of correspondence truth in favour of truth internal to a lexicon represents both a rejection of standard forms of scientific realism, as well as an attempt to present a relativistic position which avoids familiar objections to relativism about truth.

While I have not attempted to develop connections between Kuhn's ontological relativism and recent trends in contemporary analytic philosophy, it should be clear that significant parallels exist between his views and other philosophical positions currently being defended. Here one might mention Putnam's internal realism, some contemporary forms of pragmatism,[42] as well as certain antirealist tendencies deriving from the later Wittgenstein. Given the prominence of such positions within the current philosophical scene, there seems little reason to expect that the relativistic stance characteristic of Kuhn's later work will meet with as much controversy as his original discussion encountered.

Notes

1. E.g., Doppelt (1982), Lakatos (1978b, pp. 90-1), Popper (1970, pp. 55-6) and Siegel (1987).
2. E.g., Davidson (1984), Kitcher (1978), Scheffler (1967) and Shapere (1984c).
3. In writings after 1970, Kuhn laid increasing emphasis on the role of rational factors in scientific change and denied wholesale methodological variation with paradigm (e.g., Kuhn, 1977c). As for incommensurability, in later work Kuhn denied radical variation of conceptual scheme, and restricted translation failure to localized subsets of the vocabulary used by theories. The charge of conceptual relativism is explicitly rebutted in his (1983).
4. For the distinction between rationality, conceptual and ontological relativism, see Chapter 1.
5. Cf. (1970a, pp. 148-50). Note that, whereas I prefer to speak of different forms of incommensurability, Kuhn in fact presents them as 'aspects' (1970a, p. 150) of the same thing, as factors 'collectively' leading to incommensurability (1970a, p. 148). Thus, he writes as if the three factors which constitute incommensurability must all occur at once, which coheres well with his original model on which changes at all three levels occur in the course of revolutionary change of paradigm. Nevertheless, I take the three different factors to be capable of occurring separately, and hence speak of different forms rather than aspects of incommensurability.
6. Cf. Doppelt (1982), Laudan (1984), Siegel (1987, pp. 51-4), and Shapere (1984b, pp. 35-6).
7. For variation of meaning and reference, see Scheffler (1967, pp. 58-64), Devitt (1979), Putnam (1975b). On conceptual relativism, see Davidson (1984), Kitcher (1978) and Putnam (1981).

8. Cf. Popper (1994, pp. 34-5, 54-8).
9. Cf. Kuhn (1970a, pp. 184-5, 199-200) and (1970b, pp. 259-66).
10. E.g., Davidson (1984), Kitcher (1978).
11. The doctrine of conceptual relativism is perhaps more plausibly associated with the work of Paul Feyerabend, who endorsed a more radical form of meaning variance and incommensurability than did Kuhn (cf. Feyerabend, 1981b).
12. Implications of meaning variance such as those indicated in the text have been widely associated with both Kuhn's and Feyerabend's versions of the incommensurability thesis. However, as I noted in Chapter 2, there are significant differences between Kuhn's and Feyerabend's versions of the incommensurability thesis. Most notably, the latter was an exclusively semantic thesis which changed little from its initial introduction. As we saw above, Kuhn's version of the thesis originally included methodological and perceptual variation between paradigms, in addition to variation of conceptual apparatus.
13. Shapere (1984b, p. 35, 1984c, p. 67), cf. Scheffler (1967, p. 82).
14. For detailed criticism of Davidson's objections, as well as related objections due to Putnam (1981), see Chapters 5 and 6.
15. E.g., Kuhn (1970b, p. 267) and (1977d, p. 506).
16. Davidson argues that conceptual relativism rests on the metaphor of different points of view, which, paradoxically, makes sense 'only if there is a common coordinate system on which to plot them' (1984, p. 184). The paradox arises for Kuhn because he actually tells us about incommensurable concepts: 'Kuhn', Davidson writes, 'is brilliant at saying what things were like before the revolution using — what else? — our post-revolutionary idiom' (1984, p. 184). Putnam makes a similar point, when he says that "To tell us that Galileo had 'incommensurable' notions and then to go on to describe them at length is totally incoherent" (1981, pp. 114-5).
17. For details of how Kuhn's local incommensurability thesis meets this and related objections, see Chapter 5.
18. For example, following the passage quoted in the text in which Kuhn compares paradigm change with interplanetary space travel, Kuhn goes on to say that 'Of course, nothing of quite that sort does occur: there is no geographical transformation; outside the laboratory everyday affairs usually continue as before' (1970a, p. 111).
19. See, for example, Musgrave (1979), Nola (1980a) and Scheffler (1967).
20. See, for example, Brown (1983a, pp. 19-20), Devitt (1984, p. 137) and Mandelbaum (1982, pp. 50-2).

21. In his lengthy treatment of Kuhn's metaphysical standpoint, Hoyningen-Huene draws an explicit parallel between Kuhn and Kant: 'For both Kant and Kuhn, epistemic *subjects* are co-constitutive of [the phenomenal world]'. Drawing an analogy with Kant's idea of a thing-in-itself, Hoyningen-Huene contrasts the phenomenal world of a scientist with 'the world-in-itself', which is both invariant and unknowable. See Hoyningen-Huene (1993, pp. 32-5).
22. See, for example, (1979, p. 417), (1987, p. 19), (1991b, p. 19).
23. Cf. (1983), (1990), (1991a).
24. While Kuhn ordinarily used 'lexicon' to refer to a structured vocabulary, he later extended its use by speaking of the lexicon as a mental module which stores a set of kind terms (1991a, pp. 11-2, 1993, p. 315).
25. It is important to note that the requirement of sameness of taxonomic structure across lexicons is meant by Kuhn to be stronger than a merely extensionalist requirement that the taxonomic categories of different classificatory schemes have the same items in their extension. The extensions of such categories must not only be specified as objects belonging in the extension; they must also be represented in some way as constituting a natural kind (1983, p. 676). Presumably, this requires that there must be some minimal retention of sortal or categorial vocabulary across taxonomic systems. However, Kuhn appears to hold that the same kinds may be picked out within different systems of classification, even though no criteria of categorization are shared across classificatory system (1983, pp. 681-3). For discussion of this issue, see my (1994, pp. 95-100).
26. Kuhn has developed two examples of such definitional interdependence at length. In his (1983, pp. 675-6), he argues that such phlogistic terminology as 'dephlogisticated air' and 'phlogistication' depend semantically on the concept of phlogiston, which depends in turn on such concepts as that of a chemical principle. He also argues that such Newtonian terms as 'force' and 'mass' have a similar semantic interdependence (1983, p. 677, 1990, pp. 301-8).
27. E.g., Putnam (1975c) and Kripke (1980).
28. See Fine (1975) and Devitt (1979).
29. See Enç (1976), Kroon (1985) and Nola (1980b).
30. Hacking (1979, pp. 229-30), (1983, pp. 109-11), (1993, pp. 277, 306).
31. I have argued in my (1994, p. 201) that this is incoherent. If there are facts of the matter which make for the reality of low level kinds, then there must also be facts of the matter about such kinds

which generate higher level kinds (*pace* the transcendental nominalist).

32. Cf. Kuhn (1991b, pp. 20-1), where he disagrees with the view that 'though social concepts shape the world to which they are applied, concepts of the natural world do not', and argues instead that, while 'Hesperus and Phosphorus are the same *planet* ... it is only under that description, only as planets, that they can be recognized as one and the same'.
33. Similarly, Hoyningen-Huene remarks that 'One might reply to Hacking that Kuhn's position ought to be placed *between* nominalism and realism, as the similarity relations of which concepts are constituted contain both genetically subject-sided *and* genetically object-sided moments' (1993, p. 76, note 52).
34. Exactly what Kuhn's metaphysical stance is remains somewhat difficult to establish. While on a number of occasions he has described his stance as Kantian, at one point he rejects Kant's 'things-in-themselves' (1979, p. 418), and at another he accepts that there is 'something permanent, fixed, and stable', which is 'like Kant's *Ding an sich*' (1991a, p. 12). What does seem clear, though, is that Kuhn wishes to reject 'the one big mind-independent world about which scientists were once said to discover the truth' (1992, p. 20), and that he thinks that 'no sense can be made of the notion of reality as it has ordinarily functioned in philosophy of science' (1992, p. 14).
35. While Kuhn wishes to relegate the mind independent reality in itself to the status of an epistemically inaccessible Kantian substrait, it seems clear that such reality must be the ultimate source of sensory input. For the very idea of the empirical revisability of categorial schemes requires the existence of an external source for sensory input which is independent of human conceptual and theoretical activity.
36. Cf. 'One often hears that successive theories grow ever closer to, or approximiate more and more closely to, the truth ... Perhaps there is some other way of salvaging the notion of 'truth' for application to whole theories, but this one will not do. There is, I think, no theory-independent way to reconstruct phrases like 'really there'; the notion of a match between the ontology of a theory and its "real" counterpart in nature now seems to me illusive in principle' (1970a, p. 206).
37. Cf. (1991a, p. 6), (1992, p. 14), (1993, p. 330).
38. Cf. (1991a, pp. 8-9), (1993, pp. 330-1).
39. Cf. (1991a, p. 8). More specifically, Kuhn argues that 'something like a redundancy theory of truth' is necessary in order 'to require choice between acceptance and rejection of a statement or a theory

in the face of evidence'. In connection with this point, Kuhn refers without elaboration to Horwich (1990). Since Horwich argues that his minimalist conception of truth is consistent with scientific realism, it might, at first blush, seem mistaken to think that such a view might be conjoined with Kuhn's antirealism. However, Horwich's point is not simply that minimalism is consistent with scientific realism, but that it is philosophically neutral. Thus, it may very well be consistent with Kuhn's antirealist metaphysical stance.

40. Because Kuhn connects truth internal to a lexicon with rational assertability, the question arises whether he would wish to distinguish between a true claim and one which is evidentially well justified but false. Nothing he says clearly decides this question one way or the other. But there would appear to be no reason why he could not embrace Putnam's (1981) conception of truth as idealized rational justification by relativizing such justification to lexicon. In this way, Kuhn could avoid identifying truth with mere rational justification.
41. This point would need to be qualified to take into account Kuhn's idea of local incommensurability, according to which there may be shared vocabulary across semantically variant theories. Presumably, the notion of truth must be applicable to statements couched in such shared vocabulary, and must therefore be applicable in comparison between theories.
42. It is not without relevance here that Richard Rorty at one point says that the form of pragmatism he defends might be called 'left-wing Kuhnianism' (1991, p. 38).

4 Taxonomic incommensurability

4.1 Introduction

In later years, Thomas Kuhn developed a refined version of the thesis of the incommensurability of alternative scientific theories. This version of the thesis involves differences between the taxonomic categories which scientific theories employ. I call it the thesis of 'taxonomic incommensurability'. The taxonomic incommensurability thesis is in several respects superior to earlier versions. However, Kuhn associates a number of antirealist claims about truth and reality with the thesis. I will argue that these claims do not follow from taxonomic incommensurability, which is instead consistent with a full blooded form of scientific realism.

Along with Paul Feyerabend, Kuhn is well known for having argued that rival or successive scientific theories are incommensurable in the sense of being unable to be compared by means of common standards of evaluation. It is less well known that Kuhn's views on this topic underwent a continuous series of changes after their original presentation in *The Structure of Scientific Revolutions*. Kuhn originally presented incommensurability as conceptual, methodological and perceptual disparity between paradigms, resulting in communication breakdown and rational undecidability of paradigm debate. At a later stage, he restricted incommensurability to the semantic relationship of untranslatability between theories, which he claimed to be similar to Quinean indeterminacy of translation. Later still, Kuhn came to treat incommensurability as translation failure between interdefined clusters of terms within the special vocabulary used by theories.

This chapter is organized as follows. In Section 4.2, I examine Kuhn's idea that scientific revolutions are characterized by change in the taxonomic structure which scientific theories impose upon the world. In Section 4.3, I consider Kuhn's claim that change of structure gives rise, at the semantic level, to localized translation failure between interdefined subsets of terms. Section 4.4 traces this untranslatability to a relation of non-overlap which Kuhn claims to hold between natural kinds. In Section 4.5, I critically examine Kuhn's claim that incommensurability entails the falsity of the realist idea of progress as increase of truth about a fixed set of entities. Section 4.6 criticizes Kuhn's rejection of the correspondence theory of truth. And in Section 4.7 I suggest that the scientific realist need find little to object to in the thesis of taxonomic incommensurability.

4.2 Taxonomic change

In the original presentation of his model of theory change in *The Structure of Scientific Revolutions*, Kuhn placed great emphasis on the non-cumulative nature of revolutionary scientific change. One aspect of such change which has assumed particular importance in later developments of his position is change of taxonomy. According to Kuhn, scientific revolutions are characterized by changes in the taxonomic schemes by means of which theories classify the entities in their domains of application.

Before addressing the issue of taxonomic change, I will briefly sketch Kuhn's view of the nature of taxonomic schemes and categories. Kuhn makes frequent use of historical examples, such as the astronomical categories of *planet* and *star*, and the chemical categories of *compound* and *mixture*. His examples reveal that scientific theories classify the objects and phenomena to which they apply into a variety of categories. Such categories contain items which theories group together on the basis of characteristic properties or behaviour which they have in common. Because theories typically classify their domains into a number of different categories, such theoretical classification requires a taxonomic system which contains multiple categories.

Kuhn suggests that change of such taxonomic systems is what typifies scientific revolutions (Kuhn, 1987). He notes that the criteria which define taxonomic categories change during a scientific revolution. However, since such criteria may also vary during normal science, the characteristics of revolutionary change must lie elsewhere:

> What characterizes revolutions is ... change in several of the taxonomic categories prerequisite to scientific descriptions and generalizations. That change ... is an adjustment not only of criteria relevant to categorization, but also of the way in which objects and situations are distributed among preexisting categories. (1987, pp. 19-20)

Revolutionary scientific change is not restricted, therefore, to changes in the claims theories make about the members of shared categories of entities. Rather, such change alters the very system of classification by means of which the membership of such categories is determined, with consequent alterations in both the criteria of classification and in the membership of categories.

One of Kuhn's standard examples of taxonomic change is drawn from the transition between Ptolemaic and Copernican astronomy:

> Before [the transition] occurred, the sun and moon were planets, the earth was not. After it, the earth was a planet, like Mars and Jupiter; the sun was a star; and the moon was a new sort of body, a satellite. (1987, p. 8)

In this passage, as elsewhere, Kuhn writes as if the entities themselves undergo change, rather than the taxonomic system; e.g., the sun was a planet, later it was a star. What he presumably means, though, is that while the sun was once classified as a planet, it was later classified as a star.

The transition to Copernican astronomy illustrates a number of features of the sort of taxonomic change Kuhn has in mind. First, there is a fixed set of entities — in this case, the set of heavenly bodies — which constitutes a common domain of objects that is shared between different systems of classification.[1] Second, the change of taxonomy is not a wholesale change of taxonomic scheme, since many of the older categories are preserved in the later classification. Third, change of taxonomy involves the shift of objects, or sets of objects,[2] between categories, as well as the introduction of some new categories. Fourth, as a result of such reclassification, entities which were formerly considered to be unlike each other are taken to be members of the same category after a revolution.

Such taxonomic change has a number of important consequences at the semantic level. Occasionally, major change of ontology or addition of new categories may result in the introduction of novel vocabulary, which varies semantically from previous vocabulary. However, in many cases the original vocabulary is preserved through change of taxonomy, and is therefore subject to change of meaning. Where a change affects the criteria by means of which a category term is applied, such change may alter the sense of the term. But in cases in which objects are also transferred from one taxonomic category to another, the retained terms may undergo change of extension as well.

4.3 Local holism and untranslatability

The semantic variance associated with taxonomic change lies at the heart of incommensurability. Instead of total communication breakdown, Kuhn argues for failure of exact translation between subsets of interdefined terms within the special language of theories. Such failure of translation is due to a certain 'local holism'.

According to Kuhn, revolutionary change of taxonomic structure, unlike piecemeal normal scientific change, proceeds in a holistic fashion. This is due to transfer of items between categories in taxonomic change:

> Since such redistribution always involves more than one category and since those categories are interdefined, this sort of alteration is necessarily holistic. That holism ... is rooted in the nature of language, for the criteria relevant to categorization are *ipso facto* the criteria that attach the names of those categories to the world. (1987, p. 20)

The holistic nature of taxonomic change is reflected, at the semantic level, by the interdefinition of the terms which refer to taxonomic categories. For taxonomic kind terms receive their definition within an integrated conceptual structure in which a number of different concepts are semantically interconnected.

As a result of the holistic interdefinition of terms, it may prove impossible to translate names for the taxonomic categories defined by one theory by means of the terms of another theory. One example discussed by Kuhn is the case of phlogistic versus oxygen chemistry. While much of the language used by proponents of the phlogiston theory is still in use, 'a small group of terms remains for which the modern chemical vocabulary offers no equivalent' (1983, p. 675). Terms such as 'phlogiston', 'dephlogisticated air' and 'principle' form a cluster of conceptually related terms which cannot be defined on the basis of the special vocabulary of the oxygen theory: 'they constitute an interrelated or interdefined set that must be acquired together, as a whole, before any of them can be used, applied to natural phenomena' (1983, p. 676).

As a result of translation failure due to the holistic interdefinition of category terms, incommensurability emerges as a localized phenomenon, restricted to narrow subsets of terms within alternative theories. The resulting version of the incommensurability thesis is an improvement on earlier versions of the thesis. On its basis, for example, it is possible to meet Shapere's objection that incommensurable theories cannot constitute rivals (Shapere, 1984b, p. 45, 1984c, p. 73), since there is sufficient semantic common ground between theories to sustain conflict between them (cf. Kuhn 1983, p. 671). Moreover, it is possible to meet objections due to Davidson (1984) and Putnam (1981) that the incommensurability thesis illegitimately presupposes the translatability of untranslatable terms. For, given the distinction between shared semantically stable vocabulary and an untranslatable core of terms, there is no need to translate untranslatable expressions in arguing for incommensurability (see Chapter 5).

4.4 Natural kinds and the no-overlap principle

Kuhn's most recent treatment of incommensurability is characterized by an increasing emphasis on the semantics of natural kind terms. Kuhn now argues that terms from one taxonomic structure fail to be translatable into another due to certain restrictions governing relations between natural kinds. The restrictions derive from what Kuhn calls the 'no-overlap principle'. Before I discuss this principle, however, I will introduce Kuhn's idea of a lexicon.

Where Kuhn once spoke of paradigms, he now tends to speak of lexicons or lexical structures. Kuhn sometimes describes the lexicon as a mental module which stores concepts and vocabulary (1993, pp. 315, 329). More typically, the lexicon is a structured vocabulary of kind terms, which represents a taxonomy of natural kinds (1983, pp. 682-3, 1991a, pp. 4-5). Kuhn claims that successful communication does not require speakers to use the same criteria in applying terms to the world. It requires only that speakers operate with 'homologous lexical structures', with a structured vocabulary which incorporates the same taxonomic system (1983, p. 683). Analogously, for translation to succeed from the lexicon of one theory into another, theories need only share lexical taxonomy; if they do not, they are incommensurable.

Kuhn insists that purely extensional constraints on translation are inadequate, since translation which preserves reference may fail to preserve crucial aspects of meaning (1983, p. 679). Yet, his claim that homology of lexical structure suffices for translation may seem to suggest that sameness of reference does suffice for translation. For one might think that lexicons whose terms have the same extensions must share lexical taxonomy. It is at this point, however, that Kuhn's recent emphasis on natural kinds becomes relevant. For the requirement of lexical homology is meant to insure that terms from intertranslatable lexicons refer to the same natural kind, rather than that they merely have the same extension. Since a single set of things may belong to a number of distinct natural kinds, reference to a given natural kind requires its members to be individuated qua members of that kind, rather than in a merely extensional manner. The requirement of reference to the same natural kind is, therefore, a stronger constraint than co-extensiveness.

In Kuhn's most recent writings on the subject, the requirement of reference to the same natural kind has become the principal ingredient of his argument for incommensurability. For Kuhn's current argument for translation failure between disparate lexical structures turns on a point about the hierarchical nature of natural kind taxonomies:

> no two kind terms ... may overlap in their referents unless they are related as species to genus. There are no dogs that are also cats, no gold rings that are also silver rings, and so on: that's what makes dogs, cats, silver, and gold each a kind. (1991a, p. 4)

In other words, members of one natural kind may only be members of another natural kind if one of the kinds is itself contained in the other. For no natural kind may include members from more than one category in a taxonomic structure, unless the kind is a higher order kind which includes members of subordinate kinds within the taxonomy. Since this requirement precludes overlap between the membership of kinds, Kuhn calls it the no-overlap principle.

How the no-overlap principle leads to untranslatability may be illustrated by means of Kuhn's example of celestial taxonomy. Suppose one sought to translate the Ptolemaic term 'planet' into the lexicon of Copernican astronomy. In addition to planets classified as such by Copernican astronomy, the Ptolemaic category *planet* includes the sun and the moon. Translating the Ptolemaic term 'planet' into the Copernican lexicon would therefore require incorporation into the latter taxonomy of a single category drawn from members of three distinct Copernican categories. But such a category cannot be introduced into the Copernican taxonomy as a natural kind of the latter taxonomy. For the Ptolemaic category combines entities together as members of a single, unified kind which the Copernican scheme treats as members of distinct natural kinds.

The question must surely arise, however, of just why it is impossible to integrate a kind from one taxonomy within an alternative taxonomic scheme. The answer to this question is not completely clear, since Kuhn does not present his account of the issue in sufficient detail. Nevertheless, Kuhn does suggest that the reason has to do with the projectibility of kind terms (1993, pp. 316, 318). Because kind terms are projectible, it is a presupposition of the use of such terms that the items to which they refer are expected to display lawlike behaviour. Indeed, Kuhn takes it to be part of the meaning of a kind term that the entities to which it refers are subject to specific nomological regularities which determine their characteristic behaviour (1993, p. 317).[3]

Given the relation between the meaning of kind terms and the laws governing members of a kind, untranslatability is due to difference in laws governing kinds from rival taxonomies. More specifically, a kind from one taxonomy cannot be introduced into a rival taxonomy if members of the kind are classified by the latter taxonomy as members of distinct kinds subject to distinct sets of natural laws. For example, the Ptolemaic category *planet* cannot be introduced as a unified kind within the Copernican scheme, since members of such a category would be subject to incompatible laws which normally govern the behaviour of distinct kinds of heavenly body. Some govern the behaviour normally exhibited by stars or satellites, while others govern that displayed by planets. But, given the inability to introduce a kind from one taxonomy into the other, neither may the kind terms of one lexical structure be introduced into the rival lexicon. Thus, as a result of differences in the laws governing the kinds within different taxonomies, kind terms from one lexical taxonomy may fail to be translatable by means of a term which names a kind within a rival taxonomy.

4.5 Zeroing in on truth

Kuhn bases a number of antirealist claims on the thesis of incommensurability. Some of these have to do with truth, others with reference and reality. In the remaining sections of this chapter, I will focus on his remarks about truth, and then attempt to show why the scientific realist has nothing to fear from taxonomic incommensurability.

Kuhn has long been critical of the realist idea that the advance of science involves a steady build up of truths about a common domain of entities. Most often, Kuhn's criticism has taken the form of a historical objection based on the radical ontological change evident in the history of science. Kuhn says, for example, that in the historical transition between Aristotle, Newton and Einstein, there is 'no coherent direction of ontological development' (1970a, p. 206). Thus, as against the realist idea of the advance of science as a process of 'zeroing in on nature's real joints', Kuhn can 'see no historical evidence for a process of zeroing in' (1979, p. 418).

Kuhn's remarks suggest the following argument against the realist account of progress. In the transition between scientific theories, a radical change occurs in the descriptions of the entities (e.g., atoms, phlogiston, etc.) to which theories are ontologically committed. Hence, later theories refer to none (or perhaps few) of the entities to which earlier theories referred, so that in the transition between theories there is a radical change of reference. Thus, the advance of science can manifestly not consist in an increase of truths about a common domain of entities.

The force of this argument may, however, be significantly weakened by use of a causal theory of reference. For, to the extent that reference may be determined independently of description, as it is according to the causal theory, it need not vary with change in the descriptions given by theories of the entities in their domain. Consequently, Kuhn's historical objection fails to carry weight against the realist account of scientific advance, since change of descriptive content of theories need not be invariably accompanied by wholesale discontinuity of reference.[4]

However, Kuhn has recently offered a different objection to the realist view of progress. He dismisses realist talk 'of science's zeroing in on, getting closer and closer to, the truth' as meaningless. And he says that the fact such talk is 'meaningless is a consequence of incommensurability' (1993, p. 330). The reason for this has to do with translation failure between lexicons and the no-overlap principle:

> There is, for example, no way, even in an enriched Newtonian vocabulary, to convey the Aristotelian propositions regularly misconstrued as asserting the proportionality of force and motion or the impossibility of a void. Using our conceptual lexicon, these Aristotelian propositions cannot be expressed — they are simply ineffable — and we are barred by the no-overlap principle from access to the concepts required to express them. It follows that no shared metric is available to compare our assertions about force and motion with Aristotle's and thus to provide a basis for a claim that our (or, for that matter, his) are closer to the truth. (1993, p. 330)

In this passage, Kuhn infers from untranslatability between a pair of theories that there is no sense in which one may be closer to the truth than the other. Thus, he takes the untenability of the realist account of progress to follow from incommensurability.

But in this Kuhn seems to me to be seriously mistaken. The mistake turns on the intensional nature of translation versus the extensional nature of truth. Put simply, despite untranslatability, a pair of theories may refer to the same entities and each theory may make more or less true claims about those entities. To bring this out, I will try to make three related points.[5]

First, it is extremely implausible to suppose that conflicting theories about the same world might be in principle incapable of being more or less true than one another. Unless such theories are profoundly mistaken, to the point of failing altogether to refer to any actual entities, at least some of the terms employed by the theories must refer to at least some of the same things. For if the theories are competing theories of the same domain of phenomena, and they do not suffer from wholesale reference failure, then at least some of the entities referred to by terms of one theory must fall within the extensions of terms of the other theory. But, if this is so, then there is no reason in principle why one of the theories may not assert more truths about those entities than the other.

Second, inability to translate between theories does not entail that one theory may be no closer to the truth than another. The crucial point here is that truth depends on reference rather than sense, so that sentences may be true or false of the same things even though their terms differ in sense. Given the possibility of non-synonymous co-referential expressions, terms from non-intertranslatable theories may nevertheless have the same extension. Hence, it may be possible for theories to assert a variety of true or false claims of a common set of entities, to which the terms of both theories refer despite failure of translation. But such a possibility insures that one theory may assert a greater number of truths about the shared set of things than the other does, so that it may approximate the truth more closely than the other.[6]

The thrust of these two points is that the realist idea of advance on the truth is not undermined by translation failure between theories. But Kuhn's objection was not just that theories cannot advance on truth: it was also that there is no basis for judging them to do so. For Kuhn claims that untranslatability between lexicons entails that theories are unable to be compared for closeness to truth.

Yet Kuhn's objection to such comparison is unconvincing. According to Kuhn, propositions from incommensurable theories cannot be compared as approximations to the truth, since the propositions of one such theory cannot be formulated within the lexicon of another such theory (1993, p. 330). But it is not necessary to formulate propositions within the lexicon of a single theory in order to compare them for truth. The lexicon of a theory is the special vocabulary of a theory which constitutes a local fragment of an embracing natural language As such, the lexicons of alternative theories are situated within the context of a background language, which contains a variety of vocabularies with special areas of application. Given the containment of alternative lexicons within a natural language, the background natural language may serve as metalanguage for the lexicons, which may be treated as object languages. Employing the natural language as metalanguage, it may then be said of some object linguistic sentence from a given lexicon that it is true while saying of another object linguistic sentence from another lexicon that it is false. It is possible, in this manner, to compare the content of incommensurable theories with respect to degree of truth without the need to translate from one into the other. Of course, such comparisons are fallible and theory laden. But that, surely, is a different issue.

4.6 Lexicons and truth

Kuhn has often objected to the idea that theories may be true in the sense of corresponding to reality, arguing for example that 'the notion of a match between the ontology of a theory and its "real" counterpart in nature [is] illusive in principle' (1970a, p. 206). In recent work, Kuhn continued to oppose the correspondence theory (1991a, p. 6, 1993, p. 330), though he granted a crucial role to a weaker conception of truth, similar to a redundancy conception (1991a, p. 8). In what follows, I will focus on Kuhn's claim that a lexicon cannot itself be true or false.

Kuhn's later denial of correspondence between theory and reality takes the form of a denial that lexicons may be true or false. Kuhn concedes, however, that the notion of truth has a legitimate role within the context of a lexicon:

> Each lexicon makes possible a corresponding form of life within which the truth or falsity of propositions may be both claimed and rationally justified ... With the Aristotelian lexicon in place it does make sense to speak of the truth or falsity of Aristotelian assertions ... but the truth values arrived at need have no bearing on the truth or falsity of apparently similar assertions made with the Newtonian lexicon. (1993, pp. 330-1)

On the conception of truth which emerges, truth is internal to lexicon in the sense that its use is restricted to assessing claims made within the context of a lexicon. As such, its scope is severely limited: neither is the truth of claims made in one lexicon relevant to that of claims made in another, nor may the concept of truth be applied to a lexicon itself.[7]

As for the relation between lexicon and reality, Kuhn says that 'lexicons are not ... the sorts of things that can be true or false' (1993, p. 330). Their 'logical status', he says, 'like that of word-meanings in general, is that of convention' (1993, p. 330); 'the justification of lexicons or lexical change can only be pragmatic' (1993, p. 331). Moreover, lexicons deal with experience in different ways:

> Some ways are better suited to some purposes, some to others. But none is to be accepted as true or rejected as false; none gives privileged access to a real, as against an invented, world. The ways of being-in-the-world which a lexicon provides are not candidates for true/false. (1991a, p. 12)

Thus, while the notion of truth has a function within a lexicon, there is no sense in which a lexicon may itself be true. Rather than being true or false, a lexicon has the status of a linguistic convention which may be judged on the basis of how well it serves a particular purpose rather than how well it reflects reality.

Such an internalist conception of truth has profoundly antirealist consequences. It entails that scientific theories are unable to be true reflections of reality and that the advance of science fails to lead to an increase in truths known about reality. Without wishing to claim that the correspondence theory of truth applies unproblematically to scientific theories, I wish to object to Kuhn's antirealist treatment of the truth status of lexicons.

Let me begin, though, with a point of agreement. Kuhn claims that lexicons are neither true nor false, and that they have the status of conventions. A lexicon, as defined by Kuhn, is a 'structured vocabulary', a set of words. It is not words, or sets of words, but claims made using those words, that may be true or false. Moreover, that this or that sound or sequence of letters should represent a particular semantic content is, at base, a matter of linguistic convention. Thus, Kuhn is right to deny that lexicons have truth value and to assert their conventional status.

Trouble begins, however, when Kuhn concludes from this that theories may not truly reflect reality. Kuhn appears to suggest, for example, that theories are unable to correspond to reality because of the conventional status of lexicons (1993, p. 330). But the two issues are really quite separate: for, in spite of the fact that words acquire meaning by convention, the truth of empirical claims made using words may still depend on the way things stand in the world. Thus, while theories may be expressed using the resources of a conventional lexicon, nothing follows from this about the nature of the truth of theories. To think otherwise is to confuse the language in which a claim is expressed with the claim itself.

Connected with this is another problem involving the conventional status of lexicons. Kuhn writes as if their conventionality makes truth internal to lexicon, so that no question may arise of whether theory corresponds to reality. But such emphasis on conventionality distorts the fact that lexicons play an important theoretical role. The terms of a lexicon are, as Kuhn insists, natural kind terms, introduced in the context of a scientific theory in order to express the theory's picture of the world. Thus, a lexicon is not merely a neutral medium of expression.

The lexicon of the phlogiston theory, for example, includes such terms as 'phlogiston', 'phlogistication' and 'dephlogisticated air'. An important theoretical advance was made when it was found that the entities postulated by the phlogiston theory, the purported referents of phlogistic terminology, do not in fact exist. This suggests, however, that there is a truth of the matter about the relation between lexicon and reality. For there is a genuine question to be asked whether the entities postulated by the lexicon of a theory actually exist. But given the possibility of truth and falsity at this level, it follows that truth cannot be merely a matter internal to lexicon. The claims made using the terms of a lexicon may or may not correspond to the way the world is.

4.7 A realist remedy

The incommensurability thesis has been widely perceived as a serious threat to scientific realism. Kuhn himself associates a number of antirealist claims with the thesis. But, as I will now suggest, the realist has little to fear from taxonomic incommensurability.

Scientific realism characteristically involves four principal ingredients. The first ingredient is anti-instrumentalism: the unobservable entities postulated by scientific theories are conceived as real things, not mere predictive devices. The second is a thesis about the aim of science: the aim of scientific inquiry is to discover the truth about the world, and progress in science consists in advance toward this aim. Third, the realist adopts some version of the correspondence theory of truth, according to which what makes a statement true is that the world really is as the statement says it is. Fourth, scientific realism is a form of metaphysical realism: scientists investigate an objective reality, whose existence, structure and properties are independent of human mental activity.

I wish now briefly to argue that scientific realism is unaffected by the thesis of taxonomic incommensurability. As we saw in the previous two sections, Kuhn argues that translation failure between theories precludes convergence on truth, and he dismisses correspondence between theory and reality due to the conventionality of lexicons. However, as I have just argued, neither Kuhn's rejection of advance on truth nor his dismissal of correspondence truth may be sustained on the basis of taxonomic incommensurability. As a result, both the realist view of the aim of science and of truth emerge unscathed by incommensurability.

As for the anti-instrumentalist aspect of realism, the issue of translation between theories is an entirely separate issue from that of the reality of theoretical entities. The concepts employed by theories may evolve in the history of science regardless of whether unobservable entities exist, or whether theoretical terms are to be treated as genuinely referring expressions. At a more general level, Kuhn's picture of science as involving continual revisions of concepts and alteration of classificatory system is entirely consonant with a scientific realist account of science. For, on such an account, scientific theories are typically proposed in order to explain observable phenomena in terms of the behaviour of unobservable entities, and developing such explanatory theories involves formulating accurate concepts and classifications of such objects and phenomena. Since the development of satisfactory theory is a fallible process, subject to continuous revision in the light of empirical findings, modification of the concepts and classifications employed by theories is a permanent feature of scientific inquiry. But, given the prevalence of conceptual and classificatory change, untranslatability between theories of the kind highlighted by Kuhn may well be a regular occurrence in theory change.

Turning finally to the most fundamental level of realist commitment, the thesis of taxonomic incommensurability seems in no way to compromise the realist idea of an independent reality. Admittedly, Kuhn does on occasion say that world changes with paradigm and that the world is mind dependent. But such claims are not essential to the claims of translation failure between the vocabulary of theories. Moreover, there is no need whatsoever to suppose that the world does change with change of taxonomy. Different theories may classify the world differently, but the world remains the same. Hence, variation of taxonomic scheme is fully consistent with the mind independence aspect of realism.

More generally, the existence of conceptual change in science has no bearing on the metaphysical issue of the existence of a reality independent of human thought. Taxonomic change has no metaphysical import: the resulting failure of translation is at base a linguistic relation between theories of the same world.

Notes

1. While Kuhn holds that reality is in some sense 'mind-dependent' (Kuhn, 1990, p. 10, 1993, p. 315), the examples he gives of taxonomic change routinely involve the 'redistribution' of a common set of entities among 'preexisting categories'.
2. For transfer of sets of objects between categories, cf. "Dalton's atomic theory ... implied a new view of chemical combination with the result that the line separating the referents of the terms 'mixture' and 'compound' shifted; alloys were compounds before Dalton, mixtures after" (1970b, p. 269).
3. This connection between the meaning of terms used by theories and the laws postulated by theories is most evident in Kuhn (1990, pp. 301-8), where he illustrates the semantic dependence of Newtonian 'force' and 'mass' on Newton's laws of motion and gravitation.
4. I have, admittedly, overstated the causal theoretic case against radical reference change. As has been persuasively argued by a number of authors, not only must one admit reference change in science (Fine, 1975), but the causal theory must allow a role for description in determination of reference (Kroon, 1985, Nola, 1980). Despite this, the message of the causal theory is clear: given that reference is not fully determined by description, reference is not subject to radical variation in theoretical change.
5. In what follows I set aside problems with the idea of closeness to the truth which arise with regard to Popper's idea of verisimilitude. Kuhn's objection is not directed against the idea that there may be an increase in truth between theories with comparable truth content. His objection is against the idea that theories have comparable truth content.
6. Of course, as Kuhn insists, extensional identity across theories cannot be taken for granted, since reference may vary along with sense in the transition between theories. Nevertheless, there exist a range of weaker extensional relationships (e.g., extensional overlap, partial denotation, co-reference of term tokens) on the basis of which comparative judgement of truth content may be

made. For discussion, see Field (1973), Kitcher (1978) and Martin (1971).

7. Lest such an internalist conception of truth appear to unduly relativize truth to lexicon, Kuhn is at pains to deny that the truth of a shared set of propositions varies with lexicon. Owing to untranslatability between lexicons, there are no such shared propositions. Thus, Kuhn says, ‘it is effability, not truth, that my view relativizes to worlds and practices’ (1993, p. 336).

Part III

UNTRANSLATABILITY

5 In defence of untranslatability

5.1 Introduction

This chapter addresses criticisms of the concept of untranslatability which Davidson and Putnam have raised against the incommensurability thesis. The main themes of the criticism are present in the following extract from Putnam (1981):

> The incommensurability thesis is the thesis that terms used in another culture, say, the term 'temperature' as used by a seventeenth-century scientist, cannot be equated in meaning or reference with any terms or expressions we possess ... [I]f this thesis were really true then we could not translate other languages — or even past stages of our own language — at all. And if we cannot interpret organisms' noises at all, then we have no grounds for regarding them as thinkers, speakers, or even persons. In short, if Feyerabend (and Kuhn at his most incommensurable) were right, then members of other cultures, including seventeenth-century scientists, would be conceptualizable by us only as animals producing responses to stimuli (including noises that curiously resemble English or Italian). To tell us that Galileo had 'incommensurable' notions and then to go on to describe them at length is totally incoherent. (1981, pp. 114-5)

The central objection is that it is incoherent to talk about what is untranslatable. Three lines of argument may be distinguished with regard to this alleged incoherence. One argument is direct: it is incoherent to express the content of an untranslatable language within the language into which it is untranslatable. The other two are indirect arguments which assume translation is necessary for understanding. First: ideas expressed in an untranslatable language are incomprehensible, so claiming to understand them is incoherent. Second: it is incoherent to conceive the speaker of an untranslatable language as having a language at all. The direct argument will be dealt with in Section 5.2, and the indirect arguments in Section 5.3.

In addition, Davidson (1984) argues that languagehood is inextricable from translation. He claims that a 'dogma of a dualism of scheme and reality' which fallaciously separates language from translation underlies the incommensurability thesis. His attack on the dualism will be considered in Sections 5.4 to 5.6.

5.2 The direct incoherence argument

Putnam defines 'incommensurability' by saying that 'terms used in another culture ... cannot be equated in meaning or reference with any terms or expressions we possess'. Given this definition, the direct incoherence argument is embodied in the last sentence of the quote: "To tell us that Galileo had 'incommensurable' notions and then to go on to describe them at length is totally incoherent". For if Galileo's ideas are untranslatable into our language, then they cannot be expressed using our language, and it contradicts the claim of untranslatability to do so.

Davidson puts the point in the form of a paradox (1984, pp. 183-4). 'We are encouraged', he says, to 'imagine we understand massive conceptual change' by the use of examples, but 'the changes and the contrasts can be explained and described using the equipment of a single language' (1984, p. 183). 'Kuhn', he adds, 'is brilliant at saying what things were like before the revolution using — what else? — our post-revolutionary idiom' (1984, p. 184). The paradox is that the meaning expressed by the terms of an untranslatable language should be expressed in the very language into which translation allegedly fails.

Putnam and Davidson's remarks suggest the following argument. Suppose it is argued in language L that L* is untranslatable into L. Suppose as well that the argument in L employs examples from L* in the sense that it expresses the meaning of terms taken from L*. It follows from the latter that L* is translatable into L, for that is what expressing the meaning of terms from L* in L amounts to. But then the argument itself translates from L* into L in the course of arguing that L* is not translatable into L. If the argument is correct, then it is possible to translate from L* into L, so the conclusion is false. If the conclusion is correct, then it is impossible to translate from L* into L, so the argument is incorrect. Such an argument is incoherent.

This argument is sound but its scope is limited. Rather than being a general objection to untranslatability, it is a meta-argument to the effect that one form of untranslatability argument is self refuting. Nothing follows from that about untranslatability itself. It is not even a general objection to all arguments for untranslatability. At most, it is a criticism of arguments in which untranslatability is argued for in the language into which translation fails. It does not apply if the language of argument and the untranslatable languages are distinct.[1] In fact, it only applies to arguments which employ examples. Arguments which do not express the meaning of untranslatable expressions are immune to such criticism. As it is not fully general, the argument fails to show untranslatability to be incoherent. So it cannot be brought to bear on any particular untranslatability claim unless specifically shown to apply to it.

Of course, Putnam and Davidson employ the objection because they assume incommensurability falls within the ambit of the argument. They assume the language into which an untranslatable theory fails to be translatable is the language in which the argument for incommensurability is couched. Instead of translation failure between delimited theoretical terminologies, they identify the language into which translation fails with language as a whole.

This interpretation is explicit in Putnam's definition of 'the incommensurability thesis [as] the thesis that terms used in another culture ... cannot be equated in meaning or reference with any terms or expressions we possess'. And it is evident in the inference he draws: 'if this thesis were really true then we could not translate other languages ... at all'. When Davidson notes Kuhn's paradoxical use of 'our post-revolutionary idiom' to discuss pre-revolutionary science he assumes that the modern language into which out of date theory fails to translate is contemporary English. Davidson also takes the language into which translation fails to be a total language because he discusses incommensurability in the context of complete translation failure (1984, pp. 190-1). As Davidson and Putnam interpret incommensurability, the language of argument and the language into which translation fails are one and the same.

Given such an interpretation, it remains to note that Kuhn and Feyerabend use examples extensively. Since they use examples in arguing for incommensurability, their argument for untranslatability is open to the charge of incoherence. For if the language into which translation fails is the very language in which they argue for untranslatability, then their use of examples is indeed incoherent.[2]

This objection could be met by denying that Kuhn and Feyerabend express the meaning of the examples they discuss. One might claim that they give only approximate or partial translations. But this would be a misrepresentation. Kuhn and Feyerabend's exposition of the meaning of expressions is what shows them to be untranslatable in the first place.

It must be denied instead that the language into which translation fails is the language of argument. So it must be denied that incommensurability entails untranslatability into a total language. This accords fully with the thesis of incommensurability, since the incommensurability of scientific theories is not a relation between total languages. It is a relation between the languages of theories, and the language specific to a theory is only a part of a language. Incommensurability is due to semantic differences in the terminology of theories: the terminology employed by a theory cannot be translated into the terminology of a theory with which it is incommensurable. Instead of untranslatability into a total language, it is a case of translation failure between sublanguages within language as a whole.

That the untranslatability is limited is evident from Kuhn and Feyerabend's discussions of the theories they take to be incommensurable. They do not claim translation failure into a total language, since they are concerned with semantic analysis of the vocabulary the theories employ.[3]

Kuhn makes the point explicitly in responding to the Davidson-Putnam argument (1983, pp. 669-71). He advocates 'local' incommensurability, which is untranslatability between subsets of the terms used by pairs of theories. This involves localized semantic difference within the context of shared everyday and scientific language:

> Most of the terms common to ... two [incommensurable] theories function the same way in both; their meanings ... are preserved; their translation is simply homophonic. Only for a small subgroup of (usually interdefined) terms and for sentences containing them do problems of translatability arise. (1983, pp. 670-1)

So he does not even claim full translation failure between the special languages of theories: untranslatability is restricted to a central complex of interdefined terms.

The situation is similar with Feyerabend, who holds that the basic principles of a theory preclude the concepts of a theory with which it is incommensurable: 'the conditions of concept formation in one theory forbid the formation of the basic concepts of the other' (1978, p. 69).

The resultant untranslatability affects more than a central complex of terms. Yet it is still a relation between the languages of theories, rather than total languages.[4]

The picture of language which emerges is of natural language as a conglomerate of terminologies or local idioms with special areas of application. Untranslatability between theoretical languages constitutes a relation between sublanguages within a total language. Rather than untranslatability into a total language as assumed by Davidson and Putnam, what is at issue is localized translation failure between sublanguages contained in an encompassing language.

Thus the language into which the vocabulary of a theory fails to be translatable may be distinct from the language of argument. For the argument that a pair of sublanguages is not intertranslatable can be couched in a portion of language distinct from the language into which translation fails. Theoretical sublanguages may themselves be the topic of a discussion carried out within some other part of the language.

Thus consider two languages TL and TL* associated with two theories. Suppose that TL and TL* are sublanguages of a broader natural language L. It is possible to use L as a metalanguage to speak about the semantic relations between TL and TL*. In particular, it may be argued in L that a term t* of TL* cannot be translated into TL. Such an argument need not be formulated in TL, for it can be formulated in L. Using L as metalanguage, t* can be referred to and shown to be indefinable in TL without being expressed in TL. Nor is there any need in the course of the argument to express the meaning of t* in TL. For t* may be defined in L used as a metalanguage for TL without expressing the meaning of t* in TL.[5]

In sum, the direct incoherence argument does not apply to the incommensurability thesis. Since the untranslatability in question is a relation between theoretical sublanguages, and since such sublanguages may be discussed within a metalanguage, no incoherence attaches to the untranslatability argument.

5.3 Translation and interpretation

The Putnam passage suggests two arguments which do not proceed strictly in terms of translation. Both involve the assumption that translation is necessary for interpretation. This assumption is implicit in Putnam's inference from 'we could not translate ... at all' to 'we cannot interpret organisms' noises at all'.

Discussion of incommensurability is supposed to be incoherent because of such inability to interpret. The first argument is that if a language is untranslatable, then the ideas expressed in the language cannot be understood, so 'to describe [incommensurable notions] at length is totally incoherent'. The second is that speakers of an untranslatable language cannot be known to have a language, and 'would be conceptualizable by us only as animals producing responses to stimuli'.

It must be asked what Putnam means by 'interpret'. To say that translation failure entails inability to 'interpret organisms' noises' suggests that the meaning of untranslatable expressions cannot be understood. So to interpret an expression is presumably to understand what the meaning of the expression is. But it is unclear how interpretation is related to translation.

Putnam may assume that interpretation of a speaker who shares one's own language constitutes homophonic translation from the speaker's idiolect into one's own idiolect. If such domestic interpretation is assumed to be a form of translation, then it is natural to take interpretation of a foreign language as a form of translation as well. Interpretation of a foreign language would then consist in translating foreign expressions into a home language and understanding their home language equivalents. Thus conceived, failure to translate immediately entails failure of interpretation.

This translational sense of interpretation can be construed in two ways. If translation must be exact, interpretation of a foreign expression would consist in understanding an exact equivalent in a home language. If translation may be loose, interpretation may consist in understanding a loose rendering of a foreign expression.

If 'interpret' were given the first reading, Putnam's inference would fail. It does not follow from failure of exact translation that the content of speakers' utterances cannot be understood. For that to follow, it would have to be the case that exact translation is a necessary condition for understanding such content. But there is no reason to assume failure of exact translation to entail that a language cannot be understood at all. Such failure neither precludes the production of a gloss or loose translation, nor does it prevent the language from being learned directly.

To take interpretation in the second way as loose translation is to implausibly exaggerate incommensurability. Untranslatability of theories in the sense relevant to incommensurability does not entail a total lack of common semantic features: expressions of untranslatable languages may share aspects of reference and even meaning. Though 'dephlogisticated air' cannot be translated into the oxygen theory, some of its tokens co-refer with 'oxygen'. If 'interpretation' is taken in a loose sense, Putnam's denial of interpretation is stronger than licensed by incommensurability.

In the context of the argument interpretation cannot be taken to consist in translation. Interpretation must be separable from translation. Though in some cases interpretation may depend on translation, it cannot have translation as a constitutive component. To interpret an expression must be, quite simply, to understand what it means. And to understand an expression is not to translate it, nor is understanding restricted to what is expressed in a home language. Rather, to understand consists simply in knowing the meaning of an expression, whatever language it belongs to.

Putnam's inference from failure to translate to failure to interpret does not require that interpretation consist in translation. That inference can be made if translation is assumed to be a necessary prerequisite of interpreting a foreign expression. To say that translation is necessary for interpretation is distinct from saying that it is a component of interpretation.

The assumption that translation is necessary for interpretation is a restrictive assumption about the nature of understanding. As distinct from taking interpretation to be itself a form of translation, it takes understanding to be limited to expressions couched in one's home language. If the assumption were true, we would be unable to come to know the meaning of an expression not translatable into our language.

Let us now consider the first of Putnam's two arguments. It derives immediately from the assumption that translation is necessary for interpretation. Suppose that there is a language which we are unable to translate. Then, by the assumption, we cannot understand what is expressed in the language. And in that case we cannot know what ideas are expressed by the speakers of such a language. But advocates of the incommensurability thesis do claim to know what expressions of untranslatable languages mean. Thus they say both that the expressions cannot be translated and that they know what the expressions mean. But this is incoherent: for if the expressions cannot be translated, their meanings cannot be known; and if the meanings are known, then the expressions can be translated.

Given the assumption of the necessity of translation, the conclusion of incoherence no doubt follows. However, the assumption is itself implausible. For understanding a foreign expression need not consist in understanding its translational equivalent within one's home language. Bilingual speakers do not translate 'in their heads' while conversing in a foreign language, so a bilingual may understand a foreign expression not translatable into his home language. Moreover, if a foreign language must be translated before it may be understood, then no language could ever have been translated in the first place. Still worse, if understanding a new language really did require translation into a prior language, it would be impossible to learn one's own first language. In any case, it is as a matter of fact unnecessary to translate in order to learn a second language, since it is possible to learn a new language by the method of direct immersion. For these reasons we may conclude that understanding a foreign language is not contingent upon translation and that the first argument may be rejected.

This rebuttal is patterned on the responses of Kuhn (1983) and Feyerabend (1987), who claim that the language of a theory incommensurable with one's own can be understood. Feyerabend rebuts Putnam by pointing out that 'we can learn a language or a culture from scratch, as a child learns them, without detour through our native tongue' (1987, p. 76). Kuhn distinguishes between translation of a language and interpretation of an initially unintelligible language. He characterizes interpretation as follows:

> Unlike the translator, the interpreter may initially command only a single language. At the start, the text on which he or she works consists in whole or in part of unintelligible noises or inscriptions ... If the interpreter succeeds, what he or she has in the first instance done is learn a new language ... whether that language can be translated into the one with which the interpreter began is an open question. Acquiring a new language is not the same as translating from it into one's own. Success with the first does not imply success with the second. (1983, pp. 672-3)

This distinction enables Kuhn to rebut Putnam as Feyerabend does: an untranslatable theory may be interpreted, so there is nothing incoherent about claiming to understand the meaning of untranslatable expressions.[6]

Let us turn to Putnam's second argument, which is that untranslatability prevents language attribution. It too assumes translation to be necessary for interpretation. From this it follows that if a speaker's utterances cannot be translated, then it cannot be known what the utterances mean. And if no meaning can be attributed to the utterances of a speaker, then there is no evidence that the speaker has a language. But advocates of incommensurability describe speakers as having untranslatable languages and they attribute meanings to the speakers of such languages. But that is incoherent: for if utterances cannot be translated there is no evidence the speaker has a language; and if meaning is attributed to the utterances, that presupposes the speaker does have a language.

Our discussion of the first argument disposes of this argument's initial premise. For if translation is unnecessary then the meaning of untranslatable utterances can be known. However, we may also question the inference from inability to interpret a speaker's utterances to lack of evidence for language attribution. This inference is apparent in Putnam's remark that:

> if we cannot interpret organisms' noises at all, then we have no grounds for regarding them as thinkers, speakers, or even persons ... members of other cultures ... would be conceptualizable by us only as animals producing responses to stimuli. (1981, pp. 114-5)

That argument would succeed if it were true that an untranslatable language cannot be recognized as a language. For it is indeed incoherent to deny possession of a language to an organism while saying of that organism that it possesses concepts which it expresses in language. What should be questioned is whether a speaker whose language we are unable to translate cannot be known to possess a language.

Putnam apparently assumes that if the meaning of sounds or inscriptions cannot be interpreted then there is no reason to take the organism which produces them to have a language. Davidson takes a similar view when he asks us to reflect 'on the close relations between language and the attribution of attitudes':

> On the one hand, it is clear that speech requires a multitude of finely discriminated intentions and beliefs ... On the other hand, it seems unlikely that we can intelligibly attribute attitudes as complex as these to a speaker unless we can translate his words into ours. There can be no doubt that the relation between being able to translate someone's language and being able to describe his attitudes is very close. (1984, p. 186)

With both Putnam and Davidson, the suggestion appears to be that knowledge of semantic content or propositional attitude is required to justify language attribution.

This suggestion is surely mistaken. Why should knowledge of semantic content be necessary for language recognition? Surely, formal and contextual features count for something. Codes may be recognized as codes without being broken. Fragments of dead languages may be recognized as such prior to translation. Travellers recognize native speech as the local tongue without understanding it.

Why must psychological content be determined to identify behaviour as linguistic? In many social and physical settings the observed behaviour of humans is identifiable as linguistic without access to attitude or meaning. In any case, mental state need not be entirely inscrutable in the absence of knowledge of a language. The rough character of attitude or meaning can be known from observation of non-linguistic aspects of behaviour.

Even if there were no way to determine the presence of language without access to attitude or meaning, it would still not follow that an untranslatable language could not be identified as a language. The presumed necessity of content ascription by means of translation presupposes the necessity of translation for interpretation. To say that a speaker's meanings or attitudes can only be known if the speaker's language can be translated is to assume the only way to understand is via translation. But the possibility of direct understanding or acquisition of a language means that meaning and belief are interpretable without translation. A bilingual may determine psychological and semantic content for speakers of an untranslatable language without translating back into a home language.

In any case, the problem of recognizing language is largely irrelevant to incommensurability. A rival theorist is not an organism whose possession of a language is in question. Scientists with untranslatable theories may share a natural language. So the problem of whether a rival theorist possesses a language is resolved prior to discussion of theory. Nor is it as if the discovery of semantic variance between theories throws into question the status of a scientist as a speaker of a language. For shared use of a background language is a precondition of narrowing a linguistic difference down to difference of theory.

This completes criticism of Putnam's two arguments. I will now briefly consider a related argument which derives from Davidson's discussion of interpretative charity (1984, pp. 195-7).[7] Davidson applies the principle of charity to the problem of radical interpretation. The problem is how to interpret meaning without independent access to belief: 'a man's speech cannot be interpreted except by someone who knows a good deal about what the speaker believes ... and ... fine distinctions between beliefs are impossible without understood speech' (1984, p. 195). He assumes that 'the basic evidence for a theory of radical interpretation ... [is] the attitude of accepting as true, directed to sentences'. But such evidence does not determine meaning: 'if we merely know that someone holds a certain sentence to be true, we know neither what he means by the sentence nor what belief his holding it true represents' (1984, p. 196). Charity is invoked to extract meaning from the thin evidence of sentences held true.

To determine meaning, assumptions must be made about belief: 'if all we know is what sentences a speaker holds true, and we cannot assume that his language is our own, then we cannot take even a first step towards interpretation without knowing or assuming a great deal about the speaker's beliefs' (1984, p. 196). Belief attribution should be governed by charity. The rough idea is for the agent to come out on the whole as a believer of truths:

> We get a first approximation to a finished theory by assigning to sentences of a speaker conditions of truth that actually obtain (in our opinion) just when the speaker holds those sentences true. The guiding policy is to do this as far as possible, subject to considerations of simplicity, hunches about the effects of social conditioning, and of course our common-sense, or scientific, knowledge of explicable error. (1984, p. 196)

The principle of charity is justified because the agreement it provides is a precondition of interpretation:

> Since charity is not an option, but a condition of having a workable theory, it is meaningless to suggest that we might fall into massive error by endorsing it. Until we have successfully established a systematic correlation of sentences held true with sentences held true, there are no mistakes to make. Charity is forced on us; whether we like it or not, if we want to understand others, we must count them right in most matters. (1984, p. 197)

The connections Davidson draws between interpretation, translation and charity seem to license the following inferences. Since charity involves taking sentences of our language which we hold true as the content of alien utterances, charity implies translation. Since charity is necessary for interpretation, successful interpretation entails translation. Therefore, interpretation of an agent is inconsistent with translation failure. Thus to interpret a scientist as having a theory untranslatable into one's own is incoherent.

In effect, Davidson's use of the principle of charity combines Putnam's two arguments. In accordance with the first argument, charity makes translation necessary for interpretation. In accordance with the second, it makes translation necessary for interpreting an agent as a speaker. Two objections may be raised against this use of the principle of charity.

In the first place, the link between charity and translation must be severed. Just as interpretation does not require translation, interpretative charity does not require translation. Davidson assumes that charitable interpretation of an agent assigns truth conditions in a home language to sentences of an alien language. But while such charity might be generally advisable, it is not necessary. Charity may be applied directly within the alien language. Charity may be incorporated into the direct method of language acquisition. In learning a language directly without translating the interpreter can, and perhaps should, assign maximum plausible truth conditions as well as reasonable belief. Interpretation seeks coherence and assigns plausible truth values whether or not it results in translation.

In the second place, charity is unsuitable for theoretical discourse. The principle of charity can be refined in various ways to allow for varying degrees of error. But the general principle of assigning maximal truth is unacceptable as a principle of interpretation when applied to theoretical languages. Maximal assignment of truth to the statements of a scientific theory overlooks the possibility of large scale error. But the history of science abounds with theories that have been profoundly mistaken. Moreover, there are compelling epistemological reasons to take a fallibilist stance towards all theories, past and present. Surely, in the interpretation of scientific language no assumption about the truth of theoretical assertions should be made.[8]

Now, against this second objection, it might be argued that attribution of massive error makes behaviour unintelligible. That is, to deny of an agent that any of its beliefs are true is to make it inexplicable how it manages to engage in successful action. But to say that a theory is totally or mostly false is not to say that the entirety of an agent's beliefs are false. Moreover, a false theory can have true consequences and be put to practical use. And a theory which is strictly false but nearly or approximately true may serve as a guide for action.

The general policy of overall interpretative charity towards speakers should not be enjoined upon the interpreter of theoretical discourse. For the purpose of interpreting theoretical discourse, we are not therefore obliged by the principle of charity to impose translational equivalences upon scientific theories. So the forcing move from charity to intertheoretic translatability may be rejected. The possibility of interpretation does not rule out translation failure between theories.

5.4 The scheme-content dualism

There is another side to Putnam's claim that we have no reason to take uninterpretable organisms as 'thinkers, speakers, or even persons'. Namely, uninterpretable linguistic activity is evidentially indistinguishable from non-linguistic behaviour. The point is clearer with Davidson, whose arguments in its favour we will consider in the following two sections:

> nothing ... could count as evidence that some form of activity could not be interpreted in our language that was not at the same time evidence that that form of activity was not speech behaviour. (1984, p. 185)

The point against untranslatability is this: for neither an untranslatable language nor for non-linguistic behaviour can semantic content be given in our language; so inability to translate is indeterminate between being evidence that a language is untranslatable and that it is not a language at all.

As Davidson himself notes, to conclude that no evidence could show an untranslatable language to be a language 'comes to little more than making translatability into a familiar tongue a criterion of languagehood' (1984, p. 186). Rather than assuming translatability to be a necessary condition of languagehood, Davidson argues that language is neither conceivable nor recognizable as such independently of translation.

The central argument of Davidson's (1984) is directed against 'the dualism of conceptual scheme and empirical content' which underlies the conception of language as independent of translation. This 'dualism' posits an opposition between language, which embodies a conceptual system, and reality, upon which that system imposes order. The opposition of scheme versus content bypasses translation and characterizes language as something bearing the scheme-content relation to reality. Because this severs language from translation, Davidson must dispose of the dualism in order to show that evidence for an untranslatable language is indeterminate.

According to Davidson, the scheme-content dualism disconnects languagehood from translation as follows:

> something is a language, and associated with a conceptual scheme, whether we can translate it or not, if it stands in a certain relation (predicting, organizing, facing, or fitting) to experience (nature, reality, sensory promptings) ... The images and metaphors fall into two main groups: conceptual schemes (languages) either *organize* something, or they *fit* it (as in 'he warps his scientific heritage to fit his ... sensory promptings'). The first group contains also *systematize*, *divide up* (the stream of experience); further examples of the second group are *predict*, *account for*, *face* (the tribunal of experience). As for the entities that get organized, or which the scheme must fit ... either it is reality (the universe, the world, nature), or it is experience (the passing show, surface irritations, sensory promptings, sense-data, the given). (1984, pp. 191-2)

Such a relation gives substance to languagehood not contingent upon an interlinguistic relation of translatability. Identification of a language need not therefore involve translation, but may be based on evidence of the right sort of relation between putative linguistic behaviour and the world. Thus the dualism allows a language to be recognized as such without translation into a home language.

Davidson gives a dual analysis of the scheme-content relation: either schemes organize reality or experience, or they fit reality or experience. The accent with the first pair of relations is on the taxonomic function of language; with the second it is on its predictive or explanatory function. Davidson argues against the organizing idea that it does not give translation independent content to the idea of a language. He argues against the idea of language fitting reality that it separates truth from translation and leads illegitimately to the idea of a true but untranslatable language.

5.5 Schemes organize the world

The organizing idea is that something which is a language is recognizable as such because of its classificatory function. Translation fails because languages arrange things differently.

Against this version of the dualism, Davidson first notes that only pluralities can be organized:

> We cannot attach a clear meaning to the notion of organizing a single object (the world, nature, etc.) unless that object is understood to contain or consist in other objects. Someone who sets out to organize a closet arranges the things in it. (1984, p. 192)

He then argues that it can only be determined that a language organizes things differently if the language can on the whole be translated:

> A language may contain simple predicates whose extensions are matched by no simple predicates, or even by any predicates at all, in some other language. What enables us to make this point in particular cases is an ontology common to the two languages, with concepts that individuate the same objects. We can be clear about breakdowns in translation when they are local enough, for a background of generally successful translation provides what is needed to make the failures intelligible. But we were after larger game: we wanted to make sense of there being a language we

> could not translate at all. Or, to put the point differently, we were looking for a criterion of languagehood that did not depend on, or entail, translatability into a familiar idiom. I suggest that the image of organizing the closet of nature will not supply such a criterion. (1984, p. 192)

So, while admitting extensional variance between languages, Davidson denies that 'organizing the closet of nature' gives translation independent content to languagehood.

Extensional variance raises the possibility of translation failure. Davidson's tactic is to play down its scope. Rather than argue against semantic differences between languages, he argues that translation failure must be limited if it is to be intelligible: 'we can be clear about breakdowns in translation when they are local enough'. But this point is no objection to incommensurability, which is at most local translation failure. Theoretical sublanguages are embedded in larger languages, so translation between theories may well fail against 'a background of generally successful [albeit homophonic] translation'.

Davidson's crucial assumption is that it is necessary to translate to determine that a language divides the world differently. This supports his conclusion that translation failure is intelligible only if it is local and occurs in the context of broad translational success. Of course, if either the assumption or the conclusion were true, then the idea of organizing reality would not offer a means independent of translation for recognizing a language.

But the assumption begs the question at issue. It may be true that to find out that the classificatory systems of languages differ, the languages must be understood. But Davidson simply assumes that translation is necessary for understanding another language and the classificatory system it embodies.

To assume this is to lose sight of the purpose of the argument. Davidson is arguing that the idea of organizing reality gives no translation independent content to the notion of being a language. To show this he has to argue that there is no way to determine whether a language organizes reality without translation. But he simply assumes this. Surely, in the context of arguing that translation is necessary for the determination of classificatory difference, it begs the question to assume that translation is the only way to find out about such difference.

Davidson concludes that the 'image of organizing the closet of nature' does not enable sense to be made of total translation failure. This conclusion bespeaks a certain verificationism.[9] For it assumes that failure to specify a test for the presence of an untranslatable language entails that no content has been given to the concept of such a language.

Davidson's verificationism is evident in his inference from the intelligibility of only local translation failure to the unintelligibility of total failure. He allows that 'we can be clear about breakdowns in translation when they are local enough'. And he claims that general success in translation is what makes such breakdowns 'intelligible'. Davidson's point is that untranslatable linguistic material can only be known to be language if translation failure occurs in the context of overall translation of the language. Otherwise there would be no semantic evidence that the untranslatable material is linguistic. From this Davidson infers that sense has failed to be made of total failure: 'But we were after larger game: we wanted to make sense of there being a language we could not translate at all.'

The inference appears to be based on the following reasoning. The idea that language organizes reality can only be applied to the local case given background success in translating the language. Therefore the organizing idea does not yield a test for determining the presence of a totally untranslatable language. So that idea does not give meaning to the concept of such a language. This final inference assumes that meaning is only bestowed upon concepts if a means of verification is specified.

The problem with this can best be seen from Davidson's alternative formulation of his conclusion:

> Or, to put the point differently, we were looking for a criterion of languagehood that did not depend on, or entail, translatability into a familiar idiom. I suggest that the image of organizing the closet of nature will not supply such a criterion. (1984, p. 192)

By 'criterion' Davidson seems to mean a test for language, not an account of what being a language consists in. He concludes that because the criterion is inapplicable without translation no sense has been made of full untranslatability.

But the 'image of organizing the closet of nature' specifies a function which a language may perform. This is a criterion of being a language, as opposed to a criterion for recognizing one.[10] It gives content to the notion of being an untranslatable language: viz., such a language organizes the world differently. Such a criterion of languagehood gives content to the notion of being an untranslatable language whether or not it can verifiably be fulfilled.

Such verificationism imposes a fallacious constraint on meaning. To impart meaning to a concept is not contingent upon coming up with a test for applying it. For it is possible to specify mistaken tests for applying concepts. What enables this point to be made with respect to a given concept is a grasp of its content which is independent of such tests.

Even if this were not the case, Davidson's attack would still be beside the point. That we do not understand the notion of total untranslatability is no objection to the idea of an untranslatable language. Even if we have no conception of what total untranslatability involves, no existence claim follows from that about such languages. Neither from inability to verify the existence of a totally untranslatable language, nor from inability to give content to the concept of such a language, does it follow that no such language exists.

5.6 Schemes fit experience or reality

On the second version of the dualism, a conceptual scheme or a language enables us to deal with the world by explaining and predicting facts. Schemes are a way of 'coping with (or fitting or facing) experience' (1984, p. 193). Such metaphors emphasize prediction rather than classification, and take us 'from the referential apparatus of language ... to whole sentences':

> It is sentences that predict (or are used to predict), sentences that cope or deal with things, that fit our sensory promptings, that can be compared or confronted with the evidence. (1984, p. 193)

The relation between the two versions of the dualism appears to be this: schemes which organize the world differently provide alternative ways of coping with experience. Since it is 'sentences that cope' and the 'referential apparatus' from which sentences are built varies with scheme, sentences from alternative schemes may be untranslatable and yet deal adequately with the world.

Davidson first argues that the idea of fitting experience reduces to that of being true. Schemes account for all the evidence:

> a theory may be borne out by the available evidence and yet be false. But what is in view here is not just actually available evidence; it is the totality of possible sensory evidence past, present, and future. (1984, p. 193)

To deal with all such evidence is just to be true: 'for a theory to fit or face up to the totality of possible sensory evidence is for that theory to be true'. There is no need to maintain a dichotomy between fitting all the evidence and being true:

> the notion of fitting the totality of experience, like the notion of fitting the facts, or of being true to the facts, adds nothing intelligible to the simple concept of being true. (1984, pp. 193-4)

Instead of two versions of what schemes fit we have this: 'something is an acceptable conceptual scheme or theory if it is true' (1984, p. 194). Since fitting experience or reality thus reduces to being true, 'the criterion of a conceptual scheme different from our own now becomes: largely true but not translatable'.

This raises the question of whether 'we understand the notion of truth as applied to language, independent of the notion of translation'. Davidson takes Tarski's theory of truth as constitutive of our understanding of truth. Convention T requires translation from an object language into the metalanguage in which the truth predicate is defined, so our understanding of truth depends crucially on translation. It is worth quoting Davidson's remarks in full:

> We recognize sentences like "'Snow is white' is true if and only if snow is white" to be trivially true. Yet the totality of such English sentences uniquely determines the extension of the concept of truth for English. Tarski generalized this observation and made it a test of theories of truth: according to Tarski's Convention T, a satisfactory theory of truth for a language L must entail, for every sentence s of L, a theorem of the form 's is true if and only if p' where 's' is replaced by a description of s and 'p' by s itself if L is English, and by a translation of s into English if L is not English. This isn't, of course, a definition of truth, and it doesn't hint that there is a single definition or theory that applies to languages generally. Nevertheless, Convention T suggests, though it cannot state, an important feature common to all the specialized concepts of truth. It succeeds in doing this by making essential use of the notion of translation into a language we know. Since Convention T embodies our best intuition as to how the concept of truth is used, there does not seem to be much hope for a test that a conceptual scheme is radically different from ours if that test depends on the assumption that we can divorce the notion of truth from that of translation. (1984, pp. 194-5)

Davidson's attack on the idea that schemes fit experience or reality has two steps. The first step is the reduction of the idea to that of being true. The second is the argument that truth is inextricable from translation. The two steps are linked in that the idea of an untranslatable scheme being true divorces truth from translation.

The problem with the first step is that fitting experience does not reduce to being true as far as scientific theories are concerned. Scientific theories may be, and often are, mistaken. More to the point, theories which 'fit the evidence' in the sense of being empirically adequate may be false; for a false theory may entail true predictions.

Davidson does, it is true, restrict attention to theories which fit 'the totality of possible sensory evidence past, present, future'. But this simply removes actual science from the ambit of the argument. What he says can neither be about actual science nor is his argument relevant to examples that have been put forward of untranslatable theories. For rarely, if ever, do actual theories fit all the evidence, much less all the future evidence.

Certainly, there is no need to assume purportedly untranslatable theories to be true. To take but one example, the phlogiston theory and Lavoisier's oxygen theory were both to varying degrees false. To say that a pair of theories is incommensurable carries no commitment to their truth: it is not to say that they are both untranslatable and true.

In any event, a theory which fits all 'possible sensory evidence' is not *ipso facto* true. Perhaps a theory which fits all the facts, observable and otherwise, is true; but if it fits only the 'sensory evidence', it does not follow that it is true. So even if a pair of untranslatable theories were to fit all the evidence, there would be no reason to suppose both were true: to describe such a pair as incommensurable is not therefore to say that they are true and untranslatable.

Part of the trouble is the choice of metaphor. 'Fitting the evidence' suggests empirical adequacy, which amounts to truth at an empirical level. But in any sense in which theories 'cope with experience' they need not strictly 'fit the evidence'. Even successful theories in actual science only fit the evidence imperfectly. Theories have empirical difficulties from the start and never fit all the evidence. Yet they may still 'cope with experience' in the sense of explaining and predicting phenomena, solving problems, and guiding research. To say that such theories 'fit the evidence' in any but a loose sense is mistaken. There is even less reason to say that they are true.

Since incommensurability need not be a relation between true theories, this breaks the link between the two steps of Davidson's argument. However, Davidson's Tarskian argument cannot be evaded so easily. For untranslatability implies the possibility of true but untranslatable sentences. If a sentence can be formulated in a language, then ordinarily either it or its negation is true. If a sentence cannot be translated from one language into another, then neither can its negation be so translated. Since either the sentence or its negation is true, untranslatability raises the possibility of a true but untranslatable sentence. So Davidson's attack on the separation of truth from translation must be confronted.

Davidson argues that our concept of truth is defined for English and languages translatable into English, so our grasp of the concept does not extend beyond languages intertranslatable with English. Convention T does not define a general concept of truth for unspecified languages. Rather, it defines a truth predicate for a specific language and for sentences of languages intertranslatable with it.

A theory of truth for a language which conforms with Convention T entails a set of T-sentences for the sentences of the language and their translational equivalents. Recurring to the previous quotation:

> according to Tarski's Convention T, a satisfactory theory of truth for a language L must entail, for every sentence s of L, a theorem of the form 's is true if and only if p' where 's' is replaced by a description of s and 'p' by s itself if L is English, and by a translation of s into English if L is not English. (1984, p. 194)

The set of English T-sentences defines the English truth predicate for the sentences of English and translational equivalents:

> sentences like "'Snow is white' is true if and only if snow is white" [are] trivially true ... the totality of such English sentences uniquely determines the extension of the concept of truth for English. (1984, p. 194)

Since no T-sentences can be formed in English for sentences not translatable into English, the truth predicate of English is not defined for such sentences, which fall outside its extension.

Thus our concept of truth is given by the definition of the English truth predicate which is defined exclusively for the set of English sentences and translational equivalents. Such a concept of truth cannot be understood independently of translation. For it would not be constitutive of understanding that concept to understand it as applied to untranslatable sentences: it would not be that concept if so applied.

On the face of it, this seriously undermines any notion of translation failure which depends on a translation independent concept of truth. The argument does not, however, have any implication about translation failure between parts of a single language. Translation failure between theories does not require a translation independent concept of truth. Since the languages of theories are sublanguages of a background natural language, they may be discussed within the inclusive natural language employed as metalanguage. English may function as metalanguage and the English truth predicate may be defined over its embedded sublanguages.[11] Since English contains both sublanguages there is no need to characterize truth in English for sentences not translatable into English. Hence Davidson's argument poses no threat to the thesis of untranslatability of theoretical sublanguages.

Beyond this, however, it can also be shown that Davidson's argument against the translation independent concept of truth is problematic in its own right. In the first place, the argument does not achieve its aim. It is meant to show, as against the scheme-content dualism, that something crucial to being a language (true assertion) has no content divorced from translation. But in order to show that one could not discover a language which turned out not to be translatable, it needs to be shown that a language could not be recognized as such without translation. What it purports to show instead is that truth is indefinable for untranslatable sentences. But that does not show that a language could not be identified as such from non-semantic evidence. If a language which proved resistant to translation were to be so identified, that would present *a posteriori* the existence of untranslatable truth. In denying that truth can be disjoined from translation, Davidson rules out untranslatable truth *a priori*. But no argument is offered from the connection between truth and translation to the conclusion that language is unrecognizable as such in the absence of translation. So far from showing the impossibility of such language recognition, the argument merely assumes it.

In the second place, there is an underlying tension between the purported truth-translation nexus and Davidson's concession of local translation failure. As we saw, Davidson allows that 'we can be clear about breakdowns in translation when they are local enough' (1984, p. 192). But if a sentence of a language which is on the whole translatable into English should turn out not to be so translatable, what is to be made of the possibility of its truth?

According to Davidson, the English truth predicate is undefined for any sentence untranslatable into English. So on Davidson's own account our concept of truth is inapplicable to such a sentence. Yet either such a sentence or its denial is true. Whatever sense Davidson thinks can be made of the idea of an untranslatable sentence, he seems not to allow sense to be made of its truth.

Now such isolated translation failure might be dismissed as unproblematic, since linguistic modifications may remove local untranslatability. The fact that truth conditions cannot be given for isolated sentences need not preclude sense being made of their truth.

For, suitably modified, the language may translate recalcitrant sentences and subsume them under its truth definition.

But when does it become intelligible to apply the concept of truth to such a sentence? If the sentence must await translation, problems arise with translating the truth predicate. For until such an untranslatable sentence can be translated, the truth predicate defined in its language does not have the same extension as ours. If our concept of truth can be applied to such a sentence prior to the requisite alteration of our language, then our truth predicate can be applied to sentences for which no T-sentence in our language can be formed.

In any case, to translate by altering a language is not strictly translation at all. If a sentence may only be translated by changing a language, then it cannot be translated into the unchanged language. But linguistic boundaries are fluid and arbitrary. No rules dictate when a fragment of a language becomes part of another or how large such a fragment may be. In principle, nothing prevents one language being appended in its entirety onto another. To permit application of the truth predicate to sentences translatable by linguistic modification amounts to making the possession of truth value depend on whether a sentence belongs to our language. But to have a truth value is not merely contingent upon belonging to our language. Nor does a sentence acquire truth conditions only upon entry into our language.

In the third place, at least a *prima facie* case can be made that truth is separable from translation. Suppose one were to protest against Davidson that the concept of truth does not depend on translation. The Tarskian schema "'s' is true if and only if p" supplies a structural feature of truth which does not merely consist in a specification of the extension of 'true' for English. It is a constraint on the concept of truth such that nothing counts as a truth predicate unless the sentence of which truth is predicated and the statement of truth conditions are equivalent. As against Davidson, the suggestion is that there is a general concept of truth of which the truth predicates of particular languages are special cases.

To give some content to this claim, let us consider how one might come to recognize a truth predicate for an untranslatable language. Consider a field linguist whom we may imagine to have encountered and mastered an alien language, call it 'Alien', which fails to translate into the linguist's home language, say English. What is to prevent such a linguist from recognizing an Alien predicate whose use in Alien corresponds to the behaviour in English of the predicate 'is true'? Suppose the linguist identifies a predicate 'T' of Alien such that appending 'T' to a named Alien sentence 's' yields a sentence "'s' is T" which is assertable when and only when 's' is assertable. Provided the linguist understands what 's' means and understands that "'s' is T" is materially equivalent to 's', what reason could there be not to take 'T' as the truth predicate for Alien?

Davidson's argument suggests the following objection to this proposal. Suppose the linguist reports in English, as regards the Alien sentence 's', that 's' is true. What does the linguist's report "'s' is true" mean? Since truth conditions cannot be given for 's' in English, the English truth predicate cannot be used to say that 's' is true. So to say in English that 's' is true must mean that 's' is true-in-Alien, not true-in-English. But what does "'s' is true-in-Alien" mean in English? 'True-in-Alien' is indefinable in English because no Alien truth conditions are specifiable in English.

To give sense to saying "'s' is true-in-Alien" in English one might say that 'true-in-Alien' is English for the Alien truth predicate. The Alien truth predicate and the English truth predicate have similar functions in their respective languages. Each predicate behaves disquotationally: the result of appending either predicate to a sentence is a sentence assertable in identical circumstances to the original. In virtue of this formal resemblance both predicates instantiate a general truth concept for particular languages, and 'true-in-Alien' can be used in English to translate the Alien truth predicate.

It may be objected that the notion of 'true-in-Alien' is inconsistent with a semantic conception of truth. Since no truth condition can be given for 's' in English, what it is to say "'s' is true-in-Alien" in English cannot be defined in English.

Now, we may grant that the extension of the truth predicate for a language is defined within the language by its T-sentences. No extensional specification of 'true-in-Alien' can be given in English using T-sentences since Alien is untranslatable into English. But it does not follow that no content can be given to 'true-in-Alien' in English. For the fact that the function of the Alien predicate is analogous to that of English 'true' enables 'true-in-Alien' to be defined as an English word for the Alien predicate which performs the same function in Alien as 'true' does in English.

It might further be objected that the Alien truth predicate is not recognizable as such if it differs extensionally from English 'true'. It is not in virtue of disquotation that a truth predicate is identifiable as such. In order to identify a truth predicate, its extension must be determined. To identify such an extension as the extension of a truth predicate, it must be the same extension as the extension of the English truth predicate.

As against this, the way the imagined linguist recognizes the Alien truth predicate is precisely the same way in which the truth predicate for English is identified. Given that the linguist understands Alien and recognizes a predicate of Alien whose behaviour conforms to Tarski's schema, nothing further is required for recognizing a truth predicate. The objection reduces, in effect, to the previously criticized assumption that translation is necessary for understanding a language.

Appendix: Translation and languagehood

According to a view such as Davidson's, something which we might have reason to think is a language is not proven to be such until it has been translated. I will try to show, to the contrary, that it is necessary to appeal to factors which are independent of translation in order to establish that it is indeed a language which has been translated in the first place. If this is right, it follows that proof of languagehood, so far from depending on translation, is in fact logically prior to translation.

Let me briefly clarify the view I seek to challenge. The view is not that one is unable to have good grounds for holding that something is a language prior to translating it. For it may allow that there may be strong grounds for taking untranslated inscriptions, sounds or activity to be linguistic. The view, rather, is that such grounds can yield at best only a *prima facie* case for languagehood. Translation alone provides a criterion of being a language.

This view depends on a contrast between translation as criterion of languagehood and translation independent evidence for languagehood. Translation — the rendering of words or sentences of one language by means of words or sentences the same in meaning in another language — is taken to constitute definitive evidence for languagehood. Non-translational evidence, on the other hand, consists in non-semantic or pragmatic features of purportedly linguistic material.

The latter sort of evidence may include facts about the social setting in which speechlike behaviour is observed or the physical environment in which apparent inscriptions or symbols are found. It may also include formal aspects of the material, which indicate the presence of syntactic structure, or of morphological or phonetic properties. There is much that such evidence can include, but it excludes semantic information such as reports of the meaning of a given word or sentence, for that would be to invoke translation.

The contrast between translation and translation independent evidence of languagehood seems to mark a genuine difference. A translation of a language tells us such things as what its words and sentences mean, and it presupposes that what is translated is a language. This contrasts sharply with the situation in which evidence is proposed for taking untranslated sounds or inscriptions to be linguistic. Real as the contrast is, however, it cannot bear the weight placed on it by the position we are considering.

The trouble is that the claim that a language has been successfully translated is a claim which itself stands in need of evidence. Translation may fail and it may fail in various ways. It is possible not only to mistranslate, but — and this is of most relevance to the issue of language recognition — it is even possible to mistakenly identify material as linguistic and propose a translation for what is not in fact a language. The possibility of misidentification and mistranslation reveals translation to be a theoretical enterprise. As such, it must be supported by evidence and, like all theoretical undertakings, is fallible.

Consequently, any purported translation must be capable of being supported by evidence that it is indeed a translation of something linguistic. Such evidence cannot itself appeal to semantic information without begging the question. It would not do, for example, to defend translation of a sentence P of a language L into our language by saying that P in L means the same as our sentence Q, for that would presuppose the correctness of the translation to have been established already. Nor would it do to defend the translation of P as Q by claiming that such a translation is consistent with the translations of other sentences of L which have already been given. For that would presuppose the legitimacy of the translation of the other sentences, and indeed of their identification as linguistic. It follows, therefore, that evidence for translation must ultimately depend on factors which are independent of translation.

Unless non-translational evidence can be put forward there is no reason to take a purported translation to be a legitimate rendering of something linguistic into our language. Hence translation independent evidence must be employed to defend translation, which cannot therefore play the role in identifying language that has been claimed for it.

Notes

1. For example, it might be argued in a metalanguage that a pair of object languages is not intertranslatable without expressing untranslatable content in either object language.
2. Even their use of examples independently of such arguments would be incoherent. For if the examples cannot be expressed in our language, then they cannot be expressed in any discussion couched in our language.

3. See Kuhn on Newton and Einstein (1970a, pp. 101-2), phlogiston versus oxygen (1983a, pp. 675-6); Feyerabend on impetus and momentum (1981b, pp. 62-9), and classical physics versus general relativity and quantum mechanics (1981c).
4. Feyerabend does not restrict incommensurability to scientific theories: languages, world views, frameworks and forms of life may also be incommensurable (cf. 1987, p. 81, 1981a, p. 16, 1975, p. 269). But such broader application of the concept of incommensurability does not imply that the language into which the vocabulary of incommensurable theories is untranslatable is a total natural language.
5. For an example of a discussion of untranslatability which has this form, see Feyerabend's discussion of 'impetus' (1981b, pp. 65-6). He mentions 'impetus' and gives its meaning as defined in the impetus theory; then he shows that such a definition cannot be formulated on the basis of the principles of Newtonian mechanics. This is a point about the semantic limitations of the language of Newtonian mechanics, and the meaning of 'impetus' is not expressed in that language anywhere in the argument. The discussion is couched in English used as a metalanguage, so the language of argument and the language into which 'impetus' fails to be translatable are distinct.
6. This rebuttal may be further supported by noting that the untranslatable language to be interpreted in the case of an incommensurable theory is not a total language. For what is at issue is untranslatability within a single language, and what must be interpreted is an unknown area of that language. Interpretation of theoretical terminology untranslatable into one's own theory is therefore not the radical project of learning a completely unknown language without the benefit of any common language.
7. I say 'derives' advisedly. Davidson puts the principle of charity to a different use. However, the argument discussed in the text follows immediately from Davidson's analysis of interpretative charity. He uses the principle against partial translation failure and concludes that no sharp distinction between difference of language and of belief can be drawn (1984, p. 197).
8. Davidson may intend to exempt theory from maximal assignment of truth, for he does say we should assign truth 'subject to considerations of ... common-sense, or scientific, knowledge of explicable error' (1984, p. 196). But he fails to elaborate the point.

9. A number of authors have noted Davidson's implicit verificationism here: among them Rorty (1982, pp. 5-6) and Blackburn (1984, p. 61).
10. Clearly, it cannot be a sufficient condition of being a language, but it is perhaps necessary.
11. For example, an English T-sentence for a sentence of the impetus theory may be formulated as follows: 'Projectile bodies have impetus' is true if and only if projectile bodies have impetus.

6 Incommensurability, translation and understanding

6.1 Introduction

As scientific theories are altered and replaced, the concepts employed by theories also change. New concepts are introduced and old concepts undergo modification. Such conceptual change manifests itself, at the semantic level, in difference in the meaning of the vocabulary of theories. New terms with new meanings are introduced, and old terms shift their meaning in the transition between theories. Conceptual change is an integral part of theory change, and semantic variance between theories is the result.

The idea that meaning shifts with theory change has led to the thesis that theories may be incommensurable with one another. Kuhn and Feyerabend have argued that the languages of some semantically variant theories fail to be fully intertranslatable, and that the content of such theories cannot be directly compared. For without being expressed in synonymous vocabulary, no consequence of one theory can assert or deny a statement the same in meaning as a consequence of the other. Theories whose content is incomparable because of such translation failure are said by Kuhn and Feyerabend to be incommensurable.

The standard reponse to the thesis has been to deny the incomparability of semantically variant theories by pointing to various relations of common reference between their terms.[1] Such relations enable the content of theories to be compared, since statements from rival theories whose constituent terms refer to the same things may enter into conflict or agreement with one another. And since the terms of theories may have the same reference without being synonymous, the content of such theories may be compared even in the absence of the shared meaning which is required for translation. Thus, contrary to Kuhn and Feyerabend, translation failure between theories does not entail incomparability of content.[2]

Since comparison must take place in some language, the question arises in which language theories which fail to be intertranslatable may be compared. The key here is to distinguish the special terminology or sublanguage employed by a theory from the background natural language in which it is embedded. Translation failure of the kind relevant to incommensurability involves an inability to translate between localized theoretical sublanguages within the context of a shared background language.[3]

Given the containment of such sublanguages within an encompassing background language, the background language may function as metalanguage for the sublanguages. As such, analysis of semantic features of the vocabulary of the embedded sublanguages, treated as object languages, may be conducted in the background language.[4] Comparison of the content of theories may therefore take place in a portion of the background language (possibly including one or both theoretical sublanguages), which may be employed as metalanguage to discuss the referential relations between the terms of theories.[5]

In sum, an advocate of referential comparison is free to endorse the claim of untranslatability between theories.[6] However, any attempt to accommodate untranslatability must face serious objections with which the claim has been confronted. Thus, in this chapter I will address the issue of how it is possible to understand the language of an incommensurable theory. My aim here is to defend the idea of translation failure against the objection that it incoherently precludes understanding. As such, the argument of this chapter continues and further develops the argument in Section 5.3.

6.2 Understanding and failure to translate

Translation may seem intimately related to understanding. Indeed, one might think that it is necessary for understanding, or that understanding a foreign language constitutes translation into a native language. But if understanding is in some way contingent on translation, Kuhn and Feyerabend have no business claiming to understand untranslatable concepts. For the claim that one can both understand and yet fail to translate would be incoherent.

This objection is raised by Putnam, who claims that proponents of theories incommensurable with ours 'would be conceptualizable by us only as animals producing responses to stimuli', so that "to tell us that Galileo had 'incommensurable' notions *and then to go on to describe them at length* is totally incoherent" (1981, pp. 114-5).[7] Kuhn and Feyerabend have replied to Putnam by distinguishing learning a language from translation, and by arguing that the former may succeed though the latter fails. Feyerabend remarks that 'we can learn a language or a culture from scratch, as a child learns them, without detour through our native language' (1987, p. 76). And Kuhn claims that 'acquiring a new language is not the same as translating from it into one's own. Success with the first does not imply success with the second' (1983, pp. 672-3). Both authors therefore distinguish understanding what is said in a foreign language from translating it into one's own. And both hold that the possibility of understanding without translation removes the threat of incoherence. In what follows I seek to defend their use of this distinction.

6.3 Translation and understanding

To translate from one language into another is to express in one language what is said in the other. This involves the formulation of sentences in one language which have the same meaning as sentences of the other. Translation from one language into another requires that the former be translatable into the latter. Translatability depends on the existence of certain semantic relations between languages. In particular, it depends on whether the home language has the semantic resources required to formulate expressions with the same meaning as expressions of the target language.

The requirement of sameness of meaning reflects the need for translation in the relevant sense to be semantically exact. For although in practice translation between natural languages is often approximate, the incommensurability thesis at most denies exact translation.[8] However, the requirement does not imply that translation must be word for word. A complex expression or phrase may be synonymous with a single word and translate it exactly.[9]

By contrast, understanding is a relation between a speaker and a language; it involves no relation between languages. To understand something said in a language is to know what it means, and to arrive at knowledge of the meaning of an utterance requires a minimal competence in the language. For example, to determine the meaning of a sentence a speaker must employ knowledge of the syntax and semantics of the language to which the sentence belongs. As such, understanding what is said in a language is a cognitive relation between a speaker and a language. Neither translation nor any other interlinguistic relation enters into it.

On such a characterization, translation and understanding are distinct relationships. Translatability involves semantic relations between languages, whereas understanding is a cognitive relation between a speaker and a language. Given this, one language might be untranslatable into another which lacks the requisite semantic resources, and yet a speaker of one might understand the other. The semantic limits of a language need impose no limitation on a speaker's capacity to understand another language, so translation might fail while understanding succeeds.

6.4 Language learning and bilingualism

That translation is indeed unnecessary for understanding is suggested by reflection on the acquisition of language. Children do not enter the world equipped with a natural language. When they acquire their mother tongue they do not translate it, but rather learn to understand it directly. Similarly, adults may acquire a second language as children do their first. They may immerse themselves in a foreign language and learn it by the direct method from native speakers. So too a field linguist can acquire the unknown language of a primitive people, without the aid of an interpreter or translation manual. Nor need the acquisition of such a language proceed via translation into the linguist's home language, for the linguist too may employ a direct approach.

Further support for the independence of understanding from translation derives from reflection on bilingualism. The bilingual is a speaker with full native competence in two languages. Such speakers need not translate into a home language in order to understand. For with full native competence the bilingual understands both languages equally well. It is not as if such understanding requires translation back and forth inside the speaker's head. Moreover, the notion of a home language is inapplicable to the bilingual case, for with full native competence in both languages neither merits the status of home language.

The cases of direct language acquisition and bilingualism suggest that understanding a second language requires no mediation by a first language. The independence of understanding from translation, which thus emerges in turn suggests that one can understand a language without translation. There need, therefore, be no incoherence in claiming to understand an untranslatable language.

6.5 The place of direct language learning

I will devote the rest of the discussion to objections which might be raised against the separation of understanding from translation. The first objection stems from the idea that learning a natural language differs significantly from learning the special language of a theory. The project of learning a natural language is a monumental undertaking, whereas learning the language of a theory is a localized activity which occurs within the context of a background natural language. Hence, it might be denied that it is necessary to learn the language of a theory by the method of direct language learning.

An objection of this kind has been made by Peter Achinstein, who takes incommensurability to imply that 'a person could not learn a theory by having it explained to him using any words whose meanings he understands before he learns the theory' (1968, p. 97). Against this, he argues as follows:

> The only thing I can do is try to learn the meanings *extra-linguistically*. I must watch what those who use the theory do in their laboratories, the sorts of items to which they apply their terms, and so forth. I must learn each new theory like a child first learning language (rather than like someone learning more of his own language or a second language after learning a first one). Perhaps it would be possible (though, I suspect, exceedingly difficult) to learn scientific theories this way. What I find unacceptable is the consequence that they *must* be learned this way. In actual practice at least some if not most terms in a new theory are explained to those learning the theory by using words whose meanings the learners already know. (1968, p. 97)

Here Achinstein does not deny that the terms of a theory could be learned as a child learns its first language. What he objects to is the idea that there should be no other way to learn such terms.

However, one might equally well object that child language learning is irrelevant. For there is a fundamental difference between learning the everyday language of middle sized physical objects and learning the technical vocabulary of laboratory and theory. One might, therefore, go further than Achinstein and deny that the child language learning model applies to learning the language of a theory.

The lesson to be drawn from such objections is, however, a minimal one. Namely, there is an important disanalogy between learning a natural language and learning the language of a theory. The two projects differ in that acquiring the language of an untranslatable theory is not as radical an undertaking as that of learning an entire natural language from scratch. For, as noted in Section 6.1, incommensurability is not a failure to translate between natural languages, but between theoretical sublanguages which may be embedded within the same natural language.

Advocates of incommensurable theories may share a common natural language within which their semantical differences are localized. The task of acquiring a new theoretical sublanguage is therefore the more restricted one of learning a new vocabulary or a new idiom within one's own natural language. Sharing a natural language enables rival theorists to make use of a common language in acquiring the new portion of their language. This is not to say that there is no need to acquire terms of the untranslatable language directly, but rather that the method of direct language acquisition may be employed in favourable circumstances because the background language is shared.

Now, it might be objected that, given a shared natural language, anything expressible in one theory but not in a rival theory might be expressed in some portion of the encompassing natural language. In that case, no non-translational form of understanding is involved; for what is expressed in the one theory may be translated into a natural language known to advocates of the rival theory.

In reply to this objection, two cases need to be distinguished. It might happen that what is inexpressible in the rival theory can be expressed in a portion of the background natural language. In this first case, it is indeed unnecessary — albeit possible — to understand without translation. But there is no guarantee that such a situation will always obtain. What is expressible in the first theory may not be expressible in terms independent of that theory. In such a situation, what is expressible in the theory is not translatable into either the rival theory or the surrounding natural language. In this second case, therefore, the vocabulary of the theory can only be acquired directly, by learning it in the context of the theory. For understanding cannot be achieved via translation into the shared natural language.

6.6 The principle of effability

I will now consider an objection to the separation of understanding from translation which derives from the so-called 'principle of effability'.[10] The principle expresses the intuition that anything that can be thought can be said. To apply the principle to our problem, it may be stated in the following strong form: anything that can be thought can be said in any natural language.

The objection is that, according to the principle of effability, as so stated, understanding entails translation. For if one can understand something, one can think it. So if one can understand something said in a foreign language, it can be said in any language, and in particular it can be said in our language. Thus any understandable foreign language is translatable.

The strong statement of the principle assumes languages have unlimited expressive capacities. Yet the contrary assumption is not obviously false. It might well be that languages have semantic limits which prevent propositions sayable in one language from being expressed in another. This suggests that the effability principle should be weakened to: anything which can be thought can be said in some natural language. But, so weakened, the principle cannot sustain the objection to the translation-understanding distinction, since translation would no longer follow from understanding.

There is, however, a way to retain the strong version of the principle without weakening it in this way. The principle can be supplemented with the assumption that natural languages are infinitely enrichable. That would mean that anything sayable in one language is sayable in any other if, where necessary, the vocabulary of the other language is suitably extended.

There is much to be said for the view that natural languages are infinitely enrichable. For there seems to be no fact of the matter about where to draw the line between concurrent natural languages or between past and present stages of the same natural language. The actual divisions between natural languages rest on convention and historical accident. And such divisions as there are tend to be fluid, with terminological innovation frequently being based on inter-linguistic borrowing. Because there are no definite boundaries to natural languages, there are no limits to the alterations which may be made to such languages, so anything thinkable can be said in a natural language.

The strong principle of effability may, therefore, be conceded, provided that the assumption of infinite enrichability is made as well. Yet such a concession is entirely trivial. The assumption of infinite enrichability implies unlimited expressibility. And anything expressible in some language is translatable into a language with unlimited expressive capacities.

There is no need, though, to make a similar concession with respect to the more limited idioms or sublanguages which make up language as a whole. It is consistent with the concession of unlimited expressibility for natural languages to deny such expressibility for at least some subsections of natural languages. So while we may concede the principle of effability at the level of natural languages with no definite boundaries, the principle breaks down when it is applied to the more restricted sublanguages which such languages contain.

Here it might seem that if natural languages lack definite boundaries, their embedded sublanguages must, for similar reasons, lack such limits. Conversely, it might seem that if sublanguages have limits, such limits must give rise to limits on natural languages. Hence, it might be objected that effability must be uniformly either asserted or denied for both sublanguages and natural languages.

Such an objection fails, however, since it assumes indefinite natural language boundaries to be incompatible with definite sublinguistic boundaries. A natural language is a composite, which contains a multitude of localized vocabularies with special areas of application. While such vocabularies may change in various ways, whole new vocabularies may be incorporated into the natural language. Thus, even if a given sublanguage were subject to limits, the containing natural language need have no boundaries, since it may grow by the accretion of new vocabulary. Nor does the absence of definite boundaries on the containing language imply that the contained sublanguage can have no limits. For it may be possible to isolate a portion of a language which constitutes one of its special vocabularies; and since it is designed for a specific context, the vocabulary may be subject to certain limitations.

In particular, there appear to be limits on the terminology which can be introduced within the context of a theory. These limits are set by the ontology of a theory and by the laws purported to govern the entities postulated by the ontology of the theory. Such limits arise because of the inability to introduce into the ontology of a theory entities whose nature or behaviour is incompatible with the ontology or the laws of the theory. Limits on the types of entity to which a theory may be committed lead to limits on the vocabulary which can be introduced in the context of the theory. For a term cannot be introduced into the vocabulary of a theory, as a putatively referring expression of the theory, if the entity, to which it purports to refer, does not exist according to the theory. Hence, the vocabulary employed in the context of a theory can be treated as a restricted sublanguage which cannot be extended without limitation.

6.7 The principle of charity

Finally, I will consider an objection which stems from the principle of interpretative charity, which advises us to attribute maximal truth when interpreting the speech and behaviour of others. The need for charity about true belief is thought to arise from the close connection between meaning and belief. We need to know what speakers' words mean to find out what they believe, and we cannot find out what they mean without finding out what they believe. In interpreting what speakers of an unknown language say, one way to discover what their words mean is to get a prior fix on their beliefs. If we charitably attribute to speakers of such a language beliefs which we would ourselves hold in the circumstances in which they find themselves, then we can use such beliefs to fix the meaning of their words.[11]

The objection arises as follows. It assumes charity to be necessary for interpretation. Interpretation is assumed to be how one comes to understand speech in an unknown language. Hence, charity is necessary for understanding. Charity involves the attribution of true beliefs to a speaker of the unknown language using sentences of our language which we hold true. But such attribution constitutes translation, for it equates utterances in the unknown language with sentences of our language. Hence, translation is necessary for understanding. Thus, the principle of charity makes understanding contingent on translation, and therefore the separation between translation and understanding is inconsistent with the principle of charity.

There are a number of things to be said in reply to such an appeal to charity. In the first place, there is no need to accept the purported link between charity and translation which licenses the inference from understanding to translation. For there is no reason why charity must involve the attribution of truth using sentences of our language. Charity may be incorporated into the direct language learning approach in the form of the assumption that, translatable or not, what speakers of an unknown language say is on the whole true. Charitable interpretation need not, therefore, result in translation, so that charity might enable one to understand a language not translatable into one's own.

There is, however, a deeper problem with charity which undercuts such direct use of charitable truth attribution. The major difficulty facing any appeal to charity in the present context centers on the epistemological unsoundness of charity as a policy for the interpretation of theoretical discourse. No matter how well motivated charity is with respect to commonsense belief, the policy of attributing maximal truth to theoretical belief is unwarranted, for reasons which are entirely standard.

For a start, while the history of science is a success story which is without parallel, it is in fact the history of good false theories which have been overthrown by better false theories. Not only does this undermine the advice to treat past theories as by and large true, it also suggests that we should resist the dictates of charity for present day theories. For the vicissitudes of past theories license the expectation that today's theories will, in time, meet with a similar fate at the hands of future science.

Such a fallibilist attitude towards theories is reinforced by reflection on standard epistemological difficulties concerning the nature of empirical support. The combined weight of the problems of induction, underdetermination of theory by data, theory ladenness of observation and the Quine-Duhem thesis severely weakens the appeal of any unconditional assumption of the truth of theories. For, while the acceptance of a given theory may well be rationally justified, the generalized assumption of the truth of theories is not.

Thus reflection on the history of science and on the nature of empirical support reveals maximal truth attribution to theoretical belief to be unjustified. The claim that such belief must be interpreted charitably — and with it, the implication that any understandable theory is translatable — may, therefore, be rejected. Yet, given our earlier appeal to the possibility of direct language learning, such a dismissal of charity cannot be left unqualified.

It might be held that learning a language from scratch requires charity. For it might seem that, without at least a tentative attribution of truth, one would have no grounds on which to base any particular assignment of content to utterances in an unknown language. Yet, if charity is both necessary for direct language learning and inapplicable to theoretical discourse, the language employed by a theory cannot be learned directly.

To meet this problem it is not enough to disconnect charity from translation. The claim that charity can be applied directly to a language without translation is appropriate as a criticism of the view that the understanding of an untranslatable language is precluded by charity. But, given the above epistemological grounds for the rejection of charitable truth attribution, the problem now is to show that such charity is unnecessary for learning the language of a theory directly.

One option here is to appeal to a weaker version of the principle of charity on which charity is not characterized as maximal attribution of truth.[12] The principle of charity might be taken instead as the advice that, in seeking to understand the language of a theory, one should try to interpret theoretical belief as rational. Thus, in interpreting the words of a scientist, charity would license the provisional assumption that the scientist's words express beliefs which form a rational belief set. One would then seek to understand the belief set of a scientist as sensitive to the available evidence and internally coherent. To avoid imposing our own views on past scientists, one should also seek to understand such beliefs as appropriate given the intellectual and historical context within which the scientist operates.

A principle of charity which advises rational interpretation of agents is immune to the above epistemological criticism of charitable truth attribution. The charitable assumption of epistemic rationality may therefore be incorporated into the project of learning the language of a theory directly. Since such charity may be applied directly to the unknown theoretical language, the ability to arrive at an understanding of such a language does not imply that it can be translated.

6.8 Conclusion

We have been considering the view that one may understand a theory whose vocabulary is untranslatable into the special language of the theory one accepts. I have argued that, since understanding is independent of translation, no incoherence attaches to the claim that one understands a theory untranslatable into one's own. In the process, I have rejected objections based on the principles of effability and charity which deny the independence of understanding and translation. The considerations I have raised constitute a defence of the use to which Kuhn and Feyerabend have put the distinction between translation and understanding. This defence provides a basis on which to conclude that the incommensurability thesis does not incoherently preclude the possibility of understanding conceptually variant theories.

Notes

1. The response originates with Scheffler (1967), and is espoused, for example, by Putnam (1975b) and Devitt (1979). Initially stated in terms of co-reference by Scheffler, the response was later extended to a variety of relations of referential overlap by Field (1973), Kitcher (1978) and Martin (1971).
2. For convenience, rather than to erase the distinction between language and theory, I will sometimes speak of translation failure between theories instead of between the language of theories.
3. Feyerabend's version of incommensurability is more extreme than Kuhn's. The former involves variation of meaning of the observational and theoretical terms associated with a theory (Feyerabend, 1981b), whereas the latter is restricted to a localized subset of the central terms used by a theory (Kuhn, 1983). Yet in both cases the range of semantic variance is confined to the language employed

by a theory and does not extend to the natural language in which such theoretical language is embedded.

4. This point deals with the objection that arguments for incommensurability court paradox by translating the untranslatable (Davidson, 1984, pp. 183-4). In brief: it can be argued in a natural language taken as metalanguage that a pair of embedded theoretical sublanguages fails to be intertranslatable. The point is developed at greater length in Chapter 5.
5. Another option is to employ terms of one theory, possibly supplemented by vocabulary from the background language, to specify the referents of terms of the rival theory. In some cases, this strategy may only work for the tokens of rival term types (see Kitcher, 1978).
6. Indeed, recent work on the reference of terms employed by theories suggests that advocates of the referential response should embrace the untranslatability claim. For the relevant developments in the theory of reference, see Chapter 3 of my (1994), where I employ a modified causal theory of reference to show that phlogistic terminology is untranslatable into the language of the oxygen theory; see also my (1991).
7. Objections to incommensurability which raise related difficulties about communication and understanding have been made by a number of critics: e.g. Achinstein (1968, p. 97), Kitcher (1978, pp. 519-20), Scheffler (1967, pp. 16-7) and Trigg (1973, p. 101).
8. That incommensurability is the failure of exact rather than approximate translation may be seen from the similarity of the concepts which Kuhn and Feyerabend claim not to be interchangeable: e.g., Newtonian versus Einsteinian mass, impetus versus momentum, oxygen versus dephlogisticated air. For remarks explicitly bearing on this point, see Feyerabend (1975, p. 277) and Kuhn (1976, p. 191).
9. Incommensurability requires more than mere absence of single word equivalents, for the latter provides no basis for the denial of content comparability. Where exact translation succeeds in the absence of word for word equivalents, statements the same in meaning can be formulated and content unproblematically compared. See Kuhn's remark that translation need not replace 'words and phrases in the original' in a 'one-for-one' manner (1983, p. 672). The point is implicit in Feyerabend's repeated insistence that for incommensurability 'the conditions of concept formation in one theory forbid the formation of the basic concepts of the other' (1978, p. 68, note 118); cf. (1987, p. 31, 1981f, p. 154, note 54). Presumably, the inability to form a concept involves the inability

to define a term, rather than the mere absence of single word synonymy.

10. The name of the principle — though not the formulation to be employed — is due to Katz (1972, p. 19), who traces the principle to Frege and Tarski.
11. For such a view of the role of a principle of charity, see, for example, Davidson (1984, pp. 195-7).
12. Of course, a second option is to deny that charity in any form is required to learn the language of a theory directly. Whether this option is plausible or not, it is unnecessary to develop it here in order to meet the present objection.

Part IV

RATIONALITY

7 The problem of rational theory choice

7.1 Introduction

The problem of rational theory choice is the problem of whether choice of theory by a scientist may be objectively rational in the absence of an invariant scientific method. In this chapter I offer a solution to the problem, but the solution I propose may come as something of a surprise. For I wish to argue that the work of the very authors who have put the rationality of such choice in question, Thomas Kuhn and Paul Feyerabend, contains all that is needed to solve the problem.

The problem of rational scientific theory choice is a problem which was generated out of the clash between the two major twentieth century traditions in the philosophy of science. On the one hand, there is the empiricist tradition in the philosophy of science, which includes logical positivism and falsificationism, and which holds that science is governed by a single scientific method, invariant throughout history and the various branches of science. On the other hand, there is the more recent historical approach to philosophy of science, the main advocates of which have been Kuhn and Feyerabend, which takes the practice of science to vary with historical time period, theoretical context, and scientific discipline. In contrast with the former, the latter allows that there may be variation in scientific methodology throughout the history of science, and between different branches of science.

The question of whether scientists' choice of theory may be rational arose in the wake of widespread rejection of empiricist models of science during the 1950s and 1960s. According to the empiricist conception of science, rational acceptance of theories is governed by an invariant scientific method which is applicable throughout science. This method typically involves the use of observational data, as a basis on which to generalize to universal theories, whose logical connection with the data is either inductive or deductive in form. The principal reasons for abandoning such models have involved problems with the empirical basis of science due to the theory dependence of observation and the underdetermination of theory by data. In addition, problems of both a historical and philosophical nature have raised serious doubts about the existence of a uniform scientific method characteristic of science throughout its history.

According to empiricist philosophy of science, the acceptance of a theory by a scientist is rationally justified provided the scientist's acceptance of the theory is certified by the scientific method. For example, if a theory has attained a high degree of confirmation based on empirical evidence which supports it, then acceptance of the theory is rationally justified. Alternatively, if a theory has been submitted to severe tests without being refuted, and no other theory is as well tested, then it is rational to accept the theory. In either case, rational theory acceptance is based on objective grounds, since both observation and logical inference provide epistemically well grounded procedures of inquiry, and because such procedures jointly constitute a neutral court of appeal to which all scientists have recourse. Theory acceptance, therefore, need not be made on the basis of subjective matters of personal whim, bias or taste, since it may be based on methodological considerations, which are objective in the sense both of having properly epistemic import and being open to public scrutiny.

Advocates of the historical approach, by contrast, argue that there is no fixed scientific method, and that there is instead variation in the methodological standards employed by scientists in the evaluation of theories. Yet, in the absence of a fixed scientific method, the historical school is unable to account for the rationality and objectivity of scientific theory acceptance in the manner of empiricist philosophy of science.

This leads to the problem of rational theory choice. For if there is no fixed scientific method, then it is unclear how the choice of one theory over another can be either rational or objective. This is particularly the case if the advocates of one theory endorse one set of methodological standards, and the advocates of the rival theory endorse another set of standards. If one theory is supported by one set of standards, and the rival by another, and there is no higher set of standards, then there would appear to be no basis for a rational choice between such theories. In the end, a radical epistemological relativism may seem unavoidable, since without a fixed method to arbitrate between rival sets of methodological standards, rationality can at best depend on whatever sets of standards a scientist happens to employ.

7.2 Non-algorithmic rationality

Numerous authors have reacted to the work of the historical school by arguing that the thesis of methodological variation leads to relativism and irrationalism.[1] Recently, however, some authors have suggested that, rather than leading to relativism and irrationalism, the work of the historical school leads to a new conception of scientific rationality.[2] I wish to suggest that such a new conception of scientific rationality is already to hand, and is available within the work of the historical school. To this end, I will present four characteristic theses of the historical school, which, taken together, yield a new model of scientific rationality.

The fundamental tenet on which this new model of scientific rationality rests is one of the leading themes of historical philosophy of science. It might even be taken as the thesis which unites it into a philosophical school. This is the thesis that rational choice between conflicting scientific theories cannot in general be governed by an algorithm of theory choice. That is to say, the evaluative rules and criteria which make up the methodology of science cannot be fashioned into a single, universally acceptable, deterministic procedure, capable of being employed in a mechanical way to yield a unique choice between alternative scientific theories.

This thesis is succinctly expressed in the following quote from Kuhn's Postscript to the second edition of *The Structure of Scientific Revolutions*:

> There is no neutral algorithm for theory-choice, no systematic decision procedure which, properly applied, must lead each individual in the group to the same decision. (1970a, p. 200)

This claim of Kuhn's is a negative existential claim, and as such its truth is unable to be conclusively established. Despite the inconclusiveness of this claim, however, I suggest that it should be interpreted as a generalization based on a study of past science, which has a great deal of historical plausibility. In particular, evidence from the history of science, both of past methodological change and of repeated and prolonged disagreement throughout the history of science, indicates that no algorithm for theory choice has yet to be discovered. Moreover, in view of the complexity and variability of actual theory choice situations, it is a highly plausible conjecture that no such algorithm is ever likely to be found.

It is important to note that Kuhn actually says that there is no 'neutral' algorithm for theory choice. Presumably, the reason for this qualification is that, while it may in fact be possible to formulate an algorithm capable of uniquely determining theory choice, all such algorithms beg the question in favour of a particular theory or methodological criterion. It will simplify matters, however, to formulate this first thesis as follows:

> T^1: There is no algorithm of scientific theory choice.

Before proceeding to the second thesis, two comments are in order about T^1. First, the denial of an algorithm of theory choice should not be understood as a denial of the existence of a scientific method or of a set of methodological criteria. What T^1 denies is that there is any universal method or set of criteria which is capable of mechanically deciding between alternative theories. Second, T^1 should also not be taken to deny that there are algorithmic rules which occur in science: for even if there is no single, universal algorithm of theory choice, there may still be individual rules which function as algorithms.

7.3 Methodological pluralism

The second thesis which I propose is also principally due to Kuhn, though it is found in other authors as well.[3] According to this thesis, there is, instead of a single scientific method, an array of evaluative criteria to which scientists may appeal in choosing between theories. Kuhn lists as examples of such criteria, predictive accuracy, consistency, scope, simplicity and fertility (1977c, pp. 321-2), and he comments that such

> criteria of choice ... function not as rules, which determine choice, but as values, which influence it. (1977c, p. 331)

I will not follow Kuhn in using the term 'value' to refer to methodological criteria, though I do think Kuhn is right that there is a significant difference between those criteria which dictate the outcome of a decision and those which merely serve as a guide to choice.

In light of Kuhn's remarks, I propose the following statement of methodological pluralism as the second thesis of the present model:

> T^2: In choosing between scientific theories, scientists draw upon an array of evaluative criteria, which guide or influence rather than determine their choice of theory.

Whereas T^1 is a negative thesis which denies an algorithm of theory choice, T^2 is a positive thesis which asserts the pluralistic nature of scientific methodology. The positive thesis in T^2 is, however, complementary to the denial in T^1 of a universally applicable algorithm of theory choice. For, while there may be no algorithm of theory choice, there may nevertheless be a range of evaluative criteria, which scientists employ in deciding which theory to accept.

According to the pluralistic model of scientific methodology, scientists have at their disposal a range of criteria of theory appraisal, which jointly constitute the methodology of science. Since scientists may modify and replace methodological criteria in the advance of science, there may be variation in the set of criteria employed during the history of science. Similarly, since different branches of science may develop in different ways, there may also be methodological variation across the sciences. While it is not possible at this point to provide a complete taxonomy of such methodological criteria, the plausibility of the pluralist approach requires that at least a preliminary indication of such a taxonomy be given.

Evaluative criteria, of the sort discussed by methodological pluralists, range from general criteria and principles of theory appraisal to specific rules of experimental procedure. Examples of the former might include the criteria mentioned by Kuhn (e.g., simplicity, coherence, accuracy), as well as Popper's dictum that scientists should maximize the falsifiability of theories by avoiding *ad hoc* hypotheses. As examples of the latter, one might think of instructions for proper use of instrumentation, procedures to insure purity of samples or accuracy of measurement, and so forth. Located somewhere between the extremes of general criteria and rules of laboratory practice, one would find criteria of explanatory adequacy, such as being a well tested hypothesis, or being appropriately logically related to the phenomena to be explained, as well as norms of proper test procedure, such as repeatability and the use of experimental controls or blinds.

7.4 Two corollaries of pluralism

Turning to the two remaining elements of the model, both the third and fourth theses are, in effect, corollaries of T^2. The third thesis stems from the observation that there may be conflict between the various evaluative criteria.[4] For, while it is in principle possible for a single theory to maximally satisfy all criteria, in practice conflicting theories might each satisfy different criteria better than their rivals. Hence,

> T^3: The evaluative criteria employed in scientific theory choice may conflict in application to alternative theories.

Where such a conflict between methodological criteria occurs, the set of such criteria cannot itself uniquely dictate the outcome for choice of theory. As such, the potential for conflict between criteria further exemplifies the claim in T^1 that there is no algorithm of theory choice.

The fourth thesis derives from Feyerabend's claim that all methodological rules have limitations, and are therefore defeasible. Such defeasibility of methodological criteria is the main lesson to be learned from Feyerabend's critique of scientific method. Feyerabend is, of course, famous for having claimed in *Against Method* that, as far as the methodology of science is concerned, 'anything goes' (1975, p. 28). Yet it is often overlooked that the (non-rhetorical) force of this claim is not to deny that there are normative rules to which the practice of science conforms. Rather, it is to deny that there are any inviolable rules of scientific methodology. As such, the point of the claim that 'anything goes' is merely to jokingly concede, in case of insistence on a universal formulation of method, that, even in the absence of inviolable rules, there remains a universally applicable methodological rule — namely, that expressed by the statement 'anything goes'.

Thus, in light of Feyerabend's critique of universal method, I propose the following thesis:

T^4: No evaluative criterion employed in scientific theory choice is inviolable in all circumstances.

That thesis T^4 is also a corollary of T^2 may be seen from the fact that conflict between methodological criteria may make it necessary to decide between such criteria in order to choose between theories. But if a decision must be made on which of conflicting criteria to adhere to, then it follows that it must be possible to violate or override some criteria in favour of others.

It may at first appear that T^4 is too strong. For to say that no criterion is inviolable appears to suggest that one need not follow any rule of scientific methodology in rational choice of theory: one need not do so because no rule is binding. There are at least three points to be made in reply to this objection. First, it should be noted that it does not follow from the violability of one criterion that all criteria are violable at the same time: that there are circumstances in which a rule may be broken does not entail that no rules need be followed. Second, it is consistent with asserting the violability of rules to also assert that at least minimal adherence is required to the set of rules to which the violated rule belongs. While no single criterion need be followed, it would not be rational to accept a theory which violates all methodological criteria. Third, to assert the violability of criteria is not to assert the rationality of indiscriminate flouting of criteria. For while all criteria may be violable in some circumstances, there need nevertheless be good reasons for doing so: the circumstances must warrant such violation.

7.5 Solving the problem of theory choice

Taken together, theses T^1-T^4 constitute a non-algorithmic, pluralistic model of scientific methodology. On such a model, there is no single, universally acceptable procedure of theory appraisal capable of dictating unique choice of theory, and scientists may appeal to a variety of different criteria in defending their preferred theoretical alternative. Let us see how this model solves the problem of rational theory choice.

According to the present model, scientists confronted with a choice between alternative theories may take into account a range of different methodological criteria. One scientist might choose to accept a given theory, say the theory of continental drift in the early 20th century, because it provides the best available explanation of a broad range of phenomena (e.g., species distribution, geological pattern matching, paleoclimatological data), which the scientist regards as particularly important. A second scientist might dismiss the drift hypothesis as unacceptably *ad hoc* (e.g., due to the absence of a suitable drift mechanism) and excessively speculative. Such a scientist might favour instead the theory that the continents are permanent fixtures on the Earth's surface, which sought to explain geological phenomena without postulating any processes other than those for which there is direct empirical evidence (e.g., sedimentation, earthquakes, erosion). Yet a third scientist might reject such permanentism as an inadequate account of mountain formation, and adopt instead some version of the contracting Earth hypothesis. Contractionism derived support from physicists' claims of a cooling Earth, explained the formation of mountains as the crumpling of the Earth's crust as it gradually shrunk, and accounted for species distribution by means of the existence of land bridges between continents at earlier periods of the Earth's history.[5]

On a scenario such as this, opposing scientists adopt different geological theories on the basis of divergent assessments of the epistemic merits of the competing theories. In support of their divergent assessments, scientists appeal to a variety of evaluative criteria, such as explanatory scope, *ad hoc*ness, empirical verifiability, and support from a related discipline. In so doing, they are able to marshall supporting arguments on behalf of their favoured theories on the basis of a diverse range of methodological criteria. As a result, opposing scientists may have rational grounds for choice of theory, in spite of adopting rival theories.

There may, in other words, be rational disagreement between scientists who accept conflicting theories on the basis of different methodological considerations. This is precisely what one would expect on a non-algorithmic, pluralist conception of scientific reason. For, in the absence of a single methodological procedure able to uniquely dictate choice of theory, there is scope for scientists to arrive at a variety of divergent appraisals of the comparative strengths and weaknesses of competing theories.

As for the issue of whether divergent choice of theory may be rational in an objective sense, there seems no reason to suppose that divergent choice of theory based on variant methodological criteria need be lacking in objectivity. For, on the assumption that the rival scientists' choices are indeed made on the basis of appropriate methodological criteria, such choices would appear to be based on good reasons of a perfectly objective kind.

7.6 Relativism

It will, no doubt, be objected that the solution I have sketched to the problem of theory choice is no solution at all. One scientist rationally accepts one theory on the basis of one set of methodological criteria. Other scientists rationally accept competing theories on the basis of other methodological criteria. Such variation of rational belief with methodological criteria is nothing short of relativism.

I wish to conclude by briefly indicating why this objection seems to me to be incorrect. In the first place, it is a mistake to suppose that admitting that there may be divergent methodological grounds for conflicting choice of theory commits one to epistemic relativism. To be sure, the present conception of scientific reason contains a large measure of epistemic tolerance. But to tolerate divergence of rational belief is rather different from rendering such belief relative to operative standards. Such tolerance, moreover, is a necessity forced on us by even the most casual acquaintance with the history of science, or indeed, with intellectual life generally. The phenomenon of rational disagreement is a robust phenomenon which must be taken into account by any theory of scientific rationality.

Why, then, does the idea of rational disagreement on the basis of alternative methodological criteria so readily elicit the charge of relativism? I suggest that the answer lies with an illegitimate assumption concerning the relation between methodological criteria and rational justification. For consider what would have to be the case in order for it to follow from variation in the criteria appealed to by scientists that rational theory choice is relative to such criteria. In order for such choice to be relative to variant criteria, it would have to be the case that conformity with such criteria suffices for rational theory choice. In other words, mere accordance with operative methodological criteria would be all that is needed for acceptance of a theory to be rationally justified.

Such an assumption is untenable, however, as may be seen by reflection on the fact that not all criteria which might be employed in theory appraisal are able to provide genuine epistemic support. Appeal might, for example, be made to a purely aesthetic factor which has no bearing on the likely truth of the theory. Alternatively, use might be made of methodological criteria, which have been discredited, or which have been found wanting, as, for example, single blind drug tests have been found wanting in light of the placebo effect.[6] Cases such as these reveal that there may be deficiencies in the evaluative criteria employed by scientists, which either preclude their having probative force, or which reduce such force as they might have.

The point I am making is based on a distinction between normative and descriptive issues at the level of methodological criteria. As far as the description of actual scientific practice is concerned, scientists may in fact employ a whole range of different criteria in their appraisal of alternative theories. Yet, as for the normative dimension of such practice, the criteria which scientists actually employ need not necessarily convey epistemic support. Since criteria may be deficient, or otherwise lacking in probative force, a scientist's belief may conform with a criterion without thereby being rationally justified.

Since the charge of relativism against the present model assumes that conformity with operative criteria insures rationality, it disregards the distinction between operative criteria and criteria which convey epistemic support. Yet if we insist on distinguishing descriptive from normative issues at the level of criteria, we may assert that scientists are guided by a plurality of divergent criteria without thereby licensing the inference to epistemic relativism. In particular, the model of rationality proposed here is fully consistent with enforcing a sharp distinction between criteria which provide epistemic support and criteria which provide no such support. The present model fails, therefore, to make theory choice relative to operative criteria.

It might, finally, seem somewhat paradoxical to suppose that there may be disagreement between scientists whose beliefs are based on objective grounds. For it may seem to be part of the very concept of objectivity that it is bound up with consensus and convergence of belief. One might think, for example, that if there are objective grounds for a belief, then, necessarily, if anyone is presented with such grounds, they should accept the belief. Given such a connection between objectivity and convergent belief, how can there be objectivity if scientists disagree?

The present model of rationality requires that objectivity be conceived as separate from consensus. For if there may be rational divergence between scientists whose beliefs are objectively grounded, then objectivity evidently cannot be bound up with agreement. The seeming paradox of this idea may be alleviated, however, if the locus of objectivity is situated in the criteria of evaluation themselves, rather than in the formation of consensus. For a scientist's acceptance of a theory may be objectively grounded if it is based on appeal to methodological criteria capable of yielding genuine epistemic support. Such criteria provide objective grounds for theory acceptance since they provide epistemic support for the theory which is independent of irreducibly subjective factors, such as personal taste, whim or prejudice. Being objective, at least where rational belief is concerned, reduces to being epistemically well founded.

Notes

1. Cf. Gower (1988), Lakatos (1978b), Popper, (1970), Siegel (1987), Worrall (1988).
2. Bernstein (1983), Brown (1988), Putnam (1981).
3. Cf. Chalmers (1990), Ellis (1990), Feyerabend (1975), Laudan (1984), Newton-Smith (1981).
4. For example, Kuhn (1977c, pp. 323-4) argues that, while consistency with current theory favoured the geocentric system, considerations of simplicity tended to favour Copernicus.
5. I have drawn the general outlines of the views of the imaginary Earth scientists described here from Homer LeGrand's discussion of the situation in geology in the early twentieth century in his (1988).
6. Cf. Laudan (1984, pp. 38-9).

8 Judgement and rational theory choice

8.1 Introduction

Philosophers of science have traditionally sought an account of scientific method which might shed light on the nature of scientific rationality. Such an account of method would provide criteria for the appraisal of scientific theories, on the basis of which theory acceptance is rationally justified. Philosophers engaged in this traditional project have tended to assume that there is a single, unchanging scientific method, which operates as an algorithm to mechanically determine choice between theories.

However, recent trends in philosophy of science suggest that the traditional search for the 'one true method' is unlikely to succeed. Many recent philosophers of science reject the idea of a single scientific method in favour of a variant set of methodological criteria which do not uniquely determine choice of theory. Such pluralism initially evoked objections of relativism and irrationalism. But many philosophers now seek to understand pluralism in the light of a new concept of scientific rationality, rather than to dismiss it as relativism. Such philosophers increasingly suggest that the rationality displayed in scientific theory choice is a non-algorithmic form of rationality, on which choice of theories is not dictated by the rules of scientific method. However, in spite of such suggestions, precisely what is involved in a non-algorithmic concept of scientific rationality has yet to clearly emerge.

This paper is meant as a partial remedy to this situation. My aim is to establish a point about the nature of rationality that is given little prominence by defenders of the rationality of methodological variation. Many contemporary philosophers of science would agree with Kuhn's claim that 'there is no neutral algorithm for theory-choice' (1970a, p. 200). For it is now common to deny that there are mechanical rules which uniquely determine choice of theory. Yet it is usually left unstated that, if rationality is non-algorithmic, then rational theory choice not dictated by rules must ultimately involve an act of deliberative judgement.[1] Thus, I wish to show that a notion of judgement is a necessary component of an adequate non-algorithmic account of rational scientific theory choice.

8.2 Judgement

Before it can be argued that judgement is required by theory choice, some indication is needed of what judgement is. As a preliminary to the arguments which I will present in the next two sections, in this section I will give a rough sketch of the notion of judgement. In a later section, I will provide further analysis of judgement when I discuss the account of judgement proposed by Harold Brown.

I begin with some remarks about ordinary usage. We sometimes say, of a person who appraises a situation wisely and decides upon a suitable course of action, that their decision shows 'good judgement'. There are occasions in which someone with specialized knowledge and training in an area forms an opinion on a particular subject, basing their opinion on familiarity with the relevant facts and expertise in the general area. In such cases, we may say that they exercise 'professional judgement'. There are also cases in which an immediate decision is called for, with no time for proper evaluation of the situation at hand, in which one must make a 'snap judgement'. Sometimes, for example when a situation requires appraisal in the absence of relevant information, we may have to make a 'judgement call'.

Such idioms as these illustrate two features of judgement, as we ordinarily speak of it. First, it is typical of cases in which judgement is called for that there is some sort of decision to be made. Second, the exercise of judgement in making the decision involves an appraisal of the situation with respect to which the decision is to be made. Both of these aspects of judgement are apparent in cases in which we are faced with a choice involving a variety of potentially conflicting factors.

Practical decision making frequently provides examples of this. We are often confronted with a range of possible courses of action, no one of which is uniquely determined by relevant considerations. In such cases, we weigh up the alternatives and attempt to gauge which one is, on balance, the preferable course of action. Judgement may enter into this process at various points. We may rely on judgement in reflecting on what our aims are, as well as on which action best serves our aims. We may use judgement when we decide which of a range of relevant considerations is to be given more weight than the others. Judgement may even be employed in determining which, of all the possibly relevant factors, are to be counted as relevant considerations.

It is characteristic of circumstances which call for judgement that the considerations on the basis of which the decision is made fail to determine the outcome of the decision. This contrasts with cases in which the decision may be subsumed under an algorithmic decision procedure. In such cases, there is no role for judgement in determining the outcome. For it is precisely the function of an algorithm to remove the need for judgement. Conversely, it is characteristic of judgement that it is non-algorithmic.

But judgement is not merely the capacity to make decisions without an algorithm. It also involves the capacity to evaluate the situation in which the decision is to be made. This may include consideration of a range of information, as well as determination of the relevance and significance of various items of information. This aspect of judgement is emphasized by a number of authors. For example, Jon Elster defines 'judgement'

> as the capacity to synthesize vast and diffuse information that more or less clearly bears on the problem at hand, in such a way that no element or set of elements is given undue importance. (1983, p. 16, cited in Brown, 1988)

Here Elster suggests that judgement involves two processes, the assembly of a mass of relevant data, and the judicious appraisal of the relative significance of different pieces of data.

But it is not clear that judgement need be restricted, in the way Elster suggests, to cases involving synthesis of a broad range of data. To be sure, in cases where there is a wealth of data, use of judgement may involve evaluation of a large range of data. But there are cases in which only a small amount of data is needed, or in which relevant data is unavailable, or in which there is insufficient time to take all the relevant data into account. In such cases, judgement may still be employed, even though no great synthesis of data is required. Thus, judgement should not strictly speaking be thought of as the synthesis of a large quantity of data. Rather, judgement involves the evaluation of such data as seems appropriate in relation to the decision at hand, regardless of the quantity of data available.

To sum up what has just been said, the ability to form judgements is the ability to arrive at decisions on the basis of an evaluation of the situation with respect to which the decision is to be made. This may involve both an assessment of relevant considerations, and a determination of which considerations are relevant. To the extent that decisions based on such evaluations cannot be made by means of an algorithm, such decisions are based on judgement.

8.3 Judgement and the regress of justificatory criteria

In the next section I will argue that judgement is required in rational theory choice due to the existence within science of multiple methodological criteria. However, in this section I will argue that any appeal to criteria for rational support must rest on judgement, or lead to infinite regress. If this is right, even if the existence of multiple criteria did not require a role for judgement, appeal to methodological criteria in rational theory choice would still require the use of judgement.

The argument I will now present is that rational acceptance of theory on the basis of methodological criteria involves judgement on pain of infinite regress. Consider the decision made by a scientist to accept a theory. Suppose that the scientist makes this choice on the basis of appeal to a single methodological criterion C. Let us ask whether acceptance of the theory on the basis of C is rational. To answer this question, we must ask whether appeal to C is able to provide the scientist with rational justification. In order to show that such appeal does provide rational justification, one might appeal to a metacriterion, C*, on the basis of which appeal to criterion C may be shown to provide rational justification. But if appeal is made to a metacriterion C* to justify C, the question immediately arises of what justifies C*. If appeal is made to some meta-metacriterion, C**, then we embark on an infinite regress.[2]

But it is absurd to appeal to an infinite series of metacriteria to establish rational acceptance of a theory. Therefore, rational theory acceptance cannot be based on appeal to infinite metacriteria. Appeal to criteria must come to a halt somewhere. In particular, a judgement must be made at some stage in the justificatory process that this or that criterion is an appropriate criterion on which to base one's choice of theory. In other words, appeal to a given criterion in defence of theory choice must ultimately rest on a judgement that it is rational to appeal to this criterion. This suggests that, to the extent that a role is played by criteria in rational theory acceptance, a role must also be played by an act of judgement which does not itself rest on appeal to further criteria.[3]

It might be objected, however, that it does not follow from the infinite regress of higher order criteria that an act of judgement is necessary in order to avoid the regress. Strictly speaking, all that follows is that appeal to criteria must come to an end somewhere if the regress is to be avoided. But nothing in particular follows from this about how to end the regress. The decision to halt the regress might, for example, be based on dogmatic commitment, non-rational leap of faith, or arbitrary convention. Thus, it is consistent with the need to halt the regress of criteria that the decision to accept a theory on the basis of a criterion may rest on any number of things other than judgement.

The trouble with this objection is that, while it is indeed true that judgement is not the only way to end the regress, none of the apparent alternatives to judgement are rational. It may readily be conceded that there are numerous non-rational ways to halt the regress of justifications, such as dogmatic commitment or leap of faith. But the point of the above argument is not that the attempt to rationally support a theory must fail because it ultimately rests on non-rational commitment. Rather, the point is that the rational justification of theory on the basis of criteria must ultimately rest on a judgement of the rational acceptability of some criterion. And, while not itself justifiable by criteria, the process of judgement may nevertheless be a rational process, and acceptance of theory by appeal to criteria accepted on the basis of judgement may also be rational.

No doubt, the claim that judgement not supported by criteria rationally supports theory acceptance conflicts with engrained philosophical preconceptions. For one might be inclined to think that rationality necessarily involves criterial justification, so that judgement unsupported by criteria is necessarily non-rational. But it is by no means clear that the process of judgement can be so hastily dismissed as non-rational.

Quite the contrary, the process described in Section 8.2, of forming a judgement on the basis of relevant information in the absence of an algorithm, bears the hallmarks of a rational process. For the process of judgement characteristically involves the evaluation of relevant information, and results in a decision that is made on the basis of that information. While there may be no conclusive grounds for choice if judgement is required, judgement may nevertheless yield plausible reasons for making the decision one way rather than another. Thus, far from being beyond the pale of rationality, such a process of deliberative judgement involves the use of reason in a manner that is paradigmatic of rational decision making.

8.4 Judgement and multiple criteria of theory choice

In this section I will argue that judgement is necessary in rational theory choice due to the existence of multiple methodological criteria. In particular, because of the potential for conflict between criteria, it may be necessary to choose which criteria to weight more heavily in deciding between rival theories. Such a choice between conflicting criteria is one which requires scientists to exercise judgement.

Among philosophers who deny the existence of a fixed, universal scientific method, it is now widely assumed that there is instead a multiplicity of methodological criteria, which scientists at various times and in various contexts employ in the appraisal of theories. Standard examples of such methodological criteria include empirical adequacy, testability, explanatory power, simplicity, coherence and fertility. Not all such criteria need be employed throughout all periods of the history of science, for there has been considerable variation in operative methodological criteria. Nor need all the criteria operative at a given time be satisfied by any acceptable scientific theory, since there may be circumstances in which failure to satisfy certain criteria is justified.[4] Thus, while there is no single scientific method, there is nevertheless a partially shifting array of individually defeasible methodological criteria, which broadly constitutes the methodology of science.

In accordance with this view of the methodology of science, let us suppose that a scientist faced with a choice between theories has an array of methodological criteria to draw upon in deciding which theory to accept. In appraising such rival theories, the scientist considers whether each theory satisfies the various criteria. In certain conditions, the decision to adopt one theory over another may be unproblematic. For example, one theory might satisfy all or most of the criteria while its rival satisfies none or very few of them.

Problems arise if rival theories satisfy different criteria. For the various methodological criteria may fail to be mutually consistent in application. One theory might be simpler than another, while the other is more empirically adequate. Or, of two empirically adequate theories, one might be more fertile than the other, while the other has greater coherence.[5] In such a situation, methodological criteria fail to uniquely determine choice of theory.

Where different criteria favour different theories, a scientist choosing between alternative theories is faced with a choice between conflicting methodological criteria. For in order to choose between the theories on the basis of methodological criteria, the scientist must also decide which criteria to base the choice of theory on. In such a situation, the scientist must determine which of the conflicting criteria is to be weighted more heavily than the other. But such a decision between methodological criteria is not itself one that is able to be made on the basis of appeal to methodological criteria.

To see that this is so, consider how an attempt to decide between criteria by appeal to criteria might proceed. In the first place, the decision to accord greater weight to one criterion than another cannot be made on the basis of appeal to the very criterion to which greater weight is given, since that would simply beg the question in favour of that criterion. In the second place, the decision to favour a given criterion cannot be based on appeal to other criteria. For the criteria in question are not metacriteria which apply to criteria, but object level criteria which apply to theories. In the third place, even if a given criterion did support some criterion over another, the problem of deciding between conflicting criteria would not be removed. For suppose that coherence favours a theory which is simple over one which is empirically adequate. To choose the simpler one on that basis would require coherence to be accorded greater weight than empirical adequacy. But that in turn requires that a decision be made to favour one criterion over another, which was the original problem.

Since the decision between criteria cannot be made by appeal to criteria themselves, it is tempting to conclude that such a decision can only be made on the basis of judgement. For, if the decision may not be made on the basis of criteria, it may seem that a scientist's only recourse is to reflect, in a manner not governed by criteria, on which criteria are of greater significance in the circumstances. Such deliberations can only be made on a case by case basis, they demand thorough competence in the relevant scientific discipline, and the decisions arrived at may vary from scientist to scientist. Thus, the decision between conflicting criteria would appear to be characteristic of the kind of decision in which judgement is called for.

However, to conclude from this that judgement is necessary in the decision between criteria would be to overlook a possibility which remains for a defender of algorithmic accounts of theory choice. For it might be objected that judgement is unnecessary in case of conflicting criteria, since it is always possible to formulate an algorithm for choosing between conflicting criteria. Thus, while the choice between rival theories may require a decision on which of conflicting criteria to accord priority, there might be a higher order rule which decides between the conflicting criteria.

One might, for example, propose the following rule: if two theories are equally empirically adequate, choose the simpler; otherwise, choose the one with greater empirical adequacy. It might even be possible to formulate a complex higher order rule, which defines an ordering over criteria in such a way that any potential conflict is decided by relations of dominance between criteria. Where such a higher order algorithm is available, the choice of which criterion to grant priority is fully determined by the rule. It appears, therefore, that judgement is unnecessary in the choice between conflicting criteria, for the choice may be dictated by means of a higher order algorithm.

In reply to this objection, it suffices to note that, while it may very well be possible to formulate a higher order algorithm able to decide between conflicting criteria, the decision to adopt such an algorithm cannot itself ultimately be determined by an algorithm. For even where a higher order algorithm is available, there is a genuine question whether the algorithm should be adopted, since the mere availability of such an algorithm does not itself constitute a positive justification for using it. Thus, use of such an algorithm must rest at some level on a prior appraisal of the relative significance of the various methodological criteria. But such an appraisal cannot ultimately be based on an algorithm, for it can always be asked why use of any particular algorithm is justified.

It remains only to conclude, from the need for prior appraisal of criteria, that the adoption of any higher order algorithm requires judgement. More specifically, since the decision to adopt a higher order algorithm rests on a non-algorithmic appraisal of methodological criteria, such a decision therefore involves a judgement, not determined by rules, of the relative significance of the criteria. Thus, even if it is possible to formulate a higher order algorithm able to decide between conflicting criteria, it still does not follow that judgement is unnecessary in such a case.

8.5 Brown's theory of judgement

The arguments I have given in the preceding two sections show that judgement must be employed in the use of methodological criteria, and therefore plays a necessary role in rational choice between theories. In this section I will further develop the idea of judgement by discussing the account of judgement proposed by Harold Brown in his book *Rationality* (1988).

Brown sets the notion of judgement within the context of an agent centered model of rationality, on which the notion of rational agency rather than that of rational belief is taken as fundamental. What is crucial to rationality, for Brown, is not 'the logical relations between ... evidence and ... belief', but 'the way in which an agent deals with evidence in arriving at a belief' (1988, p. 185). Rationality is not something which attaches to belief in virtue of objective features of what is believed. Rather, rationality attaches to agents in virtue of the capacities which they exercise in forming their beliefs.

On Brown's model of rationality, the most fundamental capacity of a rational agent is the capacity to exercise judgement. Rationality cannot be fully analyzed as conformity with rules, since one can be rational in the absence of rules. Indeed, it is precisely where rules are lacking that rationality is most needed, and under such circumstances the rational agent must exercise judgement (1988, p. 185). But rationality not fully governed by rules does not reduce to unconstrained individual judgement. Rationality has an essentially social nature, as a result of which, rather than being constrained by rules, judgement is constrained by interaction with other rational agents. In order for a belief based on judgement to be rational, it must be subjected to evaluation, though not necessarily approval, at the hands of those who have the relevant expertise. Thus, Brown somewhat paradoxically concludes, 'Robinson Crusoe alone on his island could exercise judgement, but he would not be able to achieve rationality' (1988, p. 187).[6]

Brown characterizes judgement as 'the ability to evaluate a situation, assess evidence and come to a reasonable decision without following rules' (1988, p. 137). Brown does not, of course, deny that much human thought and behaviour is governed by rules (1988, pp. 139, 186). Nor does he deny that it may be rational to follow appropriate rules when such rules are available (1988, p. 184). His point, rather, is that:

> we do have an ability to think and reason beyond the range that is captured in our ability to follow rules. We exercise this ability when we are creating rules, when we modify existing rules, and when we recognize that we have an unusual case at hand, and decide how to deal with it. (1988, p. 156)

Thus, in Brown's view, while we are capable of reasoning in a rule governed manner, situations may arise in which our reasoning cannot proceed in accordance with rules. In such cases, we make use of our capacity for judgement.

While judgement is not rule governed, however, it is subject to an important constraint. Judgement requires expertise. In order to exercise judgement in some matter, one must have expertise in the area and be well informed about the specific details of the situation in question (1988, p. 146). Given the need for expertise, the ability to make judgements in an area is a learned ability that requires training (1988, p. 146), and having the ability to exercise judgement is having a certain kind of skill (1988, p. 165). However, since even the most skillful and well informed expert can arrive at erroneous conclusions, the capacity to make judgements must be viewed as a fallible capacity (1988, p. 144).

In sum, according to Brown, judgement is a fallible, acquired capacity to make decisions, on the basis of expert knowledge, without following explicit rules. Such a capacity is well suited for the role played by judgement in rational theory choice for which I have argued in the preceding two sections. For the capacity to form a judgement, in a manner that is not determined by rules, is itself a capacity to make decisions which are potentially rational. Thus, the decision, based on judgement, to choose a theory on the basis of appeal to a given methodological criterion, or set of such criteria, is capable of being a rational decision. Given this, the necessity for judgement in theory choice need not detract in the least from the rationality of such choice.

8.6 Judgement and subjectivity

I will conclude this paper by considering an objection to the idea that judgement plays a role in rational theory choice. The objection is that appeal to judgement brings an irreducibly subjective element into theory choice, which undermines rationality.

The objection arises from the fact that judgement is not grounded in criteria. For if, as I argued in Sections 8.3 and 8.4, judgement comes into rationality because appeal to criteria cannot ultimately be based on higher order criteria, then choice of theory would appear to rest ultimately on an act of judgement that is not supported by criteria. But, if this is so, theory choice would appear to be based on a fundamentally subjective act, and is therefore unable to be rational. For if no objective criterion may be appealed to in support of the act of judgement, there can be no objective grounds for theory choice.

This objection depends on two assumptions about objectivity and rationality. First, the objection assumes that if choice of theory rests on irreducibly subjective factors, then theory choice cannot be rational. Second, the objection also assumes that removal of subjective factors requires that theory choice be based on objective methodological criteria. Of these two assumptions, I will challenge the second, since appeal to criteria does not seem to be the only way to remove subjective factors, while irreducible subjectivity does seem to threaten rationality.

Before contesting this assumption, it is worth considering what lies behind it. The underlying thought is that appeal to methodological criteria avoids undue subjectivity in theory choice, since methodological criteria provide objective grounds for such choice. Part of the explanation of the objectivity of criteria is that they are formulated in public language and, unlike private experiences, are open for public inspection. As a result, the question of whether a theory satisfies a criterion is not a matter to be decided on the basis of subjective intuition, but is open to public scrutiny. Another aspect of the objectivity of criteria has to do with their normative force. The reason scientists ought to seek theories which satisfy methodological criteria is not, at base, purely subjective. Rather, such criteria are normatively binding on scientists because theories fulfilling such criteria advance the epistemic aims of science, such as growth of knowledge or predictive reliability. Because methodological criteria are thus public and directed toward the aims of science, appeal to criteria in support of a theory insures that the theory is not adopted for irreducibly subjective reasons.

But while appeal to objective criteria is one way to avoid irreducible subjectivity, it is a mistake to assume that it is the only way. As Brown points out in his discussion of rational judgement, despite not being rule governed, judgement may be subject to constraints. Two examples of such constraints are incorporated into his original model: first, it is a condition of being able to exercise judgement that one have expertise in the relevant area; second, for a belief based on judgement to be rational, it must be subjected to evaluation by others with the relevant expertise. Of course, neither judgement based on expertise nor critical appraisal by a group of experts can guarantee that a belief is infallible or true. Such constraints can, however, serve to prevent the choice of one theory over another from being based on unduly subjective considerations. In light of this, I conclude that the objection from subjectivity is unfounded, since judgement not grounded on criteria need be neither irreducibly subjective nor a threat to rationality.

Notes

1. A notable exception is Newton-Smith, who explicitly incorporates a role for judgement into his model of scientific rationality (1981, pp. 232-5, 270).
2. While the argument in the text is evidently formally analogous to the one which leads to the Pyrrhonian problem of the criterion, it is important to note that it is not here put to sceptical use. Contrary to scepticism, I assume that we are capable of both knowledge and rational belief. Rather than raise sceptical doubts, the regress of criteria is here used to

establish a feature of criterially justified rational belief, viz., that it requires judgement. I do not, therefore, appeal to judgement as a solution to the problem of the criterion.

3. A formally analogous argument shows that application of criterion C to theory T rests on judgement. For how is it determined that T satisfies C? Appeal may be made to a metacriterion C* which shows that T satisfies C. But the question arises whether C satisfies C*. Infinite regress ensues if appeal is made to a C** to justify application of C* to C.
4. For example, it may be rational to accept (or, at least, to pursue) a recently introduced theory which has yet to be established empirically, or which has only been established in a narrow domain, provided that it promises to satisfy other criteria or to become empirically adequate.
5. Kuhn provides an example of a similar case (1977c, pp. 323-4). Prior to Kepler, he says, Copernican astronomy was no more empirically accurate than the Ptolemaic system; and while the Ptolemaic scored better on the criterion of consistency, the Copernican rated higher with respect to the criterion of simplicity.
6. Brown has recently modified his position to avoid this consequence. Where he formerly held social evaluation to be necessary for rationality, he now allows that logic and observation also constrain individual judgement, and may yield rational beliefs without social interaction (Brown, 1994).

Part V

NATURALISM

9 Rationality, relativism and methodological pluralism

9.1 Introduction

It is now commonplace for philosophers of science to deny the existence of a universal scientific method. Influential authors such as Chalmers, Ellis, Feyerabend, Kuhn, Laudan and Newton-Smith all reject appeals to a unified methodology.[1] Instead, they claim that inspection of actual scientific practice, and of the history of science, reveals that use is made of a variety of methodological principles. Thus, those who deny universal method usually combine their denial with methodological pluralism.

Despite being commonplace, however, the denial of universal methodology is not as yet uncontroversial. This is in part because, in the view of many philosophers, the denial of a fixed scientific method has seemed the first step down a short road to epistemological relativism. During the 1960s and early 1970s, disagreement on this score pitched Kuhn and Feyerabend against the likes of Popper, Lakatos and Scheffler.[2] More recently, the relativistic consequences of the denial of universal method have been forcefully urged against Chalmers, Doppelt and Laudan by Gower, Siegel and Worrall respectively.[3]

There is no doubt that the pluralist denial of universal scientific method has seemed relativistic to many who have considered the idea. It does not appear to have been widely appreciated, however, that there is no necessary connection between relativism and the denial of universal method. While a philosopher who denies universal method may also embrace relativism, the denial of universal method does not itself entail relativism. Thus, it is completely open for the methodological pluralist to argue that there may be objective methodological reasons for theory choice despite absence of universal method.

In this chapter I will argue that relativism about scientific rationality does not follow either from methodological pluralism or from the pluralists' denial of universal method. In Section 9.2, I briefly contrast the idea of uniformity of method with methodological pluralism. In Section 9.3, I define a form of relativism about rational scientific belief which makes rationality depend on contextually variant methodological standards. In Section 9.4, I argue that the denial of universal method does not lead to relativism of rational scientific belief. In Section 9.5, I argue that relativity of rational belief does not follow from variation of methodological standards alone, but requires a further, objectionable assumption to the effect that compliance with such standards ensures rationality. In Section 9.6, I consider objections to the effect that rationality is relative because rationality just is compliance with operative standards. I conclude, in Section 9.7, by sketching a view of rational theory choice as akin to practical decision making, on which rationality is objective even without fixed method.

9.2 Uniformity versus plurality of method

Philosophers have traditionally believed in the existence of a uniform scientific method, which scientists throughout the history of science have employed in all branches of science. They have been divided, however, on the nature of this method. In this century, the main division has been between defenders of an inductive methodology and Popperian advocates of a falsificationist methodology. According to inductivists, scientific method consists in the empirical confirmation of theories which are arrived at by means of an inductive inference from observational data. According to Popper, the method of science is the rigorous attempt to falsify theories which are conjectural explanations of facts that constitute problems in the light of our prior expectations and theories. Despite being somewhat idealized, both inductivist and falsificationist accounts were meant as articulations of the fundamental methodology underlying scientific practice.

However, the existence of a uniform methodology became doubtful in the middle of this century as widespread methodological, semantic and perceptual variation in science was recognized. Philosophers argued that observation is theory laden and that there is no observation language free of theory, so that neither observation nor observation language could provide a neutral basis for an invariant scientific method. Of greater significance was the attack mounted by Kuhn and Feyerabend on the idea of a unique and unchanging methodology of science. Initially, Kuhn argued that the methodological standards employed by scientists vary with prevailing scientific paradigm.[4] He later added that science is characterized by a partly shifting set of guiding values, which fail to uniquely determine choice of scientific theory.[5] Kuhn's rejection of a fixed method was complemented by Feyerabend's criticism of traditional views of methodology. Feyerabend claimed, not merely that scientists have frequently violated methodological rules, but that in many cases it was rational for them to do so.[6] The outcome of Feyerabend's critique of method is similar to that of Kuhn's attack on fixed method. For, if Feyerabend is right, there can be no fixed set of methodological rules that is both applicable in all circumstances and universally binding.

Rejection of a fixed, universal method has become increasingly widespread among philosophers of science. It is now widely assumed that there is a plurality of methodological standards, which scientists at various times and in various contexts employ in the appraisal of theories. Not all standards have been employed throughout the history of science, since there has been variation in operative methodological standards. Nor need all the standards operative at a given time be satisfied by any acceptable scientific theory, since there may be circumstances in which failure to satisfy certain standards is justified. Thus, while there is no single scientific method, there is nevertheless a partially shifting array of individually defeasible methodological standards, which broadly constitutes the methodology of science.

9.3 Rationality relativism

In this section, I will present a version of epistemological relativism on which scientific rationality depends on variant methodological standards. As it is often understood, relativism is the view that what it is rational to do or believe depends on the standards which are accepted in a given context. Somewhat more specifically, the form of relativism of relevance in the present context holds that what theory it is rational for a scientist to accept depends on the methodological standards which are operative in a given context. This is the form of relativism which I referred to as 'rationality relativism' in Chapter 1.

The central thesis of rationality relativism is that rational theory acceptance is relative to operative standards. The acceptance by a scientist of a scientific theory is rationally justified if it is supported by appeal to the methodological standards which are operative in the context in which the scientist is situated. In other words, the rationality of scientific belief depends on the methodological standards which scientists working in a given context employ in deciding whether to accept theories. As a consequence of the dependence of rational theory acceptance on operative methodological standards, scientific rationality is relative to operative standards. For, if all that is required for rational theory acceptance is compliance with operative standards, then rationality of scientific belief varies relative to operative standards. Thus, if rival theories satisfy alternative sets of standards, and such alternative sets of standards are operative in different contexts, which theory it is rational to accept is relative to scientific context.

The clarity of the doctrine of rationality relativism rests on that of the notions of a methodological standard and of a context. Methodological pluralists have argued for diversity in scientific methodology by pointing to a broad array of methods and criteria employed in science.[7] These range from low level rules for the use of apparatus, to constraints on tests (e.g., experimental controls), criteria of explanatory adequacy and regulative ideals for scientific theorizing (e.g., simplicity, coherence). What all such methodological factors have in common is that they may serve as standards of rationality to which appeal may be made in justifying belief in theories which are accepted on their basis. However, given variation of standards, the standards to which appeal is made may vary with context. For example, operative methodological standards may vary with the tradition of scientific research or theoretical background, with belief system or conceptual scheme, or, more broadly, with the general intellectual or cultural heritage of a historical time period or national culture.

An example of rationality relativism is the relativistic doctrine frequently attributed to Kuhn in *The Structure of Scientific Revolutions*.[8] On Kuhn's view, the standards which scientists employ to evaluate solutions to scientific puzzles vary with the paradigm which is accepted by a community of scientists.[9] Moreover, apart from the standards operative within a paradigm, there are no higher evaluative standards to which appeal can be made when a choice is made between rival paradigms.[10] Given the lack of higher standards able to provide objective grounds for the choice between competing paradigms, the decision to switch from one paradigm to another is akin to a non-rational leap of faith, or a religious conversion. However, since each paradigm provides its own internal standards, what is rational for a scientist working within the paradigm to believe depends on the standards internal to the paradigm. Thus, due to the absence of extraparadigmatic standards governing paradigm choice and the variation of standards internal to paradigms, Kuhn has sometimes been taken as an irrationalist about paradigm choice and a relativist about the beliefs scientists accept on the basis of their paradigms.[11]

9.4 Does the denial of universal method entail rationality relativism?

It is sometimes claimed that the denial of a universal scientific method leads directly to rationality relativism. Thus, Worrall objects to the view proposed by Laudan in *Science and Values* by arguing that 'either there is an invariant core ... of methodological principles or everything is open to change'; without such an invariant core Laudan's 'model collapses into relativism'.[12] Similarly, Gower describes Chalmers' rejection of a universal, ahistorical methodology as 'sceptical relativism about scientific method'.[13] If such authors as Worrall and Gower are right, then the only alternative to a methodological stabilism is relativism about scientific rationality.

It is, however, not at all clear that the denial of a universal scientific method does lead directly to relativism. In the first place, it is important to note that to deny a universal method is not to deny that there may be methodological standards which are independent of particular theories. Even if no universal method exists, there may still be extratheoretic methodological standards, which are applicable to opposing theories and yet subject to continuous evolution throughout the history of science. For example, the standard of qualitative conformity with experience might gradually have been displaced by the standard of quantitatively precise predictive accuracy.[14] Inductivist strictures against the postulation of theoretical entities were dropped as the hypothetico-deductive method of testing theoretical hypotheses was developed.[15] And the standard requiring deterministic explanations of physical phenomena has given way to allow for statistical ones.[16] If such overriding yet changing standards exist, then it may nevertheless be possible to decide between conflicting theories on the basis of standards which are independent of theory. Given such independent standards, the short route to relativism, via contextually variant standards, is no longer available.

Of course, such an appeal to variant theory independent standards will not appease the critic who insists on methodological invariance if relativism is to be avoided. For it might be argued that, even if there are extratheoretic standards operative in science, variation of such standards results in relativism. Given that there are no ultimate, fixed standards, to which appeal may be made in comparing variant extratheoretic standards, there is no objective basis for believing theories conforming with one set of such standards, as opposed to ones which conform to some other set.[17]

Here a number of points may be made in reply to the stabilist critic. First, as Laudan notes against Worrall, even if the existence of an invariant methodology were established, that would not answer the relativist. For the relativist claims not that 'standards change but that — whether changing or unchanging — ... standards have no independent, non-question-begging rationale or foundation'.[18] Consequently, to answer the relativist, it does not suffice to establish methodological invariance. For what is required is a rational justification of methodological standards, and such justification cannot be provided merely by showing that the method employed by science is invariant.

Second, it might conceivably happen that a theory is produced which scores best on all or most of the extratheoretic standards which have been employed throughout the evolution of the methodology of science. Alternatively, while there might be a number of different sets of standards operative at a given time, it might be that all of these sets of standards are best satisfied by a single theory.[19] Even in the absence of a universal, invariant method, a theory which performs better than its rivals in either of these ways would clearly appear to be superior to its rivals by objective criteria. It is not therefore the case that the decision to accept a theory in the absence of a universal method is unable to be objectively grounded.

But the most important point to be made against the stabilist is this. As has been frequently urged by methodological pluralists, it is possible to make improvements in the methodology of science.[20] It may, for example, be discovered that a particular methodological standard is unsound, even though it was formerly taken to be a crucial component of methodology. It is arguable that the ideal of circular orbits in planetary astronomy is a standard which was rightly discarded during the transition to heliocentric astronomy. Similarly, Laudan has argued that drug testing methodology was improved by the introduction of double blind tests as a result of the discovery of the placebo effect.[21]

Even if it is impossible to isolate any fixed methodological standard which has been employed throughout the history of science, it may still be the case that methodological improvements do emerge from the practice of science. For even if there is no single component of methodology which remains stable, there may nevertheless be enough that is fixed at any one time to enable scientists to establish that one methodological approach is an advance over another. Thus if scientific methodology is viewed as a part of an evolving conception of how best to inquire into the world, the denial of a fixed method can avoid relativism about scientific rationality.

9.5 Does methodological pluralism entail rationality relativism?

While it may be conceded that denial of a universal method does not entail relativism, it might nevertheless be thought that the thesis of a plurality of methods carries a strong presumption of relativism. Thus, in this section I will consider the question whether a plurality of methodological standards leads to rationality relativism. I will argue that, for relativism to follow from a plurality of standards, it is necessary to assume that mere compliance with accepted standards suffices for rationality. But this assumption fails to take into account the normative nature of rationality, which ensures that mere compliance with standards does not suffice for rationality.

Let us suppose, then, that the claim of the methodological pluralist is that, rather than a fixed method or set of methods, the methodology of science constitutes a variant set of methodological standards. Given this, it is also tempting to suppose that operative methodological standards vary from context to context within science. For if there have been changes in accepted methodology throughout the history of science, then the standards which have been operative in one historical context may differ from those operative in another such context. But this suggests that what it is rational for a scientist to believe varies with context because there has been variation of standards relative to context. And this in turn suggests that scientific rationality is relative to contextually variant standards. Thus, the thesis of methodological pluralism seems to collapse into rationality relativism.

However, to determine whether methodological pluralism does lead to rationality relativism, as this suggests, it is necessary to consider the relation between rationality and methodological standards with some care. In particular, it is important to ask whether variation of operative methodological standards really does imply that rationality varies relative to such standards. There are good reasons to think that it does not.

To see this, note that the claim that different methodological standards are operative in different contexts is rather different from the claim that what is rational to believe depends on contextually variant standards. The first claim says simply that operative standards vary, whereas the second says that rationality depends on such standards. The two claims are hardly equivalent: to say that the standards employed in justifying beliefs vary from context to context is not to say that beliefs so justified are in fact rational. Nor does the claim that rationality is relative to variant standards follow from the claim that operative standards vary with context: for even if operative standards do vary with context, rationality might not.

What is necessary for rationality relativism to follow from variation of operative standards is an additional assumption to the effect that rational belief consists in conformity with operative standards.[22] For if rational belief were to consist simply in conformity with operative standards, then such belief would be relative to the standards operative in a given context. It is at precisely this point, however, that the inference from methodological pluralism to rationality relativism breaks down.

The problem is that the assumption that rationality consists in conformity with operative standards is itself objectionable, and need not be accepted by an advocate of methodological pluralism. For a belief might receive positive appraisal by appeal to some standard, and yet fail to be rational due to a deficiency in the standard. In particular, while a given methodological standard might achieve currency in a community, conformity by a belief with the standard might fail to bestow on the belief the intended degree of evidential or other rational support. A standard might, for example, be insufficiently demanding, so that beliefs which conform with it are as likely to be true as they are to be false. In such a case, conformity with the standard is no indication of truth, and therefore provides no basis for accepting a belief as true.

The possibility that an accepted standard may fail to be epistemically probative means that there is a genuine question which may be raised as to whether a given standard does indeed provide a basis for rational belief. For if conformity with a standard might have no bearing on the epistemic status of a belief, it may always be asked whether a particular standard does indeed yield rational support. Yet, given that such a question can legitimately be raised about the epistemic merits of a standard, it seems clear that mere conformity with an accepted standard does not suffice for a belief to be rational.

The point that a belief which complies with an operative standard may fail to be rational depends on a distinction which needs to be made between descriptive and normative considerations. The claim that a given standard is employed to appraise beliefs is a descriptive claim about which standards are, as a matter of fact, employed to evaluate beliefs. But such a descriptive claim about actual evaluative procedures does not entail the further normative claim that a belief which complies with such a standard is rationally justified. For that to follow, it would have to be the case that beliefs complying with such standards are indeed worthy of credence.

Yet, as shown by the possibility of deficient standards, it may very well happen that beliefs warranted by accepted standards fall short of rational belief worthiness. Given this potential gap between operative standards and normative rationality, mere adherence to operative standards does not necessarily provide beliefs with rational justification. It is therefore possible to advocate plurality of operative methodological standards without thereby being committed to relativism of rational belief.

9.6 Some relativist objections to normative rationality

Against what I have just argued, the relativist may object that the distinction between the normative and the descriptive is bogus: no higher epistemic authority exists than actual evaluative standards, hence no genuine distinction can be drawn between operative standards and standards which provide rational support. This objection may be developed in several different directions. I will briefly indicate three forms which the objection might take and then respond to each in turn.

First, it might be argued that methodological standards have the status of mere norms of behaviour accepted by particular human social groups; so that such standards are merely operative standards about which no question of genuine normative rationality can arise. Second, one might object that it is impossible to adopt an objective stance outside all standards from which to adjudicate the rationality of accepted evaluative standards. There can therefore be no higher court of appeal than the standards which are in fact accepted by a given community. Thus the distinction between genuine rationality and mere compliance with standards cannot be employed without begging the question in favour of some operative set of standards. Third, if, as Barnes and Bloor (1982) suggest, no criteria of rationality can be objectively grounded, the distinction between normative rationality and mere compliance with operative standards must collapse.

The first objection is that methodological standards function as mere norms of behaviour which happen to be adopted by a particular human group. As such, methodological standards have no special status, since the adoption of one set of behavioural norms as opposed to another is a matter of convention. Behavioural norms are adopted for reasons of social acceptability and practical convenience, and there is no sense in which one set of norms can be said to be more objectively correct than any other such set.[23] Given this, no question can arise as to whether a given methodological standard, or set of methodological standards, really does lead to rationally well founded belief: since they are mere norms, no question of rightness or wrongness applies to them.

In effect, this objection reduces rationality to conformity with conventionally accepted standards. Such a reduction of rationality to the merely conventional would permit rationality relativism to be inferred from methodological variation, since it implies that rationality does indeed consist in conformity with operative standards. Yet it is difficult to take such reductionism seriously, since rationality and convention do not necessarily coincide.

The point may be illustrated by an example drawn from the moral sphere. It is sometimes said that morality is merely a matter of social convention, so that what is morally right or wrong is simply a matter of what is conventionally accepted as such in a given society. But such a reduction of morality to convention removes the possibility of moral criticism of conventionally accepted practices. For, on such a view, if capital punishment, torture or racial discrimination are accepted practices within a society, then such practices are morally acceptable. Yet, if this were so, it would be impossible for a critic of such practices to argue that they are morally unacceptable despite being endorsed by convention. But such moral critique of accepted practices is in fact one significant way in which changes in social convention are sometimes brought about. The appeal made by such successful critique to moral considerations appears to show that morality cannot be a mere matter of convention.

A similar point applies to the reduction of rationality to convention. Rationality cannot be identified with conventional standards because such standards can be mistaken. As we saw in the previous section, a genuine question may be raised as to the epistemic adequacy of a methodological standard. In particular, it may be asked whether beliefs complying with such standards are in fact worthy of belief. But such a question could hardly be legitimately raised if rational belief were merely a matter of adherence to conventional standards. Thus, rationality of belief does not reduce to conformity with conventionally accepted standards.

Turning to the second objection, the point here is that it is impossible to transcend accepted standards by adopting a neutral perspective from which to evaluate standards. Thus, any attempt to criticize a given standard by showing that it fails to provide rational support necessarily begs the question in favour of some other standard which is presupposed by the criticism.

The thrust of this objection is that we can never be in a position to apply the distinction between the normative and the descriptive to any actual methodological standards. The objection rests on the assumption that it is necessary to adopt a standpoint external to all standards in order to evaluate the merits of any particular standard. Yet this assumption is surely mistaken.

There is no need to extricate ourselves from all standards to appraise any one of them. For a standard may be appraised by means of other standards. More particularly, it may be possible to evaluate the epistemic merits of a standard from within a set of operative standards and accepted beliefs which are held constant for the purposes of evaluation. An example of this is the case of double blind drug testing, which is discussed by Laudan (1984, pp. 38-9). Initially, controlled tests were employed, in which a drug was given to a group of patients but not to the control group. But some patients report improvement merely by being given a drug as a result of the placebo effect. To avoid the effect, single blind tests were employed whereby some patients were given an inactive substance. Later, double blind tests were introduced to prevent doctors conveying their expectations to patients.

The development of double blind tests involves evaluation of drug testing methodology against a background of beliefs and standards, which are presupposed at least for the purposes of evaluation. The shift from one form of test to another is propelled by a number of relevant beliefs, including beliefs in the existence of the placebo effect and in the unconscious communication of doctors' expectations to patients. It is also in part determined by standards which govern the nature of evidential support in science. At a general level, for example, the process of refinement of drug testing standards is driven by the methodological principle that acceptable theoretical hypotheses should be subjected to rigorous empirical tests. More specific standards are operative as well, such as standards of adequacy of empirical tests, for example the standard which dictates that extraneous causal influences be screened out in the testing process.

The case of double blind tests illustrates how a standard may be submitted to critical appraisal from within a system of beliefs and operative standards. Thus, epistemic evaluation of standards does not require the total renunciation of all standards. Given the possibility of evaluation of standards relative to a presupposed epistemic and methodological background, it therefore follows that the distinction between normative rationality and operative standards is one which is available to us without requiring the ability to transcend all standards.

This brings us to the third objection, for the relativist may now reply, with Barnes and Bloor, that there are no standards which enjoy a privileged epistemic status permitting them to serve as arbiter in the evaluation of other standards.[24] It may very well be possible to evaluate a given standard relative to a set of background standards. But there is nothing which gives the background standards a justification which the evaluated standard lacks. Such standards are just as much in need of justification as the standard under evaluation. Yet all justification must rest on ultimate assumptions for which no further reason may be given. At a fundamental level, therefore, all standards are rationally unjustified. Thus, in the end, there is no basis for the distinction between those standards which provide genuine rational support and those which are merely operative.

Unlike the preceding objection, this one demands that justification be given, not of any particular standard, but of the entire practice of epistemic justification. For if lack of ultimate justification means that no particular standard is rationally justified, then the practice of rational justification by appeal to standards is itself brought into question. Yet it would clearly be impossible to justify the practice of appeal to standards by appeal to some further set of standards. For to appeal to further standards in this context would simply be to beg the question, since such an appeal would be an instance of the very practice which needs to be justified. It may therefore be said that an ultimate justification of the practice of rational justification is itself impossible.[25]

But this is no major concession to relativism. For it is one thing to allow that the practice of justifying beliefs by appeal to standards cannot itself be provided with a non-circular justification. It is quite another thing to deny the distinction between standards which provide genuine rational support and those which do not. For while rationality cannot itself be justified without going in a circle, it does not follow that one standard of rationality provides the same degree of rational justification as any other standard that may be proposed.

It might, however, be thought that, since all standards are ultimately unjustified, it follows that no standard is any more justified than any other. This would be to assume that having an ultimate justification is a necessary condition for a standard to have a higher degree of rational justification than another. But to make such an assumption would be to impose an excessively high constraint on rationality, since it would be to demand something that is patently impossible. In particular, it would be to demand that a standard of rationality be provided with a justification that does not itself depend on any ultimately unjustified assumptions.

While detailed criticism of this demand lies beyond the scope of this chapter, such a stringent constraint on rationality may be rejected as involving a mistaken conception of the nature of rational justification. Rationality is not to be conceived as a transcendent state which lies beyond the reach of our epistemic practices. On the contrary, rationality is an epistemic state accessible to ordinary human agents as a result of following certain processes of belief formation. Thus, unlike truth in the metaphysical realist sense,[26] rationality is a state which may be determined — albeit fallibly — to obtain or not to obtain from within the perspective of our epistemic practices.

Given that there may be no ultimate justification of standards, the only possible form of justification must be justification that is internal to a set of epistemic practices. That is, the only possible means of justification of a standard must be by way of the evaluation of a standard with respect to an ongoing system of standards and beliefs, which operate as the presupposed background of the evaluation. Yet, as we saw with the previous objection, we certainly are able to distinguish between standards which provide genuine rational support and those which do not from within an ongoing system of standards.

In view of our ability to operate in practice with this distinction, I conclude that the distinction between normative rationality and mere conformity with operative standards is one that is available to the methodological pluralist. Given the availability of this distinction, the pluralist may assert the variation of methodological standards without falling into rationality relativism. For the pluralist need not accept that mere conformity with operative standards is sufficient for rational acceptance.

9.7 A sketch of objective rationality without universal standards

Given the distinction between compliance with standards and normative rationality, the denial of universal methodological rules does not entail that rationality depends on standards operative in a given context. As a result, methodological pluralism falls short of a rationality relativism on which scientific rationality depends on contextually variant standards. The question remains, however, whether there can be anything objective about rationality in the absence of invariant methodological standards. I will conclude by briefly sketching the requisite notion of rationality.

It might be supposed that for rationality to be objective all rational thinkers would have to proceed from the same considerations to the same conclusions. In other words, one might assume that for rationality to be objective, there must be some universal component of rationality which leads to convergence of rational belief. Yet, if instead of a universal scientific method there is a plurality of standards, the thinking of rational scientists would not converge in the required manner. Guided by divergent methodological standards, scientists confronted with alternative theories may disagree in choice of theory, and may accept the same theory for different reasons. Thus, without universal method, it may seem that science fails to be objective.

It is, however, mistaken to assume that objectivity requires convergence of rational opinion. What is required to insure objectivity in rational theory choice is not agreement, but the absence of irreducibly subjective factors, such as personal interest or idiosyncracy, cultural bias, emotive reaction, and individual taste. The role of such factors may be avoided in scientific decision making provided that decisions are based on appeal to intersubjectively available methodological standards. Without a universal method, decisions based on methodological standards may be objective, even though they do not result in uniformity of theory choice.

What is evidently needed to account for such objectively rational divergence of opinion is a theory of rationality on which scientists need not be led by the same factors to accept the same theories. Rather, confronted with alternative theories, scientists may differentially evaluate both the relevance and the relative importance of a multitude of methodologically significant features of theories. For example, they may take into account such potentially conflicting standards as explanatory breadth, simplicity, consistency with the data, and predictive accuracy. For a variety of legitimate reasons, scientists may choose to place more or less weight on some factors than on others. As a result of their variant appraisal of the importance of such factors, scientists may arrive by rational means at conflicting choices of theory.

The theory of rationality required to deal with divergence of rational theory choice is one according to which such choice is akin to decision making in practical matters. We are accustomed to rational agents who make different choices in similar situations because they value certain ends more than others, and because they weigh up the costs and benefits of their actions in diverse ways. In order to see divergent theory choice as rational, we must come to see scientists choosing between theories as rational agents who are faced with practical decisions, and who have considerable leeway in choosing an appropriate course of action.

On such a model, objective rationality does not require that all scientists arrive at the same choice of theory as a result of employing the same method. Rather, the objective nature of such rationality consists in the fact that the standards to which appeal is made in choice of theory are taken to be of primarily epistemic significance. Thus, a scientist who chooses a theory on the basis of such standards does not do so on irreducibly subjective grounds, as would be the case were the choice made on the basis of personal interest, bias or taste. Since such a choice may be based on standards which are not universally adhered to, or are accorded varying weights, the considerations on the basis of which the choice is made may fail to be universally compelling. Nevertheless, such standards may provide objective grounds for choice of theory, since the appeal of such standards transcends merely personal considerations, and therefore fails to be irreducibly subjective.

Notes

1. See, for example, Chalmers (1982) and (1990), Ellis (1990), Feyerabend (1975), Kuhn (1970a), Laudan (1984) and Newton-Smith (1981).
2. See, for example, Popper (1970), Lakatos (1978b), and Scheffler (1967).
3. See Chalmers (1982), Doppelt (1982), Gower (1988), Laudan (1989), Siegel (1987) and Worrall (1988) and (1989).
4. Cf. Kuhn (1970a, pp. 103-10, 148).
5. Kuhn (1977c, pp. 330-5).
6. Feyerabend (1975, p. 23).
7. I will use the term 'methodological standard' as a neutral term to refer to a variety of normative methodological devices. In fact, the literature displays a bewildering variety of methodological terminology. Writers on methodological variation speak variously, and sometimes interchangeably, of the following methodological devices: aims, canons, constraints, criteria, ends, goals, methods, norms, principles, rules, standards and values. Though there is little evidence of uniform usage in this area, and some evidence of ambiguity and confusion, it is not my task here to remedy this situation.
8. See, for example, Lakatos (1978b, pp. 90-1) and Popper (1970, p. 56).
9. Cf. Kuhn (1970a, pp. 35-42, 103, 148).
10. Cf. 'As in political revolutions, so in paradigm choice — there is no standard higher than the assent of the relevant community' (1970a, p. 94); see also (1970a, pp. 103-10, 147-59).
11. E.g., Siegel (1987, p. 54).
12. Worrall (1988, p. 275; cf. p. 274).
13. Gower (1988, p. 59).
14. As suggested by Kuhn (1977c, p. 335).
15. Cf. Laudan (1984, pp. 81-2).

16. As Newton-Smith suggests (1981, pp. 220-3).
17. This is the criticism raised by Worrall (1988) against Laudan (1984). See my discussion of the debate between Laudan and Worrall in Chapter 10.
18. Laudan (1989, p. 369). The challenge which Laudan claims is raised by relativism is exemplified, for example, in the argument of Barnes and Bloor (1982) that neither observation nor logic admit of objective underpinning.
19. This is the possibility of 'theory dominance' discussed by Laudan and Laudan (1989, pp. 225-6).
20. Cf. Laudan (1984, p. 40), (1989, p. 374) and Newton-Smith (1981, pp. 221-3).
21. Laudan (1984, pp. 38-9).
22. To be somewhat more precise, the requisite assumption is that rationality consists in conformity with operative standards, provided that such standards figure appropriately in the way in which the belief is held. For a belief which conforms with a standard might fail to be held on the basis of that standard, and might even be held on an irrational or non-rational basis. In the latter case, in spite of satisfying the standard, the belief is not held rationally. In order for such a belief to be held rationally, the satisfaction of the standard must be the reason why the belief is held.
23. The following are examples of conventional norms of behaviour: rules of the road; table manners; standard forms of greeting and introduction; ceremonial rituals (e.g., weddings and burials).
24. Barnes and Bloor emphasize that the attempt to provide a rational justification for beliefs and standards (1982, p. 27), or forms of inference (1982, pp. 40-2) must ultimately be circular. They deny that justification of such beliefs, standards and forms of inference can be given in 'absolute' or 'context-independent' terms, and they conclude that their acceptance is to be explained by their 'local credibility', rather than any 'universal' appeal which they might have (1982, pp. 27, 45-6).
25. Cf. Popper (1945, Vol. 2, pp. 230-1) for a closely analogous argument that rationalism cannot be established by argument but must rest on an 'irrational *faith in reason*' (1945, Vol. 2, p. 231). Of course, Popper does not draw relativist conclusions from this argument, but argues instead that a critical rationalist attitude is one which 'frankly admits its origin in an irrational decision' (1945, Vol. 2, p. 231).
26. Cf., 'the most important consequence of metaphysical realism is that *truth* is supposed to be *radically non-epistemic*', Putnam (1978, p. 125).

10 Normative naturalism and the challenge of relativism

10.1 Introduction

In a recent exchange,[1] John Worrall and Larry Laudan have debated the merits of the model of rational scientific change proposed by Laudan in his book *Science and Values* (1984). On the model advocated by Laudan, rational change may take place at the level of scientific theory and methodology, as well as at the level of the epistemic aims of science. Moreover, the rationality of a change which occurs at any one of these three levels may be dependent on considerations at the remaining levels. Yet, in spite of the avowedly anti-relativistic motivation of Laudan's model, Worrall criticizes Laudan for irrevocably relativizing scientific rationality to historically variant methodological standards.

In Worrall's view, epistemological relativism is inescapable for Laudan, given the latter's rejection of fixed principles of scientific methodology. However, in reply to Worrall, Laudan accuses him of failing to understand the true nature of the challenge presented by epistemic relativism. According to Laudan, the challenge of relativism is not simply to show that methodological standards are historically invariant. Rather, it is to show that such standards may be provided with a sound epistemic justification. And this challenge arises whether or not standards are subject to variation.

As against Laudan, Worrall charges that relativism, so construed, is unavoidable, since no ultimately compelling epistemic justification of any methodological standard may be given, on pain of a sceptical regress of justifications. Laudan would presumably dispute Worrall's claim that there may be no epistemic justification of standards capable of resisting the relativist challenge. For, in a separate series of publications, Laudan has recently spelled out the metamethodological position underlying his model of scientific rationality. This position, which he calls 'normative naturalism', directly addresses the issue of the epistemic justification of methodological standards. Given the apparent relevance of normative naturalism to the dispute between Laudan and Worrall, the question arises whether normative naturalism contains the resources necessary to avoid relativism.

In this chapter I will consider the debate between Laudan and Worrall in an attempt to determine whether normative naturalism is able to meet the challenge of relativism which Worrall raises against Laudan's model. The next three sections of the chapter are largely devoted to setting the stage. Section 10.2 presents Laudan's model of rationality, Section 10.3 reviews his debate with Worrall and Section 10.4 outlines normative naturalism. In subsequent sections I turn to the main purpose of the chapter. In Section 10.5 I argue that normative naturalism meets the relativist demand for justification of methodological standards, while at the same time avoiding several other forms of relativism. However, in Section 10.6 I show how a form of epistemic relativism involving a justificatory regress returns to haunt normative naturalism, as Worrall suggests. In Sections 10.7 and 10.8 I present and evaluate Laudan's likely reply to this challenge.

10.2 Laudan's *Science and Values*

I will begin with a sketch of the relevant features of the model which Laudan proposes in *Science and Values*. Laudan takes the problem of the formation of consensus in science to be one of the key issues which have divided recent philosophy of science. Roughly stated, empiricist philosophy of science (e.g., falsificationism, logical empiricism) has a ready explanation of consensus formation in terms of shared methodological rules which function as algorithms that determine choice of theory (1984, pp. 5-6). But such an account leaves little room to explain how or why scientists should ever come to disagree in choice of theory. By contrast, post-empiricist philosophers of science (e.g., Kuhn, Lakatos, Feyerabend), who reject the idea of a fixed algorithmic method, have difficulty accounting for consensus formation. For their models of science contain elements (e.g., incommensurability, underdetermination, violation of methodological rules) which suggest, not only that dissensus is widespread, but that there is no rational means of bringing it to an end (1984, pp. 16-7).

Thus, while empiricists explain consensus but have a hard time with disagreement, post-empiricists emphasize dissensus at the cost of being unable to explain how agreement is arrived at. But, Laudan argues, an adequate philosophical model of scientific rationality must explain both consensus formation and the existence of widespread disagreement. Laudan's own proposal for such a model of rationality is based on his analysis of the source of the trouble facing both empiricist and post-empiricist philosophy of science. On Laudan's analysis, the trouble stems from acceptance by both schools of thought of a common model of the nature of epistemic justification in science, which he refers to as the 'hierarchical model of justification' (1984, p. 23).

According to the hierarchical model, rational consensus formation in science is characterized by a hierarchy of three levels of possible agreement or disagreement (1984, pp. 23-6). At the base level of the hierarchy are opinions about matters of fact which relate to both observable and unobservable states of affairs. Disagreement arising about such matters of fact may be resolved at the second level of the hierarchy, which is the level of methodological rules. For, where methodological consensus exists, factual disagreement may be resolved by appealing to shared methodological rules. However, where no methodological consensus exists, first level factual disputes are unable to be decided by appeal to second level shared rules. Resolution of such disputes requires that reference be made to the third level of the hierarchy, the axiological level, which involves the aims or goals of science. For, provided that scientists share cognitive aims, agreement may be reached by deciding which methodological rule provides the best means of fulfilling their common aims.

A serious flaw in the hierarchical model emerges in the absence of shared aims (1984, pp. 42-3). For where scientists disagree about the aims of their enterprise, no appeal can be made to common goals to resolve lower level disputes about methodological or factual matters. Given that scientific disputes are to be resolved at a higher level, the hierarchical model does not possess the resources to explain resolution of disputes arising at the top of the hierarchy. Thus, the hierarchical model fails because it is unable to provide an account of how dispute at the level of aims may be rationally adjudicated.

To remedy this situation, Laudan proposes an alternative model on which cognitive aims are also brought within the range of rational appraisal (1984, pp. 62-4). Laudan sketches a 'reticulated model of scientific rationality', on which aims, methods and factual beliefs form a network of shifting and interdependent justificatory relations. On this model, justification runs up and down the hierarchy, rather than being restricted to descent from top to bottom. Thus, not only may aims justify methods and theories, but factual information may be relevant to the appraisal of methods, and theories provide constraints on appropriate cognitive goals. Furthermore, considerations about available methods may shape scientists' views about the attainability of specific cognitive goals. Given the reticulated nature of justificatory relations, changes that take place at one or more levels of the hierarchy may be warranted on the basis of factors obtaining at any other level of the hierarchy.

The main novelty of the reticulated model lies in the rational evaluability of cognitive aims. However, in the context of Worrall's objections, Laudan's views on the rational justification of methodological change are of greater significance. There is, of course, scope for rational methodological change within the hierarchical model, since it may be possible to determine which of competing methods better conduces to the fulfillment of a given cognitive aim. But the hierarchical model is unable to deal with all cases of such change, since it accords no role to first level factual considerations in the evaluation of methodology. Laudan argues that factual considerations do, however, play a major role in justifying methodological change, since such considerations are often needed in order to determine whether a given method does indeed lead to a particular aim (1984, pp. 38-9). Given such a role for factual considerations, rational methodological change may occur as the result of empirical discovery (1984, p. 39) or change in theory (1984, p. 77). There are, in addition, other possible forms of rational methodological change not available within the hierarchical model; for example, where scientists adopt a novel set of cognitive aims, it may be necessary to develop new methods suited to such aims (1984, p. 57).

10.3 Worrall versus Laudan

In his review of *Science and Values*, Worrall objects that Laudan's reticulated model 'collapses into relativism' (Worrall, 1988, p. 275); thus, while the model 'sounds just the ticket ... it is a ticket onto the rocks' (1988, p. 266). According to Worrall, Laudan's position leads to relativism because it allows wholesale change in the methodology of science.[2] As Worrall says,

> If no principles of evaluation stay fixed, then there is no 'objective viewpoint' from which we can show that progress has occurred and we can say only that progress has occurred *relative to the standards that we happen to accept now*. However this may be dressed up, it is relativism. Without fixed standards, no amount

of 'mutual adjustment ... among all three levels of scientific commitment' can avoid it. (1988, p. 274)

There is an important decision to be made: either there is an invariant core ... of methodological principles or everything is open to change ... *without* such an [invariant core, Laudan's] model collapses into relativism. (1988, p. 275)

As these quotes indicate, Worrall insists that 'laying down *fixed* principles of scientific theory appraisal is the only alternative to relativism' (1988, p. 265). Worrall does not, however, develop the point in great detail at this point.[3] But his argument appears to turn on the assumption that without a fixed methodology there may be no 'objective viewpoint' from which to judge the progressiveness of science. Presumably, the idea is that if there is a fixed methodology, which applies throughout the history of science, then the judgement that a given episode in the history of science is progressive may be based on considerations which are independent of our own particular viewpoint. But if there is no such methodology, then the judgement that a historical episode is progressive amounts at most to the judgement that it is progressive from our point of view. A judgement of the latter sort would reflect our local standards, rather than unchanging, universal standards. Thus, members of another community, who consider the same episode from the viewpoint of a different set of standards, might disagree with us about the progressiveness of that episode. Yet in the absence of independent standards, there is no sense in which we are right and they are wrong. Relative to local standards both are right, and there is no further question of rightness or wrongness which can be raised.

In his response to Worrall, Laudan challenges the assumption which lies behind Worrall's objection.[4] Where Worrall assumes that variation of methodology leads straight to relativism, Laudan argues that the issue of methodological variance versus invariance has nothing to do with relativism.

The central claim of the epistemic relativist, at least where standards and methods are concerned, is not that those standards change but that — whether changing or unchanging — those standards have no independent non-question-begging rationale or foundation. Even if man had been using exactly the same inferential principles ever since the dawn of science, the relativist would doubtless ask, and properly so, 'What is their justification?' ... the challenge of relativism is exactly the same whether the methods of science are one or many, constant or

> evolving. If we can answer that challenge, i.e., if we can show why certain methods are better than others, then we can offer a justification for the current methods of science, even if they are different from the methods of science of three centuries ago. If, on the other hand, we cannot resolve the relativist's meta-philosophical conundrum, then it will be wholly beside the point whether methods are constant or changing. (Laudan, 1989, pp. 369-70)

Laudan's point against Worrall may be summarized in the following terms. The challenge of relativism is precisely not to show that there are absolute standards which are invariant throughout the history of science. Rather, the challenge of relativism is to provide a rational justification for the methodology that science uses. This is because, even if it could be shown that the same methodology has been employed throughout the history of science, the relativist challenge may still be raised against that invariant methodology. For what rationally justifies such a methodology, as opposed to some wildly different one, can hardly be that the methodology is historically invariant: not having changed throughout history is no justification for a methodology. Thus, the problem of showing that present scientific methods are rational methods arises whether or not present methods are the same as past methods. Given this, Laudan objects against Worrall that: "Sporting bumper stickers proclaiming that 'scientists always do it the same way' is a laughably feeble response to the relativist's demand" (1989, p. 370); to respond to relativism, it "is to no avail to dig in our heels and say that 'everything's okay as long as the aims and methods of science don't change'" (1989, p. 371).

In reply to Laudan, Worrall, in effect, denies that Laudan's version of the relativist challenge can be answered.

> Relativism, as *Laudan* defines it, is inevitable. There is a potential infinite regress of justification and this means that *ultimately* the only way to avoid sceptical relativism is to dig in one's heels. (Worrall, 1989, p. 381).

In other words, Worrall is suggesting, the demand for the rational justification of methodological principles, which Laudan sees as the challenge of relativism, leads directly to an infinite regress, so that relativism deriving from that source is unavoidable. What the regress of justifications shows, according to Worrall, is that rationality is subject to intrinsic logical limitations.[5] These limits must simply be admitted:

if the sceptic really presses, then the only option is, I believe, the honest admission that *ultimately* we must stop arguing and 'dogmatically' assert certain basic principles of rationality. If Laudan is right that this honest admission entails relativism, then relativism wins. (1989, p. 383)

But while Worrall takes such 'sceptical relativism' to be unavoidable, he denies that this is the real problem posed by relativism. Instead, he continues to maintain that the real threat of relativism stems from the claim that there are no invariant standards of scientific methodology.

In summary, then, Laudan and Worrall are fundamentally at odds over the nature of the challenge presented by relativism. Worrall maintains that the challenge of relativism is to establish an invariant core of methodological principles, on the basis of which choices of theory throughout the history of science may be objectively justified. By contrast, Laudan sees relativism as leading to a demand for an account of the justification of methodological principles, which must be applicable regardless of whether such principles are subject to variation. As we have just seen, however, Worrall takes the demand for the justification of methodological principles to involve a form of relativism that is unavoidable. It remains to be seen whether Laudan's position contains the resources to meet this form of relativism. We will return to this question after discussion of Laudan's normative naturalist metamethodology.

10.4 Normative naturalism

Laudan appears not to have explicitly replied to Worrall's claim that 'relativism, as *Laudan* defines it, is inevitable' (1989, p. 381). However, it seems clear that Laudan would disagree with Worrall about the impossibility of providing a rational justification of the methods of science which meets the challenge of relativism. This is because Laudan has developed an approach to such metamethodological matters, which is designed precisely to provide a rationale for the methods of science. In this section I will present the outlines of this metamethodological view, and in the next four sections I will consider whether this view successfully meets the relativist challenge.

In a subsequent series of publications, Laudan has continued to develop the details of the metamethodological position which underlies the model of scientific rationality proposed in *Science and Values*.[6] Laudan calls this position 'normative naturalism'. The position is normative because it seeks to illuminate the nature of epistemic justification in science, and because it is prescriptive rather than merely descriptive.[7] It is naturalistic because it treats methodology as 'continuous with other sorts of theories about how the natural world is constituted' (1990a, p. 44), and 'as co-extensive with the sciences' (1990b, p. 315). And it is a metamethodological position because it is a theory about the justification of methodological rules, rather than a mere specification of such rules (cf. 1987a, p. 23 and 1990b, p. 315). As a naturalistic metamethodology, normative naturalism stands in opposition to the conventionalist metamethodology of Popper (1959, pp. 53-6) and the intuitionism previously espoused by Laudan himself (1977, pp. 158-63).[8]

The key to Laudan's normative naturalism is his analysis of the syntax and semantics of methodological rules (1987a, pp. 23-6). According to Laudan, methodological rules are to be analyzed as hypothetical imperatives stating a relation between cognitive means and ends. For example, Laudan suggests that Popper's rule against *ad hoc* hypotheses be expressed in the form of a conditional: 'if one wants to develop theories which are very risky, then one ought to avoid *ad hoc* hypotheses' (1987a, p. 24). On such an analysis, methodological rules constitute claims about how to attain particular goals, which rest on contingent facts about the way the world is. Such rules are therefore to be thought of as elliptical formulations of empirical claims about the world and how to find out about it. Accordingly, the truth of a methodological rule depends on a contingent state of affairs; in particular, it depends on there being a correlation between use of a given method of inquiry and attainment of a specific epistemic result (1987a, p. 25).[9]

On such an analysis of methodological rules, a methodology is to be conceived as, in effect, a broadly empirical theory about how to conduct inquiry (1987b, p. 349). Because of their theoretical status, methodological rules are, like scientific theories, subject to appraisal, revision, and possible replacement, as a result of empirical considerations. Moreover, in order to provide a rational justification for such rules it may be necessary to put forward empirical evidence on their behalf. Because of their hypothetical form, methodological rules presuppose the existence of connections between particular cognitive means and ends. Thus, justification of such a rule requires evidence that the means does indeed reliably conduce to the desired end.[10] In particular, it requires evidence that a correlation obtains between use of a given method and realization of the intended epistemic goal.

At the heart of Laudan's endeavour to naturalize metamethodology, therefore, lies the thesis that rules possessing normative force may be grounded in factual means-end relations. Moreover, one of the central motivations of his normative naturalism is to provide an account of the rational justification of methodological principles. Thus, one of the chief aims of normative naturalism is evidently to meet the relativist demand for an epistemologically satisfactory account of methodological justification. In the next section, I will argue, as against Worrall, that there is a clear sense in which Laudan meets the relativist challenge.

10.5 Normative naturalism and epistemic justification

As we saw in Section 10.3, Laudan and Worrall differ fundamentally on the nature of the relativist challenge. Worrall sees the challenge of relativism as a demand for invariant standards, whereas Laudan takes the challenge to be to show that methodological standards are justified. In this section, I will argue that normative naturalism meets the relativist challenge in the sense that it provides an account of the rational justification of methodological standards. However, as we also saw in Section 10.3, Worrall holds that the demand for justification leads inexorably to a relativism of ultimately indefensible principles. I will consider the ramifications of this problem in the following three sections.

According to Laudan, the relativist is rightly unimpressed by the claim that the principles of scientific methodology are historically invariant. For the relativist may always reply to such a claim, 'What is their justification?' (Laudan, 1989, p. 370). The question of how such principles are justified is precisely the question addressed by normative naturalism. The central thesis of normative naturalism in this regard is that the justificational basis of a methodological rule does not differ fundamentally from that of any other broadly empirical claim about the world. Given their hypothetical imperative form, methodological rules are justified by presenting evidence that the means-end relations which they presuppose do in fact obtain. Because such rules are, in effect, low level empirical claims, providing evidence on their behalf presents no greater obstacle than does establishing any other low level empirical claim.[11]

Laudan tends to portray methodological justification as a comparative matter.[12] While it is unclear whether methodological justification is necessarily comparative, it seems clear that it must at least in general be so. This can be seen by consideration of the prescriptive force of the rules in question. Since such rules are, in effect, recommendations on how best to achieve a desired end, what prescriptive force they possess must rest on their purportedly being the best available means to that end. Accordingly, evidence for such a rule must be evidence to the effect that it is the most effective method among the available alternatives (1987a, p. 26).

The comparative nature of methodological justification is particularly significant for the issue of relativism. For if one methodological rule can be shown to be better justified than another, then, as Laudan notes (1989, p. 370), it becomes possible to provide a rational justification for presently accepted scientific methods. In particular, if present methods can be shown to better promote our cognitive aims than previously employed methods, then we are justified in using present methods.

This point has immediate relevance to Worrall's initial objection to Laudan that the denial of methodological invariance leads straight to relativism. Given that one method (or set of methods) may have stronger evidential support than another, Worrall's argument that there may be no 'objective viewpoint' from which to judge scientific progress breaks down. For, even in the absence of an invariant method, the transition between theories may still be progressive, for example, if a later theory satisfies a rule which has been shown to lead to a given aim more reliably than did the rule satisfied by an earlier theory. There is, moreover, no need to step outside history to make objective judgements of progress: provided only that present methods are better justified than previous methods, we are perfectly entitled to look back on the history of science and judge that particular episodes were conducive to present cognitive aims. Nor need the variation of methodology land us in a relativity of judgements of progress to operative standards, since some standards are better justified than others.[13]

Normative naturalism also contrasts sharply with forms of relativism which deny a basis for rational choice between alternative methodological standards. One example of such relativism is relativism due to the conventional status of methodology, which Laudan ascribes to Popper.[14] Another example is the form of relativism often attributed to Kuhn, according to which methodological standards vary with paradigm, and there are no 'higher' standards on which to base a choice between standards.[15] On either of these views, there is no basis on which to show that one set of standards is rationally better justified than another. Yet, precisely because normative naturalism provides scope for the epistemic justification of methodological standards, normative naturalism fails to render such justification relative in either of these senses.

In sum, normative naturalism provides an account of the justification of methodological standards by means of empirical evidence for cognitive means-end connections. As such, it avoids forms of relativism which relativize judgements of progress to variant standards, or which provide for no rational justification of methodological standards. Given that normative naturalism provides an account of epistemic justification, and that it avoids such forms of relativism, there is therefore a clear sense in which normative naturalism meets the relativist challenge.

10.6 Normative naturalism and sceptical relativism

Despite having just argued that there is a clear sense in which normative naturalism meets the relativist challenge, I will now argue that there remains a sense in which normative naturalism falls prey to relativism. Specifically, I will argue that normative naturalism is subject to a sceptical regress of justifications which leads to a relativism of indefensible ultimate principles. In other words, I will argue that normative naturalism faces a severe threat of relativism, which is precisely analogous to that highlighted by Worrall's argument that the demand for justification leads to relativism. In the next section, I will consider Laudan's likely reply to this version of the relativist challenge.

Before presenting the argument, it is worth commenting briefly on the relation between scepticism and relativism. As they are usually understood, scepticism and relativism pull in opposite directions. Scepticism denies knowledge, whereas relativism makes knowledge relative to context. However, there is a form of relativism which may be derived from a classical sceptical form of argument. In particular, it may be argued along the lines of the sceptical problem of the criterion that no methodological rule or standard can be provided with an ultimately compelling rational defence. For the attempt to justify any given standard leads to an infinite regress, as the demand for justification continues to be pressed. Alternatively, it may proceed in a circle, or else grind to a halt at a standard for which no justification may be given. Yet if there is no ultimate justification for any standard, then one standard is as rationally well founded as any other. This entails the relativistic thesis that it is just as rational to proceed in accordance with one standard as any other standard that might be proposed.[16] Given the source of this form of relativism, it is not altogether devoid of significance that Worrall should refer to it as 'sceptical relativism'.

To see how such sceptical relativism arises with respect to normative naturalism, recall that methodological rules receive justification, according to normative naturalism, by means of empirical evidence of cognitive means-ends relationships. Since methodological rules are to be cast in the form of hypothetical imperatives which recommend performing a given action in order to realize a particular aim, they are to be supported by evidence to the effect that performing such an action reliably leads to the aim in question. Thus, justification of such rules rests on evidence for the existence of correlations between performing a particular kind of action and achieving a particular kind of result.

Suppose, then, that evidence has been put forward on behalf of a given methodological rule to the effect that an appropriate means-end relationship obtains. Such evidence might well provide rational support for use of the rule in pursuit of the desired aim. Nevertheless, the question immediately arises of whether acceptance of the evidence is itself rationally justified. In response to this question, further evidence might be advanced in support of acceptance of the initial evidence.[17] But, as before, this raises the question of whether acceptance of the further evidence is rational, which leads to an infinite regress. To avoid the regress, appeal might be made to the initial evidence in support of its own acceptability; but this would be to argue in a circle. Alternatively, a halt might be called at some final item of evidence for which no further justification may be given. Since neither a regress of reasons, circular argument nor dogmatic halting point provides the original evidence with rational support, it follows that the evidence advanced on behalf of the methodological rule must ultimately fail to provide it with such support. Furthermore, since a similar argument can be employed against any rule for which evidence might be proposed, it follows that one rule is as rationally well grounded as any other.

This argument shows that the normative naturalist account of epistemic justification is open to relativist attack by means of a sceptical regress of reasons. It would therefore appear that the normative naturalist account of epistemic justification does not contain the resources to meet the challenge of sceptical relativism raised by Worrall. However, it will be considered in the next section whether there is any basis on which Laudan can respond to the sceptical relativist challenge.

10.7 Blocking the sceptical relativist regress

As it happens, Laudan explicitly addresses the threat of an infinite regress in the course of his discussion of the evidential basis of methodological rules (1987a, pp. 25-6). He argues that the justificatory regress, which would ensue from questioning the evidential basis of a methodological rule, may be brought to an end by appeal to a general inductive principle of evidence. Thus, Laudan, in effect, anticipates the threat of sceptical relativism which Worrall raises against the demand for methodological justification.

According to Laudan, the threat of a regress arises against normative naturalism because of the need to justify the test procedures employed in providing empirical support for methodological rules. As he says,

> ... we could 'test' a methodological rule only by taking for granted the prior establishment of some other methodological rule, which will tell us how to test the former. And that latter rule, in its turn will presumably require for its justification some previously established methodological rule, etc. (1987a, p. 25)

Given the supposed need to empirically justify methods, how is the regress to be avoided?

Laudan proposes that what is needed to 'block the regress' is a principle of evidence, common to all methodological theories, which may serve as 'a neutral and impartial vehicle for choosing between rival methodologies' (1987a, p. 25). Such a principle is to found, Laudan suggests, in our ordinary 'inductive convictions about the appraisal of policies and strategies' (1987a, p. 25). Laudan formulates this principle as follows:

> (R_1) If actions of a particular sort, m, have consistently promoted certain cognitive ends, e, in the past, and rival actions, n, have failed to do so, then assume that future actions following the rule "if your aim is e, you ought to do m" are more likely to promote those ends than actions based on the rule "if your aim is e, you ought to do n." (1987a, p. 25)

This is an explicitly inductivist metamethodological principle, which licenses inference from the past performance of a method to the likelihood of its future success. In particular, provided there is empirical evidence that a given method is the most reliable means of achieving a given cognitive aim, it follows deductively from (R_1) that one ought to employ such a method in order to achieve that aim.

Given that (R_1) serves, in conjunction with the statement of a cognitive means-end relation, to entail a methodological rule, the justificatory role of (R_1) seems straightforward. Specifically, (R_1) provides the license for future application of empirically well founded methodological rules. The question remains, however, of how (R_1) itself is to be justified.

Laudan does present (R_1) as a principle which will 'block the regress'. This may suggest that appeal to (R_1) would prevent the sceptic from being able to generate the infinite regress. But this seems clearly false. For one may always ask for a justification of (R_1). If an argument is presented for (R_1), then the premises of the argument may be challenged, as well as the premises of any further argument which may be proposed in support of those premises, and so on, *ad infinitum*.[18]

Given that scope remains for a regress, I suggest that the purpose of (R_1) is not to eliminate altogether the possibility of generating a regress. Rather, (R_1) is presented as a general metamethodological principle, which we have compelling epistemological grounds to accept. Thus, while it remains in principle possible to generate a sceptical regress on the basis of (R_1), this possibility is not to be granted any particularly great epistemological significance. Assuming that strong grounds may be advanced in favour of (R_1), the possibility of a regress constitutes, at most, the rather abstract possibility that a persistent questioner might repeatedly press the challenge of justifying reasons. But, surely, given the logic of justification, this possibility always exists.[19] Provided that (R_1) is independently well justified, however, it does not follow that a sceptical relativism of ultimate principles is the inevitable result.

10.8 Scepticism, induction, naturalism

The remarks with which I closed the preceding section give rise to two immediate questions. First, does (R_1) possess a sound epistemic justification? Second, is it plausible to relegate the sceptical regress to the status of a mere abstract possibility? I will briefly address each of these questions in turn.

As for the issue of justification, Laudan presents two key considerations:

> (1), (R_1) is arguably assumed universally among philosophers of science, and thus has promise as a quasi-Archimedean standpoint, and (2), quite independently of the sociology of philosophical consensus, it appears to be a sound rule of learning from experience. Indeed, if (R_1) is not sound, no general rule is. (1987a, p. 26)

In support of point (1), Laudan argues that (R_1) should be acceptable to the major contemporary theories of methodology, viz., inductivism, historical philosophy of science, and Popper's falsificationism.[20] Yet, even if he is right about this, it is unclear how the existence of such a consensus among methodologists of science might serve as a warrant for (R_1): "for after all, 'the whole of [methodology]' might err".[21] Moreover, for Laudan to appeal to consensus as the epistemic basis for (R_1), would seem to commit him to a meta-metamethodological conventionalism not in keeping with his explicit rejection of conventionalism at the metamethodological level.

Both these objections miss the point, however, as is evident from Laudan's remark that (R_1) 'has promise as a quasi-Archimedean standpoint' (1987a, p. 26). Rather than philosophical consensus providing a warrant for (R_1), the existence of such consensus suggests that debate amongst philosophers over a given methodological rule is unlikely to proceed beyond (R_1). For the role of (R_1) is precisely to provide a common ground on the basis of which to forge consensus in debate about the merits of a given methodological principle. This means, first, that such debate is unlikely to degenerate into a regress of reasons; and, second, that debate is likely to focus more narrowly on the evidential credentials of the rule in question. Consensus on (R_1), therefore, does not provide the epistemic grounds for (R_1), but rather serves as neutral court of appeal which may adjudicate between rival methodologies.

This shifts the epistemic burden for (R_1) to Laudan's point (2), according to which (R_1) is 'a sound rule of learning from experience' (1987a, p. 26). What appears to be the ground for this claim is Laudan's remark that 'if (R_1) is not sound, no general rule is' (1987a, p. 26). And this appears, as Alexander Rosenberg has remarked, to be a form of the pragmatic justification of induction, according to which use of induction is pragmatically justified, since inductive inference will succeed, if any predictive method will succeed.[22] Now, as much ink as has been spilt over the problem of induction, it can hardly be supposed that the pragmatic justification of induction will command universal acceptance among philosophers of science. But Laudan's point is presumably not that this is the canonical solution to the problem of induction. Rather, what the pragmatic response establishes is a more minimal point: viz., that without at least assuming that induction works we can make no sense of learning from experience at all. For to learn from experience is precisely to be able to take past experience as a guide to the likely course of future experience.

Of course, this view of the indispensability of induction may seem to beg the question against the inductive sceptic, who demands that induction be given a non-circular justification. This brings us to the second question stated at the opening of this section. There is a parallel between refusal to provide a more substantive response to the inductive sceptic and relegation of the possibility of sceptical regress to the realm of abstract possibility. In particular, I wish to suggest that what lies behind both failures to directly resolve the problem of sceptical demand for justification is a robustly naturalistic approach to matters of epistemic justification.

More specifically, what frames Laudan's apparent refusal to provide an account of epistemic justification which would satisfy the sceptic is a rejection of the sceptic's demand for ultimate (or 'higher') justification. A concern for modes of justification over and above those employed in the practice of science is notoriously absent from the sciences. Hence, a rejection of such a demand is entirely consonant with a naturalistic insistence that the epistemic standards of the sciences provide an appropriate level of rigour for epistemology. Laudan's naturalism is therefore a crucial element in his response to sceptical attacks on epistemic justification: for it is precisely because he takes a naturalistic view of such justification that he rejects the sceptical challenge.

There is, however, more to such naturalism than a swift dismissal of scepticism in the name of science. The appearance of question begging against the sceptic may be dispelled by reflection upon a further aspect of naturalistic thinking about justification. It has often been argued that the sceptic seeks to impose inappropriate standards on the application of epistemic concepts, which constitutes an illegitimate break with the usual standards governing our ordinary use of such concepts.[23] This claim of the inappropriateness of the sceptic's demands accords well with the naturalistic view that there is no higher form of justification of the kind sought by the sceptic. Thus, in refusing to answer the sceptic's demand for ultimate justification, Laudan's insistence on ordinary modes of justification is of a piece with his naturalism.

Finally, lest it be supposed that the refusal to meet the sceptic's demand signals a significant lowering of justificatory standards, it should be noted that Laudan's naturalist metamethodology is intrinsically self-corrective. Not only is it possible on his view to refute particular methodological rules, but (R_1) itself rests on the contingent reliability of induction, and is itself therefore defeasible.[24] Given that normative naturalism, like science itself, is open to revision as a result of empirical inquiry, it can hardly be thought to set the standards too low.

10.9 Conclusion

The aim of this chapter has been to evaluate Worrall's charge of relativism against Laudan's model of scientific change in light of the latter's normative naturalist metamethodology. As we saw in Section

10.3, however, three different senses of the challenge of relativism are at issue in the debate between Laudan and Worrall. How has normative naturalism fared on each of these versions of the relativist challenge?

In the first sense, relativism threatens due to the absence of invariant methodological standards. I argued in Section 10.5 that, because of the comparative nature of the justification of methodological rules, one rule may be better justified than another, so that relativism does not follow from the denial of methodological invariance. The second sense of the relativist challenge, found in Laudan's reply to Worrall, is to provide an epistemic justification of methodological standards. However, as we saw in Sections 10.4 and 10.5, an account of the epistemological justification of methodological rules is precisely what normative naturalism offers. The third sense of the challenge owes much to scepticism, and employs a justificatory regress to induce a relativism of undefended ultimate principles. As I argued in Sections 10.6 and 10.7, sceptical relativism poses a serious threat to normative naturalism. However, as I suggested in Section 10.8, a response to such sceptical challenges is available to Laudan, by stressing the naturalistic rejection of sceptical assumptions about the nature of epistemic justification. Given the considerations that I have advanced in connection with each of these three points, I conclude that, while Worrall's sceptical relativism poses a serious threat, Laudan's normative naturalism does contain the resources to withstand the threat of relativism.

Notes

1. See Laudan (1989), and Worrall (1988) and (1989).
2. One might think that such an objection misses the mark, since Laudan's point is precisely that methodological changes can be justified relative to epistemic aims. But in fact Worrall is unimpressed by this aspect of Laudan's position. He rejects Laudan's hierarchical interpretation of the traditional model of rationality; and he dismisses 'discussion of the aims and goals of science' as 'quite unsuited to settling methodological disputes' (Worrall, 1989, p. 269).
3. But it is a recurring theme in a number of Worrall's papers (e.g., Worrall, 1985), and receives further development in his response to Laudan: 'the serious threat' of relativism, he says, comes from one who denies fixed standards and argues that 'his own principles therefore, while admittedly different from those presently accepted by science, may even become the principles

accepted by the science of the near future. So why should he now give them up?' (Worrall, 1989, p. 383).

4. It is worth remarking that, while Worrall takes Laudan to assert wholesale methodological variation in the history of science, Laudan denies that this is his position. Rather, Laudan espouses a somewhat weaker position: he claims to have shown 'that some rather central methodological principles have been abandoned or significantly altered over the course of time'; and he 'can see no grounds for holding any particular methodological rule ... to be *in principle* immune from revision' (Laudan, 1989, p. 371, note 6). While these points clearly raise important issues about methodological variation and relativism, given the substance of Laudan's reply to Worrall, the issue of whether methodological change may be comprehensive represents something of a side issue.
5. In support of the idea that rationality has logical limits, Worrall cites the treatment by Popper (1945, Vol. 2) and Bartley (1984) of the possibility of rational justification of a rationalist approach, as well as Lewis Carroll's parable of Achilles and the Tortoise.
6. Laudan (1987a), (1987b), (1987c), (1990a) and (1990b). This position also informs the remarks of the pragmatist interlocutor in the dialogue in Laudan's *Science and Relativism* (Laudan, 1990c, see especially Chapter 4).
7. Thus, unlike Lakatos, Laudan takes philosophical theory of methodology to be both a theory of rational justification and a source of prescriptive advice for scientists.
8. See Laudan (1986) for his rejection of intuitionism. I discuss this issue in somewhat more detail in Chapter 11.
9. Since it might be thought that conceptual considerations reveal that *ad hoc* modifications of theories reduce the risk of falsification, it might appear that Popper's rule against *ad hoc*ness is not the best illustration of the bearing of empirical considerations on metamethodological issues. However, it should not be assumed that exclusively empirical evidence is required for the justification of methodological rules. While Laudan is primarily concerned to argue against the view that such justification may proceed in an *a priori* fashion, he also insists that non-empirical conceptual considerations are crucial to both science and its methodology (1990a, pp. 50-1).
10. In light of the requirement that the means reliably conduce to the desired end, normative naturalism might appear to be a form of reliabilist epistemology. There do, however appear to be a number of salient differences between normative naturalism and reliabilism, at least as it is classically understood (e.g., Goldman,

1979). First, for Goldman a reliable method is one which leads reliably to truth, whereas for Laudan the cognitive ends in question are typically something other than truth. Second, reliabilism is a theory of the justification of an agent's epistemic states, whereas normative naturalism is a theory of the justification of method. Thus, rather than take a reliabilist view of individual epistemic rationality, Laudan operates with an instrumental account of rationality on which an agent's belief that an action will lead to their aim is required for the act to be rational (cf. Laudan, 1987a, p. 21).

11. As Paulo Abrantes has pointed out to me, Laudan tends to emphasize the history of science as a source of empirical data (e.g., 1987a, pp. 27-8), at the expense of, say, cognitive science or evolutionary biology, to which other naturalistic epistemologists might be inclined to look for evidence. This is presumably because, while the latter may be perfectly good sources of data regarding perceptual and inferential processes, they are less well suited as sources of data for the performance of methodological rules in selecting successful theories. Indeed, there is a good deal of *prima facie* plausibility in the thought that the history of science should be the primary source of data concerning the track record of scientific methods.
12. For example, in the following previously quoted passage he explicitly identifies an answer to the relativist challenge with the comparative appraisal of methods: 'If we can answer that challenge, i.e., if we can show why certain methods are better than others, then we can offer a justification for the current methods of science, even if they are different from the methods of science of three centuries ago' (1989, p. 370).
13. As for the point that judgements of progress depend on assumed aims, the threat of relativity to variant aims dissipates when it is recognized that aims too may be adjudicated rationally (cf. Laudan, 1984).
14. Given Popper's lifelong opposition to relativism, this claim of Laudan's may strain credibility. Nevertheless, Laudan has plausibly argued in a number of places that the conventionalist metamethodology espoused by Popper (1959, Chapter 2) relegates the standards of scientific method to a purely conventional status (see, e.g., Laudan, 1984, pp. 48-9, 1989, pp. 370-1, 1996, pp. 15-6). For further discussion, see Chapter 11.
15. Such an interpretation of Kuhn, which may be found for example in Lakatos (1978a, pp. 90-1), is suggested by combining Kuhn's claim that paradigms 'are the source of the methods, problem-field, and standards of solution' (Kuhn, 1970a, p. 103) with his

claim that 'as in political revolutions, so in paradigm choice — there is no standard higher than the assent of the relevant community' (1970a, p. 94).

16. Apart from obvious similarities to the problem of the criterion, the argument I have sketched has affinities with what Bartley calls the 'dilemma of ultimate commitment', which leads to what he terms 'ultimate relativism' (Bartley, 1984, pp. 72-3).
17. Alternatively, appeal might be made to a general principle of evidence, for example, one which supports the use of observation as a source of evidence or justifies the particular manner in which the evidence was collected. But similar considerations to those about to be presented in the text would then apply to such a general principle.
18. For simplicity, I overlook the possibility of circularity or calling a dogmatic halting point to avoid the regress.
19. By the 'logic of justification', I mean simply that justification has the premise-conclusion format of a logical argument (be it inductive or deductive): what is justified appears as conclusion, and what does the justifying appears as premise. But, since the premises of any argument constitute undefended assumptions within the context of the argument, the premises of any argument may always be questioned.
20. As Laudan notes, it is somewhat controversial to attribute acceptance of an inductive principle such as (R_1) to Popper. However, quite apart from Popper's 'whiff of inductivism' (Popper, 1974, pp. 1192-3, note 165b), it is arguable that (R_1) should be acceptable within a Popperian framework. For it could simply be said that a methodological rule, which is empirically supported by evidence of a strong correlation between cognitive means and ends, has attained a high degree of corroboration.
21. With apologies to Popper (1959, p. 29).
22. See Rosenberg (1990, p. 41).
23. Similarly, it is sometimes argued that scepticism breaks with the usual norms governing challenge to the epistemic justification of empirical claims. While at least *prima facie* grounds against a claim are ordinarily required in order to raise doubts about it, the sceptical challenge arises by pressing gratuitous demands for justification. For related discussion see Rescher (1980, pp. 169-72).
24. For the point that normative naturalism rests, in this respect, on thoroughly contingent matters, see Leplin (1990, pp. 29-30).

11 Popper's metamethodological conventionalism and the turn to naturalism

11.1 Introduction

In recent years, work in the philosophy of science has taken a turn toward naturalism. Rather than legislate for science in an *a priori* manner, philosophers of science now routinely appeal to empirical facts drawn from the history of science, and some even attempt to model their metascientific views on one or another branch of the natural sciences. Initially, the turn to naturalism seemed to signal a rejection of the normative orientation of traditional philosophy of science, since it was widely assumed that no epistemic evaluation might be based on merely descriptive matters about such things as how scientists behave. However, recent naturalistic philosophy of science has increasingly taken up the problem of how to ground normative concerns on a factual basis.

One prominent advocate of a naturalized approach to such normative concerns is Larry Laudan, who has recently developed a naturalistic approach to the epistemic justification of methodological rules. Laudan's approach is a naturalistic metamethodology, which provides a naturalistic account of the normative nature of methodology. He calls the position 'normative naturalism'. An important part of the case for Laudan's normative naturalism is his rejection of earlier metamethodological approaches. On the one hand, Laudan rejects Karl Popper's 'conventionalist' metamethodological stance on which methodological rules have the status of conventions. Laudan even goes so far as to trace the roots of contemporary epistemological relativism back to the metamethodological conventionalism of Popper and the logical empiricists. On the other hand, Laudan rejects an intuitionist metamethodology such as that of Imre Lakatos, according to which a methodology must accord with "the basic 'value judgements' of the scientific elite" regarding the rationality of past episodes in the history of science (Lakatos, 1978c, p. 124). Nor does Laudan exempt himself from his critique of intuitionism, since he retreats as well from his own earlier appeal to pretheoretical intuitions about the rationality of past science.[1]

In this chapter I will discuss the metamethodological problem of the epistemic justification of methodological rules. I will begin by examining Popper's conventionalist view of the status of methodological rules, and then briefly sketch the transition from conventionalism via intuitionism to present-day naturalism. I think that the shortcomings of intuitionism and conventionalism do more than a little to justify the current popularity of naturalistic approaches to the philosophy of science.

11.2 Popper on methodological rules as conventions

In *The Logic of Scientific Discovery* (1959), Popper writes that

> Methodological rules are here regarded as *conventions*. They might be described as the rules of the game of empirical science. They differ from the rules of pure logic rather as do the rules of chess, which few would regard as part of *pure* logic: seeing that the rules of pure logic govern transformations of linguistic formulae, the result of an inquiry into the rules of chess could perhaps be entitled 'The Logic of Chess', but hardly 'Logic' pure and simple. (1959, p. 53)

What does Popper mean when he says that methodological rules are conventions? Popper is operating with a distinction between conventions, rules of logic and statements of empirical fact.[2] A rule of logic is a formal rule governing entailments between sentences of a language. A statement of fact is a statement about the world which is made true or false by the way the world is. But a convention is neither of these kinds of things. A convention is neither a rule for deriving one sentence from another nor is it a truth valued statement about a contingent state of affairs.[3] But if a convention is neither of these things, then what is it?

Light may be shed on convention by pursuing Popper's analogy with the rules of chess. In chess, the knight moves two squares one way and one sideways. The bishop moves diagonally on squares of a single colour. Pawns move straight ahead except to take an opposing piece. Pieces are typically taken by moving a piece onto the square occupied by an opponent's piece. The game is won by checkmating the king. Checkmate occurs when a checked king is unable to move without moving into check.

The movements of chessmen and the rules governing checkmate exemplify two of the main kinds of rules found in chess. Rules of the first kind define moves which are permitted within the game of chess, and include rules for taking opposing pieces. Rules of the second kind define what it is to win or lose in the game of chess, as well as what counts as coming to a draw. We might say that rules of the first kind are rules of procedure, while rules of the second kind provide criteria of success or failure relative to the game of chess.[4]

In what sense are the rules of chess conventions? Clearly, they are not forced on us by the laws of nature: nothing physically makes us move chess pieces in the way prescribed by the rules of chess. Nor are the rules of chess descriptions of pre-existing empirical states of affairs: prior to being introduced, the rules of chess simply did not exist. Nor do the rules of chess follow from the rules of logic. Their status is quite different from any of these things.

What most clearly distinguishes the rules of chess from laws of nature, empirical claims and rules of logic is that they depend on us. The first players of chess invented its rules. Those who devised the rules of chess created the game of chess. They proposed, in more or less final form, a set of rules which constitute the rules of chess. These rules define allowable moves as well as winning and losing for the game of chess. As such, they impose constraints on, and define success with respect to, a particular form of human activity, viz., the activity known as 'playing chess'. The rules of chess are, moreover, the result of a deliberate act of volition: they were freely chosen by the inventors of chess. Thus, we may say that the reason they have the status of conventions is that they are deliberately chosen rules which are voluntarily taken to govern a particular form of human activity.

Against what I have just said, it might be objected that conventional rules are not voluntary for those who follow them. After all, there is such a thing as being against the rules. For example, it is against the rules of chess to move the king two squares forward and one sideways as one moves a knight. Given this, the rules of chess would seem to be obligatory in nature.

The reply to this objection is that the obligatory nature of conventions is at most conditional. For it is not obligatory to play the game of chess. (Or, in any case, under ordinary circumstances it is not normally obligatory to do so.) But if you wish to play chess, then you have to play by the rules of chess. If you move pieces in a way which breaks the rules of chess, or if you swipe the board clean in anger, you cease thereby to play the game of chess. In other words, the obligatory nature of the rules of chess is conditional on playing the game.

To return to the issue of the methodological rules of science, I wish to suggest that Popper takes rules of method to be conventions in both of the two senses of rule outlined above. Some of the rules Popper describes govern proper procedure in science, while others define criteria of success and failure for the 'game of science'.

Popper proposes a number of rules which define acceptable scientific procedure, the principal aim of which is to insure that false theories are removed from science. The basic rule of Popper's theory of method is that scientists are to seek explanatory hypotheses, which are rigorously tested and rejected if they fail such tests. Popper offers a number of other rules which subserve this basic rule. One example of such a rule is his rule against *ad hoc* hypotheses, which forbids the introduction into science of independently untestable auxiliary hypotheses. Another example is the rule that a hypothesis which has 'proved its mettle' by means of tests "may not be allowed to drop out without 'good reason'" (1959, pp. 53-4).

Popper also takes methodological rules to define success and failure within science. A successful move in science occurs when a falsifiable theory passes rigorous tests and may be tentatively accepted into the body of science. Popper's criterion of demarcation between science and non-science may be seen as defining failure within the context of science. For if a proposed theory is incapable of being falsified, then such a theory is to be dismissed as unscientific. Failure also occurs when a proposed theory is refuted by a negative test, since such a theory fails to qualify for acceptance into the body of science.

Given Popper's view that methodological rules have the status of conventions, the question arises of how such rules are to be evaluated. As conventions, methodological rules are unable to bear a truth value, and are therefore unable to be shown to be true. Nor would it be possible to put forward evidence which inconclusively confirms such rules. How, then, are such rules to be evaluated?

11.3 Popper on choice of method

To the objection that the rules of chess are obligatory, I replied that they are obligatory only if you wish to play the game. Does the analogous response apply in the case of Popper's proposed rules for the 'game of science'? Suppose you choose not to follow Popper's rules. Does it follow that you are not playing the 'game of science'? What happens if there is disagreement about appropriate methodological rules for science?

There is an apparent disanalogy between the games of science and chess. The practice of science existed prior to Popper's proposal of methodological rules for the game of science. Thus, unlike the conventions introduced by the inventors of chess, Popper's proposal is a proposal concerning a previously existing practice, rather than a proposal of rules on which a future practice is to be based. We might perhaps think of Popper's proposals concerning the rules of science as conjectures about what the actual methodological conventions of the 'game of science' are.[5]

The matter is further complicated, however, by the fact that Popper's proposals for the rules of science are meant to have normative force. They cannot therefore be intended as mere descriptions of actual scientific practice, which lack normative content. Thus, Popper's proposals might better be thought of as proposals of the optimal means for achieving the aims of science, since such means might fail on occasion to be implemented despite being optimal.

That this is indeed Popper's view of the matter is suggested by what he says about how choice is made between alternative proposals of methods. In *The Logic of Scientific Discovery* Popper claims that:

> The theory of method, in so far as it goes beyond the purely logical analysis of the relations between scientific statements, is concerned with *the choice of methods* — with decisions about the way in which scientific statements are to be dealt with. These decisions will of course depend in their turn upon the *aim* which we choose from among a number of possible aims. (1959, p. 49)

Popper's view appears to be that alternative sets of methodological rules may be proposed for science, and that the choice between such alternative sets of rules is to be made on the basis of an appeal to the aims of the enterprise.[6] This view of how methods are chosen with reference to aims accords well with the hierarchical model of scientific reason which Laudan attributes to empiricist philosophy of science in *Science and Values* (1984, pp. 23 ff).

According to the hierarchical model, disputes among scientists about factual matters may be resolved by appeal to shared methods. Disputes about methods are settled by determining whether proposed methods optimally conduce to the aims of science. It is this latter aspect of the hierarchical model which appears to be exemplified by Popper's remark above that choice of method depends on choice of aims. However, as Laudan shows, the hierarchical model is seriously undermined by the existence of a variety of different possible aims for science. For the possibility of alternative aims immediately gives rise to the question of how to choose between alternative aims. Yet, because aims are at the top of the hierarchy, and justification proceeds from top to bottom on this model, the hierarchical model is powerless to provide a rational account of the choice of aims (cf. Laudan, 1984, pp. 42-3).

The question for Popper, then, is whether there may be rational grounds for the choice between alternative aims. Before turning to this question, however, it is worth taking note of some related remarks which Popper makes in another context about the basis for choosing between alternative conventions. In *The Open Society and its Enemies* (1945, Vol. 1) Popper distinguishes between norms and facts, and argues that statements of norms cannot be derived from statements of facts. He says that norms have the status of conventions, but that this does not mean that they are entirely arbitrary. Nor does the fact that 'we are free to choose' between them mean that one set of norms 'is just as good as any other' (1945, Vol. 1, pp. 64-5).

> It must, of course, be admitted that the view that norms are conventional or artificial indicates that there will be a certain element of arbitrariness involved, i.e. that there may be different systems of norms between which there is not much to choose ... But artificiality by no means implies full arbitrariness. (1945, Vol. 1, p. 65)

Popper goes on to say that moral decisions differ from aesthetic decisions in point of urgency since 'many moral decisions involve the life and death of other men' (1945, Vol. 1, p. 65). Because this is so, proposed moral norms may have potential consequences on the basis of which we may judge whether to accept or reject them.

11.4 Popper on choice of aims

Given Popper's denial of the total arbitrariness of conventions in the moral context, one might expect him to hold that the choice between alternative methodological rules is similarly non-arbitrary. The question is whether he succeeds in showing that there may be a rational basis for such non-arbitrary choice.

The suspicion that Popper has little to say on this front is immediately raised by remarks he makes about the choice between conflicting views of the aims of science. Early in *The Logic of Scientific Discovery*, Popper writes that:

> My criterion of demarcation will ... have to be regarded as a *proposal for an agreement or convention*. As to the suitability of any such convention opinions may differ; and a reasonable discussion of these questions is only possible between parties having some purpose in common. The choice of that purpose must, of course, be ultimately a matter of decision, going beyond rational argument. (1959, p. 37)

If what Popper says here is taken literally, then he seems to have given up the game altogether. For if a reasonable discussion requires an agreed purpose, then it seems to follow that there can be no reasonable discussion between proponents of conflicting aims of science. Indeed, Popper appears to explicitly draw just such a non-rationalist conclusion when he states that a decision on such purposes goes 'beyond rational argument'.

The suspicion that Popper fails to account for rational choice of scientific aims is only heightened when Popper turns to the choice between the aims he favours and the aims he opposes. According to Popper, some philosophers take the aim of science to be 'a system of absolutely certain, irrevocably true statements' (1959, p. 37). Others hold that the 'essence of science' is its 'dignity', which "resides in its 'wholeness' and in its 'real truth and essentiality'" (1959, p. 38). Against such philosophers, Popper says simply that he has a different set of aims in mind. He does not defend the aims he favours 'by representing them as the true or the essential aims of science' (1959, p. 38). He says that he 'freely admit[s] that in arriving at [his] proposals [he has] been guided ... by value judgments and predilections' (1959, p. 38). He also expresses the hope that his 'proposals may be acceptable to those who value not only logical rigour but also freedom from dogmatism; who seek practical applicability, but are even more attracted by the adventure of science...' (1959, p. 38).

Such comments as these seem to indicate that Popper places great value on such things as 'logical rigour', 'freedom from dogmatism', and 'the adventure of science'. They also show that Popper takes his proposals to lead to the realization of such values, since he hopes the proposals will appeal to those who share these values. But Popper does not explain why anyone ought to embrace the values which he favours. Nor does anything he says suggest how someone who simply fails to share these value judgements might be shown to be mistaken in any objective sense.

Similar points apply to Popper's treatment of the conventionalist philosophy of science of Pierre Duhem and Henri Poincaré. Popper admits that conventionalism is a defensible doctrine, and perhaps even an internally consistent one, though he himself finds it to be 'quite unacceptable' (1959, p. 80). Conventionalists place a high value on such things as simplicity, certainty and epistemic conservatism, whereas Popper values new discoveries, falsifications and the development of bold new theories. Thus, conventionalism is based on 'an idea of science', which stems from an 'entirely different' view of the 'aims and purposes' of science from Popper's. He says that conventionalist philosophy is 'incontestable' (1959, p. 81), and that 'the only way to avoid conventionalism is by taking a decision: the decision not to apply its methods' (1959, p.

82). Yet, as far as the basis of such a decision is concerned, Popper concedes that the 'conflict with the conventionalists is not one that can be ultimately settled by a detached theoretical discussion' (1959, p. 81). Thus, Popper's view appears to be that the conflict between falsificationism and conventionalism ultimately reduces to a difference of value judgements between which rational considerations are unable to decide.

In light of Popper's talk of value judgements, predilections and the inability to decide the dispute with conventionalism by a 'detached theoretical discussion', it seems difficult to avoid the conclusion tentatively suggested by Lakatos that for Popper the choice between sets of rules ultimately reduces to 'a matter of subjective taste' (1978d, p. 144, note 8). And if this is right, then Laudan would appear to be entirely justified in laying the metamethodological blame for contemporary epistemological relativism squarely on Popper's doorstep. For it is tempting to side with Laudan when he says that, for Popper, 'There are no objective or rational grounds ... for choosing between rival cognitive values and their attendant methodologies' (1984, p. 48).

There is perhaps a way out of this bind for Popper, since he does suggest that there is a way in which methodological proposals may be evaluated on the basis of their consequences:

> there is only *one* way ... of arguing rationally in support of my proposals. This is to analyse their logical consequences: to point out their fertility — their power to elucidate the problems of the theory of knowledge. (1959, p. 38)

What form such problems might take is suggested in a later passage, in which Popper remarks that:

> [t]he philosopher ... will accept my definition as useful only if he can accept its consequences. We must satisfy him that these consequences enable us to detect inconsistencies and inadequacies in older theories of knowledge, and to trace these back to the fundamental assumptions and conventions from which they spring ... It is by this method, if by any, that methodological conventions might be justified, and might prove their value. (1959, p. 55)

Unfortunately, Popper does not explain how his methodological proposals do reveal the 'inconsistencies and inadequacies in older theories of knowledge', nor is it evident how they might do so.[7]

At a more general level, Popper's claim that his proposals are to be judged by 'their power to elucidate problems of the theory of knowledge' merely serves to raise the question of how to decide rationally whether a problem of the theory of knowledge has achieved elucidation. Different theorists of knowledge may conceive the problems of the theory of knowledge differently, and so may count different things as elucidations of its problems. Moreover, given that rival theorists of knowledge may differ with respect to their favoured epistemic aims, the judgement that a proposal yields elucidation may depend on whether the proposal sheds light on how to achieve one's favoured aims. But this would hardly show one set of aims to be preferable to another. Thus, despite Popper's talk of elucidating problems in the theory of knowledge, the question of how to choose rationally between alternative methodological rules by appeal to scientific aims appears to remain quite unresolved.

11.5 Lakatos on Popper on choice of method

Before turning to Laudan's metamethodological naturalism, I will briefly consider Lakatos's critique of Popper. For Lakatos's critique of Popper as well as his alternative metamethodology lies in the background of Laudan's turn from intuitionism to naturalism.

Lakatos claims that 'Popper never offered a theory of rational criticism of consistent conventions' (1978d, p. 144). According to Lakatos, this is because Popper, having initially failed to specify an aim for the game of science, and having eventually specified the aim as truth, failed to provide an adequate connection between the game and its ultimate purpose.[8] As a realist, Popper thinks of the aim of science as truth, or at least increasing approximation to the truth. Yet, says Lakatos, Popper provides no basis on which to determine whether adherence to a given set of methodological rules does lead to realization of the aim of science.

Not only does Popper fail to show how the falsificationist method leads to truth, it would be quite out of keeping with his general philosophical outlook for him to do so. 'Indeed', Lakatos says, 'the thesis that any such argument connecting method and success is impossible, has been a cornerstone of Popper's philosophy from 1920 to 1970' (1978d, p. 144). In this Lakatos seems to me to be completely correct. For were Popper to draw a close connection between falsificationist methodology and advance toward truth, this would be to renounce the fallibilist epistemology and anti-inductivism on which he characteristically insisted throughout his career. Were Popper, for example, to equate replacement of a falsified theory by an unfalsified but highly corroborated one with advance toward the truth, this would mean that we may know that we are advancing toward the truth. But it is just such knowledge of advance on truth which is denied by Popper's fallibilist conception of knowledge.[9] Moreover, it is precisely such a connection between corroboration and increase of verisimilitude, urged by Lakatos in his 'plea for a whiff of inductivism', which Popper explicitly rejects as having been against his intention.[10]

Yet, because Popper provides no account of how use of a method may be shown to lead to the truth, he is unable to provide a satisfactory rationale for the use of such a method. For if it is unable to be shown that use of a method does conduce to a desired end, then it is quite unclear on what basis use of such a method as a means to that end may be recommended to the exclusion of other possible methods. This objection, which Lakatos raises to Popper's failure to forge a link between method and aim, is distinct from the objection raised in the previous section that Popper provides no account of rational choice between alternative aims.

Lakatos's response to Popper's failure to connect method to the aim of science is to propose an alternative metamethodology, on which it is possible to decide between competing methodological proposals on a rational basis. Lakatos's proposal appeals to scientists' intuitions about exemplary instances of past science as arbiter between rival methodologies.[11] Lakatos says:

> let us agree provisionally on the meta-criterion that a rationality theory — or demarcation criterion — is to be rejected if it is inconsistent with accepted 'basic value judgments' of the scientific community ... if a demarcation criterion is inconsistent with the basic appraisals of the scientific élite, it should be given up. (1978d, pp. 145-6)

This is the metacriterion which Lakatos employs when he proposes that rival methodological views are to be evaluated by considering their ability to sustain rational reconstructions of the history of science. For, if correct, such methodologies should reveal as rational exemplary episodes in the history of science, which have been chosen on the basis of intuitions of the scientific élite as exemplary of rational science.[12]

The attempt to ground metamethodology on the intuitions of the scientific élite runs into trouble, however, with questions about the status of such intuitions.[13] For example, might not the intuitions of scientists about the merits of past science be mistaken? Can such intuitions be criticized? Why trust scientists' intuitions, rather than, say, those of historians or philosophers of science? What if the intuitions of scientists diverge?

One of the deepest objections to Lakatos's metamethodological intuitionism is surely that it rests on an underlying circularity. For how are we to decide the membership of the scientific élite, to whose intuitions we must appeal? If the decision on who belongs to the élite is not based on a prior methodology able to distinguish élite from run-of-the-mill scientists, the question arises of why any credence should be placed in a given choice of the scientific élite. Yet if a prior methodology is employed in choice of élite, then methodology is not grounded on prior intuitions about instances, but rather on a methodology presupposed in choice of the élite.

11.6 Laudan's normative naturalism

As noted previously, Laudan (1984) argues that the traditional conception of scientific rationality of Popper and the logical empiricists is based on a hierarchical model, according to which epistemic justification travels downward from the aims and methods of science to beliefs and theories about factual matters. Laudan argues that the hierarchical model fails to provide a rationale for the choice between conflicting aims. He proposes an alternative reticulated model on which justification proceeds in both directions: not only may justification proceed downward, but it may travel upward from base level factual and theoretical beliefs to mid level methods, and top level aims. Laudan's reticulated model is meant to provide an objective rationale for the kinds of choices of theories, methods and aims facing scientists in complex historical circumstances, which have driven writers such as Kuhn and Feyerabend to embrace some form of epistemological relativism.

In later work, Laudan has continued to develop the metamethodological stance which underlies the model of justification proposed in *Science and Values*. Laudan calls this metamethodological stance normative naturalism. It is a normative position because it concerns the nature of epistemic justification, and has prescriptive consequences. It is a form of naturalism because it treats the study of methodology as continuous with the sciences. Given its status as a naturalistic metamethodology, normative naturalism stands opposed to both Popper's conventionalist metamethodology and the intuitionism of Lakatos and Laudan's former self.

The key to normative naturalism is Laudan's analysis of the underlying logical form of methodological rules. He argues that methodological rules may be construed as hypothetical imperatives which link a given cognitive means with a desired cognitive end. For example, Popper's rule against *ad hoc* hypotheses may be expressed in the form of the conditional:

> if one wants to develop theories which are very risky, then one ought to avoid *ad hoc* hypotheses. (Laudan, 1987, p. 24)

On such an analysis, methodological rules constitute claims about how to attain particular goals, which rest on contingent facts about the way the world is. More precisely, methodological rules are empirical claims which assert the existence of correlations between use of a given method of inquiry and attainment of a specific epistemic result.

On Laudan's analysis of the form of methodological rules, a proposed methodology for science is, in effect, to be conceived as a broadly empirical theory about how to conduct inquiry. Because they have such a theoretical status, methodological rules are, like scientific theories, subject to appraisal, revision, and possible replacement, in the light of empirical considerations. Thus, to justify such rules empirical evidence may need to be presented on their behalf. Because methodological rules assert connections between particular cognitive means and ends, justification requires evidence that a given means does indeed reliably conduce to the desired end. In particular, it requires evidence that a correlation obtains between use of a given method and realization of the intended epistemic goal.

Such a naturalistic approach to the justification of method contrasts sharply with Popper's conventionalism. Since methodological rules have the status of conventions for Popper, they are not in his view substantive empirical claims which are made true or false by facts about the way the world is. Rather, such rules have the force of norms or directives which are proposed as a basis of a particular form of human activity. Instead of being treated in the manner of truth valued claims about the world, the appraisal of methodological rules turns on whether they are considered to advance previously determined aims.

Laudan's approach represents an advance on Popper's on at least two fronts. First, whereas it is not clear with Popper how to rationally decide between methods, Laudan's proposal that methodological rules be analyzed as hypothetical imperatives leads to the suggestion that such choice be based on empirical grounds. For suppose that conflicting methodological rules are proposed as each leading to the same cognitive aims. In principle, at least, it may be possible to present empirical evidence to the effect that one of the methods is a more reliable means than the other of obtaining the aim in question. Secondly, while Popper appears to place choice of aim beyond the range of rational considerations, Laudan's naturalization of methodology enables broadly empirical considerations to play a role in choice of aims. This may, for example, be seen from the fact that empirical considerations are relevant to whether suitable means exist for securing a particular end. Because of this it may be possible to exclude certain aims as unattainable given the means at our disposal. Accordingly, there may be rational grounds for choosing an apparently obtainable aim over one that is evidently unattainable.

Laudan's naturalism also has apparent advantages over the metamethodological appeal to intuitions. For instead of being based ultimately on intuitions about past science, according to Laudan methodological rules derive their epistemic warrant from empirical facts about the way the world is. Whereas intuitions, scientists' or otherwise, are an unpromising basis on which to found the justification of method, the naturalistic appeal to empirical relations between means and ends affords hope that such justification may be placed on a more secure and objective footing. For, not only may methodological rules be grounded in empirical means-ends relations, they may be subjected to critical appraisal on the basis of empirical evidence as well. Since they may be tested by means of evidence for or against the purported means-ends linkages, they are both defeasible and confirmable by empirical means. Admittedly, any such appeal to empirical facts of the matter must face the problem that observation is theory laden. But the fact that observation is theory laden hardly places such a naturalistic metamethodology in a less secure position than would an appeal to intuitions.

11.7 Conclusion

Contemporary work in philosophy of science is characterized by a great variety of naturalized approaches. I suspect that there as many different reasons for embracing naturalism as there are varieties of naturalism. To mention just a couple of related reasons, there has been widespread reaction against *a prioristic* approaches to the methodology of science, partly inspired by work in the history and sociology of science. Connected with this has been the recent rise of neo-pragmatism, belatedly following the breakdown of the analytic-synthetic distinction, which was central to logical empiricism.

Yet if the story I have sketched here of the demise of metalevel conventionalism and intuitionism and the rise of metamethodological naturalism is correct, then I hope to have added another strand to the argument for naturalism. The central problem facing any metamethodology is to explain the epistemic warrant of methodological rules. Neither conventionalist nor intuitionist metamethodology seem capable of providing an objective account of such warrant. Yet a naturalist alternative of the kind proposed by Laudan offers a promising suggestion about the nature of epistemic warrant. Thus, to cast the point in terms of relative problem solving ability, while the problem of warrant seems insuperable for the older programs of conventionalism and intuitionism, the naturalist program has the resources for a very plausible solution to the problem.

Notes

1. In his (1986), Laudan rejects the use which he had formerly made of 'our preferred pre-analytic intuitions about scientific rationality' in his (1977, pp. 160-1).
2. Cf. Popper's remark that 'only two kinds of statements exist for [positivists]: logical tautologies and empirical statements. If methodology is not logic, then [positivists] will conclude, it must be a branch of some empirical science' (1959, p. 52). Popper denies that methodology is an empirical science, and that rules of method are logical rules. Hence, his claim that methodological rules are conventions suggests they belong to some third category. However, since some positivists treated logic as conventional, for them the latter may not mark the distinction Popper requires between logical and methodological rules.
3. Against the claim that conventions have no truth value, it might be objected that it is true, for example, that in the United States cars drive on the righthand side of the road. Yet which side of the road cars drive on is surely a matter of convention. However, this is a case where the truth about which side of the road cars drive on is a truth about a convention governing traffic arrangements, rather than a truth about some pre-existing states of affairs. Popper makes a related point when he says that 'The making of a decision, the adoption of a norm or of a standard, is a fact. But the norm or standard which has been adopted, is not a fact' (Popper, 1945, Vol. 1, p. 64). For discussion of the point that conventional rules of method lack truth value, see Nola (1987, pp. 458-60).
4. In addition to rules of procedure and criteria of success and failure, one might also distinguish rules governing the construction of chesspieces, layout of chessboard, as well as rules of play governing such things as time permitted per move. Of potentially greater relevance to the methodology of science are what one might call rules of tactics, e.g., 'develop the board', 'control the center', 'protect the king'. However, such rules of tactics seem more closely analogous to heuristic rules employed within the context of discovery, which involves psychological matters which Popper takes to fall outside the ambit of 'the logic of science' (1959, p. 32).
5. Something like this is suggested by Popper's remark that it is from the consequences of his proposed definition of empirical science that 'the scientist will be able to see how far it conforms to his intuitive idea of the goal of his endeavours' (1959, p. 55). Popper's idea apparently is that scientists must judge how well falsificationist methodology accords with their understanding of the scientific enterprise.

6. That methods are to be conceived in relation to aims is further suggested by Popper's comment that: 'It is only from the consequences of my definition of empirical science, and from the methodological decisions which depend upon this definition, that the scientist will be able to see how far it conforms to his intuitive idea of the goal of his endeavours' (1959, p. 55). While what Popper says here lacks detail, the idea seems to be that a scientist may appraise Popper's methodological proposals by considering whether they advance the goals which they take to be constitutive of the goals of science. But presumably Popper would not say this unless he assumed methods are to be appraised with respect to their intended goals.
7. However, in a footnote to the above passage Popper says that he has not dealt with the issue of resolving inconsistencies in *The Logic of Scientific Discovery*. He notes that 'in an as yet unpublished work I have tried to take the critical path; and I have tried to show that the problems of both the classical and the modern theory of knowledge (from Hume via Kant to Russell and Whitehead) can be traced back to the problem of demarcation' (1959, p. 55, note 3).
8. In his reply to Lakatos, Popper disputes Lakatos's claim that the idea of truth as the aim of science was not already contained in the original presentation of his views in his (1959); cf. Popper (1974, pp. 1001-3).
9. For Popper, at most 'we may *guess* that the better corroborated theory is also one that is nearer to the truth' (1974, p. 1011).
10. Lakatos proposes corroboration as a 'measure of verisimilitude' (1978d, p. 159), where Popper sees it as a mere 'indication' thereof (1974, p. 1011).
11. In his (1987, pp. 472-3), Robert Nola argues that, particularly in his later work, Popper himself appeals to intuitions about past great science in proposing his demarcation criterion. This suggests either that Popper's conventionalism contains an element of intuitionism or that he later shifted to an intuitionist position.
12. Despite Lakatos's use of the expression 'value judgement', I follow Laudan in speaking of intuitions. The main function of 'basic value judgements' for Lakatos is to select particular episodes from the history of science as test cases for a methodology. Popper, who as we have seen also speaks of value judgements, takes such judgements to extend more widely, to include, for example, preferences about the aims of science, methodological principles and general epistemological stance. By contrast, Lakatos's value judgements have the character of normative intuitions about particular instances.
13. For discussion of some of the difficulties which arise for the appeal to intuitions, see Laudan (1986) and Nola (1987, pp. 472-5).

Bibliography

Achinstein, Peter (1968), *Concepts of Science*, Johns Hopkins University Press, Baltimore

Barnes, Barry, and Bloor, David (1982), 'Relativism, Rationalism and the Sociology of Knowledge', in M. Hollis and S. Lukes (eds), *Rationality and Relativism*, Blackwell, Oxford, pp. 21-47

Bartley, William Warren (1984), *The Retreat to Commitment*, 2nd ed., Open Court, La Salle

Bernstein, Richard (1983), *Beyond Objectivism and Relativism*, University of Pennsylvania Press, Philadelphia

Blackburn, Simon (1984), *Spreading the Word*, Oxford University Press, Oxford

Brown, Harold I. (1983a), 'Incommensurability', *Inquiry*, 26, pp. 3-29

Brown, Harold I. (1983b), 'Response to Siegel', *Synthese*, 56, pp. 91-105

Brown, Harold I. (1988), *Rationality*, Routledge, London

Brown, Harold I. (1994), 'Judgment and Reason', *Electronic Journal of Analytic Philosophy*, 2:4

Chalmers, Alan (1982), *What is this thing called Science?*, 2nd ed., Open University Press, Milton Keynes

Chalmers, Alan (1990), *Science and its Fabrication*, Open University Press, Milton Keynes

Davidson, Donald (1984), 'On The Very Idea of a Conceptual Scheme', in *Inquiries into Truth and Interpretation*, Oxford University Press, Oxford, pp. 183-198

Devitt, Michael (1979), 'Against Incommensurability', *Australasian Journal of Philosophy*, 57, pp. 29-50

Devitt, Michael (1984), *Realism and Truth*, Blackwell, Oxford

Doppelt, Gerald (1982), 'Kuhn's Epistemological Relativism: an Interpretation and Defence', in Meiland and Krausz (1982), pp. 113-146

Ellis, Brian (1990), *Truth and Objectivity*, Blackwell, Oxford

Elster, Jon (1983), *Sour Grapes*, Cambridge University Press, Cambridge

Enç, Berent (1976), 'Reference of Theoretical Terms', *Nous*, 10, pp. 261-282

Feyerabend, Paul K. (1975), *Against Method*, New Left Books, London

Feyerabend, Paul K. (1978), *Science in a Free Society*, New Left Books, London

Feyerabend, Paul K. (1981a), *Realism, Rationalism and Scientific Method: Philosophical Papers, Vol. 1*, Cambridge University Press, Cambridge

Feyerabend, Paul K. (1981b), 'Explanation, Reduction and Empiricism', in (1981a), pp. 44-96

Feyerabend, Paul K. (1981c), "On the 'Meaning' of Scientific Terms", in (1981a), pp. 97-103

Feyerabend, Paul K. (1981d), 'Reply to Criticism', in (1981a), pp. 104-131

Feyerabend, Paul K. (1981e), *Problems of Empiricism: Philosophical Papers, Vol. 2*, Cambridge University Press, Cambridge

Feyerabend, Paul K. (1981f), 'Consolations for the Specialist', in (1981e), pp. 131-167

Feyerabend, Paul K. (1987), 'Putnam on Incommensurability', *British Journal for the Philosophy of Science*, 38, pp. 75-81

Field, Hartry (1973), 'Theory Change and the Indeterminacy of Reference', *Journal of Philosophy*, 70, pp. 462-481

Fine, Arthur (1975), 'How to Compare Theories: Reference and Change', *Nous*, 9, pp. 7-24

Goldman, Alvin I. (1979), 'What is Justified Belief?', in G.J. Pappas (ed.), *Justification and Knowledge*, Reidel, Dordrecht, pp. 1-23

Gower, Barry (1988), 'Chalmers on Method', *British Journal for the Philosophy of Science*, 39, pp. 59-65

Hacking, Ian (1979), 'Review of *The Essential Tension*', *History and Theory*, 18, 223-236

Hacking, Ian (1983), *Representing and Intervening*, Cambridge University Press, Cambridge

Hacking, Ian (1993), 'Working in a New World: The Taxonomic Solution', in Horwich (1993), pp. 275-310

Horwich, Paul (1990), *Truth*, Blackwell, Oxford

Horwich, Paul (ed.) (1993), *World Changes: Thomas Kuhn and the Nature of Science*, MIT Press, Cambridge, Mass.

Hoyningen-Huene, Paul (1989), 'Idealist Elements in Thomas Kuhn's Philosophy of Science', *History of Philosophy Quarterly*, 6, pp. 393-401

Hoyningen-Huene, Paul (1993), *Reconstructing Scientific Revolutions: Thomas S. Kuhn's Philosophy of Science*, University of Chicago Press, Chicago

Katz, Jerrold J. (1972), *Semantic Theory*, Harper and Row, New York

Kitcher, Philip (1978), 'Theories, Theorists, and Theoretical Change', *The Philosophical Review*, 87, pp. 519-547

Kripke, Saul (1980), *Naming and Necessity*, Blackwell, Oxford

Kroon, Frederick W. (1985), 'Theoretical Terms and the Causal View of Reference', *Australasian Journal of Philosophy*, 63, pp. 143-166

Kuhn, Thomas S. (1970a), *The Structure of Scientific Revolutions*, 2nd ed., University of Chicago Press, Chicago

Kuhn, Thomas S. (1970b), 'Reflections on my Critics', in I. Lakatos and A.E. Musgrave (eds), *Criticism and the Growth of Knowledge*, Cambridge University Press, Cambridge, pp. 231-278

Kuhn, Thomas S. (1976), 'Theory-Change as Structure-Change: Comments on the Sneed Formalism', *Erkenntnis*, 10, pp. 179-199

Kuhn, Thomas S. (1977a), *The Essential Tension*, University of Chicago Press, Chicago

Kuhn, Thomas S. (1977b), 'Second Thoughts on Paradigms', in (1977a), pp. 293-319

Kuhn, Thomas S. (1977c), 'Objectivity, Value Judgment and Theory Choice', in (1977a), pp. 320-339

Kuhn, Thomas S. (1977d), 'Discussion', in F. Suppe (ed.) *The Structure of Scientific Theories*, University of Illinois Press, Urbana, pp. 500-517

Kuhn, Thomas S. (1979), 'Metaphor in Science', in A. Ortony (ed.), *Metaphor and Thought*, Cambridge University Press, Cambridge, pp. 409-419

Kuhn, Thomas S. (1983), 'Commensurability, Comparability, Communicability', in P.D. Asquith and T. Nickles (eds), *PSA 1982, Vol. 2*, Philosophy of Science Association, East Lansing, Michigan, pp. 669-688

Kuhn, Thomas S. (1987), 'What are Scientific Revolutions?', in *The Probabilistic Revolution, Vol. 1, Ideas in History*, L. Krüger, L.J. Daston, and M. Heidelberger (eds), MIT Press, Cambridge, Mass., pp. 7-22

Kuhn, Thomas S. (1989), 'Possible Worlds in History of Science', in S. Allen (ed.), *Possible Worlds in Humanities, Arts and Sciences*, de Gruyter, Berlin, pp. 9-32

Kuhn, Thomas S. (1990), 'Dubbing and Redubbing: the Vulnerability of Rigid Designation', in C.W. Savage (ed.), *Scientific Theories: Minnesota Studies, Vol. 14*, University of Minnesota Press, Minneapolis, pp. 298-318

Kuhn, Thomas S. (1991a), 'The Road Since Structure', *PSA 1990, Vol. 2*, A. Fine, M. Forbes and L. Wessels (eds), Philosophy of Science Association, East Lansing, Michigan, pp. 2-13

Kuhn, Thomas S. (1991b), 'The Natural and the Human Sciences', in D.R. Hiley, J.F. Bohman and R. Shusterman (eds), *The Interpretative Turn: Philosophy, Science, Culture*, Cornell University Press, Ithaca, pp. 17-24

Kuhn, Thomas S. (1992), 'The Trouble with the Historical Philosophy of Science', *Rothschild Distinguished Lecture*, Department of History of Science, Harvard University

Kuhn, Thomas S. (1993), 'Afterwords', in Horwich (1993), pp. 311-340

Lakatos, Imre (1978a), *The Methodology of Scientific Research Programmes: Philosophical Papers, Vol. 1*, Cambridge University Press, Cambridge

Lakatos, Imre (1978b), 'Falsification and the Methodology of Scientific Research Programmes', in (1978a), pp. 8-101

Lakatos, Imre (1978c), 'History of Science and its Rational Reconstructions', in (1978a), pp. 102-137

Lakatos, Imre (1978d), 'Popper on Demarcation and Induction', in (1978a), pp. 139-167

Lakatos, Imre, and Alan Musgrave (eds) (1970), *Criticism and the Growth of Knowledge*, Cambridge University Press, Cambridge

Laudan, Larry (1977), *Progress and its Problems*, University of California Press, Berkeley

Laudan, Larry (1984), *Science and Values*, University of California Press, Berkeley

Laudan, Larry (1986), 'Some Problems Facing Intuitionist Meta-Methodologies', *Synthese*, 67, pp. 115-129

Laudan, Larry (1987a), 'Progress or Rationality? The Prospects for Normative Naturalism', *American Philosophical Quarterly*, 24, pp. 19-31

Laudan, Larry (1987b), 'Methodology's Prospects', A. Fine and P. Machamer (eds), *PSA 1986, Vol. 2*, Philosophy of Science Association, East Lansing, Michigan, pp. 347-354

Laudan, Larry (1987c), 'Relativism, Naturalism and Reticulation', *Synthese*, 71, pp. 221-234

Laudan, Larry (1989), 'If It Ain't Broke, Don't Fix It', *British Journal for the Philosophy of Science*, 40, pp. 369-375

Laudan, Larry (1990a), 'Normative Naturalism', *Philosophy of Science*, 57, pp. 44-59

Laudan, Larry (1990b), 'Aim-less Epistemology?', *Studies in History and Philosophy of Science*, 21, pp. 315-322

Laudan, Larry (1990c), *Science and Relativism*, University of Chicago Press, Chicago

Laudan, Larry (1996), '"The Sins of the Fathers...": Positivist Origins of Postpositivist Relativisms', in *Beyond Positivism and Relativism: Theory, Method, and Evidence*, Westview Press, Boulder, Colorado, pp. 3-25

Laudan, Rachel and Laudan, Larry (1989), 'Dominance and the Disunity of Method: Solving the Problems of Innovation and Consensus', *Philosophy of Science*, 56, pp. 221-237

LeGrand, Homer (1988), *Drifting Continents and Shifting Theories*, Cambridge University Press, Cambridge

Leplin, Jarrett (1990), 'Renormalizing Epistemology', *Philosophy of Science*, 57, pp. 20-33

Mandelbaum, Maurice (1982), 'Subjective, Objective and Conceptual Relativisms', in Meiland and Krausz (1982), pp. 34-61

Martin, Michael (1971), 'Referential Variance and Scientific Objectivity', *British Journal for the Philosophy of Science*, 22, pp. 17-22

Masterman, Margaret (1970), 'The Nature of a Paradigm', in Lakatos and Musgrave (1970), pp. 59-90

Meiland, Jack W. and Michael Krausz (eds) (1982), *Relativism: Cognitive and Moral*, University of Notre Dame Press, Notre Dame

Musgrave, Alan E. (1979), 'How to Avoid Incommensurability', *Acta Philosophica Fennica*, 30, pp. 336-346

Newton-Smith, William H. (1981), *The Rationality of Science*, Routledge and Kegan Paul, London

Nola, Robert (1980a), '"Paradigms Lost or the World Regained" — An Excursion into Realism and Idealism in Science', *Synthese*, 45, pp. 317-350

Nola, Robert (1980b), 'Fixing the Reference of Theoretical Terms', *Philosophy of Science*, 47, pp. 505-531

Nola, Robert (1987), 'The Status of Popper's Theory of Scientific Method', *British Journal for the Philosophy of Science*, 38, pp. 441-480

Popper, Karl (1945), *The Open Society and its Enemies*, 2 Vols., Routledge, London

Popper, Karl (1959), *The Logic of Scientific Discovery*, Harper and Row, New York

Popper, Karl (1970), 'Normal Science and its Dangers', in Lakatos and Musgrave (1970), pp. 51-58

Popper, Karl (1974), 'Replies to My Critics', in P. A. Schilpp (ed.), *The Philosophy of Karl Popper, Vol. II*, La Salle, Open Court, pp. 961-1180

Popper, Karl (1994), 'The Myth of the Framework', in *The Myth of the Framework*, Routledge and Kegan Paul, London, pp. 33-64

Putnam, Hilary (1975a), *Mind, Language and Reality: Philosophical Papers, Vol. 2*, Cambridge University Press, Cambridge

Putnam, Hilary (1975b), 'Explanation and Reference', in (1975a), pp. 196-214

Putnam, Hilary (1975c), "The Meaning of 'Meaning'", in (1975a), pp. 215-271

Putnam, Hilary (1978), *Meaning and the Moral Sciences*, Routledge and Kegan Paul, London

Putnam, Hilary (1981) *Reason, Truth and History*, Cambridge University Press, Cambridge

Quine, W.V.O. (1960), *Word and Object*, MIT Press, Cambridge, Mass.

Quine, W.V.O. (1969), 'Ontological Relativity', in *Ontological Relativity and Other Essays*, Columbia University Press, New York, pp. 26-68

Quine, W.V.O. (1987), 'Indeterminacy of Translation Again', *Journal of Philosophy*, 84, pp. 5-10

Rescher, Nicholas (1980), *Scepticism: A Critical Reappraisal*, Blackwell, Oxford

Rorty, Richard (1982), 'The World Well Lost', in *Consequences of Pragmatism*, Harvester, Brighton, pp. 3-18

Rorty, Richard (1991), 'Science as Solidarity', in *Objectivity, Relativism, and Truth: Philosophical Papers, Vol. I*, Cambridge University Press, Cambridge, pp. 35-45

Rosenberg, Alexander (1990), 'Normative Naturalism and the Role of Philosophy', *Philosophy of Science*, 57, pp. 34-43

Sankey, Howard (1991), 'Translation Failure Between Theories', *Studies in History and Philosophy of Science*, 22, pp. 223-236

Sankey, Howard (1994), *The Incommensurability Thesis*, Avebury, Aldershot

Scheffler, Israel (1967), *Science and Subjectivity*, Bobbs-Merrill, Indianapolis

Shapere, Dudley (1984a), *Reason and the Search for Knowledge*, Reidel, Dordrecht

Shapere, Dudley (1984b), 'The Structure of Scientific Revolutions', in (1984a), pp. 37-48

Shapere, Dudley (1984c), 'Meaning and Scientific Change', in (1984a), pp. 58-101

Siegel, Harvey (1987), *Relativism Refuted*, Reidel, Dordrecht

Trigg, Roger (1973), *Reason and Commitment*, Cambridge University Press, Cambridge

Worrall, John (1985), 'The Background to the Forefront', in P.D. Asquith and P. Kitcher (eds), *PSA 1984, Vol. 2*, Philosophy of Science Association, East Lansing, Michigan, pp. 672-682

Worrall, John (1988), 'The Value of a Fixed Methodology', *British Journal for the Philosophy of Science* 39, pp. 263-275

Worrall, John (1989), 'Fix It and Be Damned: A Reply to Laudan', *British Journal for the Philosophy of Science*, 40, pp. 376-388

Index